Printed Matters

Historical Urban Studies

Series editors: *Jean-Luc Pinol* and *Richard Rodger*

Titles in the series include:

Power, Profit and Urban Land: Landownership in Medieval and
Early Modern Northern European Towns
edited by *Finn-Einar Eliassen* and *Geir Atle Ersland*

Cathedrals of Urban Modernity:
The First Museums of Contemporary Art, 1800–1930
J. Pedro Lorente

Advertising and the European City: Historical Perspectives
edited by *Clemens Wischermann* and *Elliott Shore*

Body and City: Histories of Urban Public Health
edited by *Sally Sheard* and *Helen Power*

Urban Governance: Britain and Beyond since 1750
edited by *Robert J. Morris* and *Richard H. Trainor*

The Artisan and the European Town, 1500–1900
edited by *Geoffrey Crossick*

Urban Fortunes: Property and Inheritance in
the Town, 1700–1900
edited by *Jon Stobart* and *Alastair Owens*

Identities in Space: Contested Terrains in the Western City since 1850
edited by *Simon Gunn* and *Robert J. Morris*

Capital Cities and their Hinterlands in Early Modern Europe
edited by *Peter Clark* and *Bernard Lepetit*

Printed Matters

Printing, publishing and urban culture
in Europe in the modern period

edited by

Malcolm Gee
and Tim Kirk

Routledge
Taylor & Francis Group

LONDON AND NEW YORK

First published 2002 by Ashgate Publishing

Reissued 2018 by Routledge
2 Park Square, Milton Park, Abingdon, Oxon, OX14 4RN
711 Third Avenue, New York, NY 10017

Routledge is an imprint of the Taylor & Francis Group, an informa business

A Library of Congress record exists under LC control number: 2001022930

Typeset by Manton Typesetters, Louth, Lincolnshire, UK.

ISBN 13: 978-1-138-72329-0 (hbk)
ISBN 13: 978-1-315-19311-3 (ebk)

MIX
Paper from
responsible sources
FSC
www.fsc.org FSC™ C013985

Printed in the United Kingdom
by Henry Ling Limited

Contents

List of Figures

General Editors' Preface

Density and proximity of buildings and people are two of the defining characteristics of the urban dimension. It is these which identify a place as uniquely urban, though the threshold for such pressure points varies from place to place. What is considered an important cluster in one context – a few hundred inhabitants or buildings on the margins of Europe – may not be considered as urban elsewhere. A third defining characteristic is functionality – the commercial or strategic position of a town or city which conveys an advantage. Over time, these functional advantages may diminish, or the balance of advantage may change within a hierarchy of towns. To understand how the relative importance of towns shifts over time and space is to grasp a set of relationships which is fundamental to the study of urban history.

Towns and cities are products of history, yet have themselves helped to shape history. As the proportion of urban dwellers has increased, so the urban dimension has proved a legitimate unit of analysis through which to understand the spectrum of human experience and to explore the cumulative memory of past generations. Though obscured by layers of economic, social and political change, the study of the urban milieu provides insights into the functioning of human relationships and, if urban historians themselves are not directly concerned with current policy studies, few contemporary concerns can be understood without reference to the historical development of towns and cities.

This longer historical perspective is essential to an understanding of social processes. Crime, housing conditions and property values, health and education, discrimination and deviance, and the formulation of regulations and social policies to deal with them were, and remain, amongst the perennial preoccupations of towns and cities – no historical period has a monopoly of these concerns. They recur in successive generations, albeit in varying mixtures and strengths; the details may differ but the central forces of class, power and authority in the city remain. If this was the case for different periods, so it was for different geographical entities and cultures. Both scientific knowledge and technical information were available across Europe and showed little respect for frontiers. Yet despite common concerns and access to broadly similar knowledge, different solutions to urban problems were proposed and adopted by towns and cities in different parts of Europe. This comparative dimension informs urban historians as to which were systematic factors and which were of a purely local nature: general and particular forces can be distinguished.

These analytical frameworks, considered in a comparative context, inform the books in this series.

Université de Tours   Jean-Luc Pinol
University of Leicester   Richard Rodger
2002

Notes on Contributors

Fay Brauer is Senior Lecturer in Art History and Theory at the University of New South Wales. She is currently working on a book entitled, *Culture's Capital: the French State, the Paris Salons and the 'Civilizing Mission'*.

Peter Fritzsche is Professor of History at the University of Illinois at Urbana-Champaign. His publications include *Reading Berlin 1900* (1996) and *Germans into Nazis* (1998). His current research focuses on comparative questions of memory and identity and vernacular uses of the past in modern Europe.

Malcolm Gee teaches Art History at the University of Northumbria. He has published widely on the history of the French art market in the early twentieth century. He is currently working on a study of artistic relations between France and Germany during the period of the Weimar Republic.

David W.S. Gray teaches Cultural History at the University of Northumbria. He is a specialist in the history of graphic illustration in nineteenth-century France and is currently working on a comprehensive critical study of the work of Gavarni.

Valerie Holman is Research Fellow in War and Culture Studies at the University of Westminster, and acts as Academic Adviser in the History of Art for the Faculty of Continuing Education at Birkbeck. Her recent publications include Valerie Holman and Debra Kelly (eds), *France at War in the Twentieth Century: Propaganda, Myth and Metaphor* (2000).

Tim Kirk teaches history at the University of Newcastle upon Tyne. He is the author of *Nazism and the Working Class in Austria* (1996) and co-editor, with Dermot Cavanagh, of *Subversion and Scurrility. Popular Discourse in Europe from 1500 to the Present* (2000).

Sarah L. Leonard recently completed her PhD in the Department of History at Brown University. She is currently completing a book entitled *The Politics of 'Immoral print': Readers, Peddlers and Police in Germany, 1820-1890*.

Debbie Lewer is Lecturer in Art History at Christie's Education, London. She has written extensively on Dada and twentieth-century art and is currently working on post-war German art.

Jean-Dominique Mellot is a senior curator at the Bibliothèque nationale de France and lecturer at the Ecole pratique des hautes études, IV section, (Paris, Sorbonne). He is a specialist in the history of the book and publishing and of religion in seventeenth- and eighteenth-century France. His numerous publications include, *L'Edition rouennaise et ses marchés (vers 1600 – vers 1730): dynamisme provincial et centralisme parisien* (1998).

Dominique Varry is Senior Lecturer in the History of the Book at the Ecole nationale supérieure des sciences de l'information et des bibliothèques (Enssib) in Lyons-Villeurbanne. He is the editor of *Histoire des bibliothèques françaises*, 3, *Les bibliothèques de la Révolution et du 19e siècle, 1789-1914*, (Paris: 1991) and co-edited *L'Europe et le livre* (1996) and *Le livre et l'historien* (1997). In recent years his research has focused on the history of the book trade in Lyon, especially in the eighteenth century.

Catherine Viollet is a researcher attached to the Institute of Modern Texts and Manuscripts (Institut des textes and Manuscripts Modernes) (CNRS, Paris – National Council for Scientific Research). She specializes in the study of the genesis of twentieth-century literary texts and is in charge of the research team on 'Genesis and Autobiography'. She edited *Genèse textuelle, identités sexuelles* (1997), and, with Philippe Lejeune, *Genèses du Je* (2000).

Preface

This book has its origins in an international interdisciplinary conference organized by the Research Group in European Urban Culture at the University of Northumbria in 1997. We should like to thank our colleagues in the group, Alex Cowan and Jill Steward, for their help then and since. Work on this project has been supported by research funds from the University of Northumbria and, in the case of Malcolm Gee, by the Leverhulme Trust, and we should like to thank them accordingly. Above all, this book would not have been possible without the encouraging interdisciplinary research culture of the Department of Historical and Critical Studies at the University of Northumbria.

Malcolm Gee and Tim Kirk

Introduction

Malcolm Gee and Tim Kirk

'All history', argues Roger Chartier, '– whether economic, social or religious – requires the study of systems of representation and the acts the systems generate. This is what makes it cultural history.'[1] Since the invention of printing in the mid-fifteenth century the production, distribution and consumption of printed matter have been the principal means through which this process of representation has taken place in European society. Chartier is one of a group of distinguished scholars whose work has transformed the previously somewhat isolated field of book history and shifted the history of printing and publishing into the centre of historical concern. It opens up new areas of reflection whose pertinence extends far beyond the France of the Ancien Régime, which has been the focus of Chartier's own research.[2]

The study of print and printing culture has naturally led historians to a concern with its urban context. The urban environment was fundamental to the development of printing from the outset, since it was in towns that the necessary combination of technical and entrepreneurial competencies were located, and where a growing demand for printed texts was to be found. During the sixteenth century the business of printing became a constituent part of European urban culture, and this development reinforced the differences between life in the town and life in the countryside. In the course of the remaining five centuries of the millennium, print conquered the world, but also remained a product intimately embedded in urban life: printed matter was manufactured, sold, and largely invented in urban centres. It permeated urban experience at every level, and formed the chief means through which ideas, values and, indeed, facts created in cities have been exported to the rest of society. To this extent print has promoted the broader urbanization of society as a whole, by spreading urban attitudes and ideas beyond the limits of the city.

It is with this urban cultural environment that the essays in this collection are primarily concerned. We have set out to demonstrate the centrality of printing and publishing to the understanding of urban culture, examined from

---

[1] Roger Chartier, *The Cultural Uses of Print in Early Modern France*, trans. Lydia G. Cohrane, Princeton, NJ: Princeton University Press, 1987, p. 11.

[2] See, for example: Chartier, *Cultural Uses*; Robert Darnton, *The Business of the Enlightenment. A Publishing History of the* Encylopédie, Cambridge, MA: Harvard University Press, 1979; and *The Literary Underground of the Old Regime*, Cambridge, MA: Harvard University Press, 1982; Henri-Jean Martin, *Histoire et pouvoirs de l'écrit*, Paris: Perrin, 1988.

a variety of disciplinary perspectives, but we have not attempted to survey European urban print culture in its entirety. Rather, the studies here focus on a number of specific urban contexts, mainly in France and Germany and in the post-1800 period, and on particular aspects of the use of print in each instance, considering a wide range of printed matter from the crafted book to the mass-circulation newspaper and the ephemeral propaganda leaflet. In doing so they engage with a number of recurrent issues which relate to this field of historical study as a whole.

One of these is the role of printing in specific urban economies. From its earliest days in Mainz, the printing business has always been closely associated with particular towns for various reasons: Frankfurt and Leipzig, Amsterdam, Leiden and Antwerp, Venice and Florence, London and Paris – and not least Lyons and Rouen, both of which were well established as centres of printing by the end of the sixteenth century. Although they were provincial towns in a country noted for the eventual dominance of the capital, both Rouen and Lyons were important urban centres in their own right in early modern Europe: Rouen as regional capital of Normandy, and Lyons at the cultural and economic crossroads of Europe. The contributions here by Jean-Dominique Mellot and Dominique Varry (Chapters 1 and 2) trace the evolution of the printing and bookselling trades in Rouen and Lyons respectively, from a golden age when the two cities operated as independent cultural centres both within their regions and in Europe as a whole, to their eventual demise and eclipse by Paris. The rise of the nation state privileged the cultural economies of cities such as London and Paris over those of other towns and cities which were central to the early development of printing. This was less the case in Germany, where the late establishment of a centralized territorial state enabled cities such as Frankfurt, Leipzig, Hamburg and Munich to continue to flourish as centres of printing and publishing. After 1871, however, Berlin was assertive in establishing itself as the cultural capital of the new Reich, a development which is reflected in the emergent popular market for the mass-circulation press and its exploitation by Berlin-based publishing houses, but is also clearly evident in the specialist field of art publishing (discussed here by Malcolm Gee in Chapter 8). European cities grew so rapidly during the nineteenth century that they were able to furnish the niche markets that made the development of the specialist periodical press possible. Specialist publications in turn promoted the further development and cohesion of cultural networks such as those involved in the *fin-de-siècle* art market. Art journals, like their counterparts in the fields of science, sport and religion, catered for urban subcommunities within the existing structures of public life.[3]

---

[3] See Jörg Requate, 'Öffentlichkeit und Medien als Gegenstand historischer Analyse', *Geschichte und Gesellschaft*, 25, 1999, pp. 5–32, here p.14. Requate refers to 'vielfältige Teilöffentlichkeiten'.

All urban networks were part of a greater urban community, whose emergent metropolitan identity was shaped by the printed paraphernalia of modern urban life. The diversity of urban tribes and their representation in print as 'types' served both to illustrate difference, but also to reaffirm the common experience of the urban environment which was necessary to recognize them. There was a long tradition of caricaturistic images of urban occupations. David Gray's contribution here (Chapter 3) deals with precisely this type of imagery. Gavarni's urban types build on an earlier tradition of '*cris de la ville*', stereotypical representations of the trades of the early modern town. Gray argues that Gavarni reinvented the genre in response to the transformation of urban life by the rapid expansion of the city in the wake of economic modernization. Enterprising businessmen realised that in the new metropolis there were new readers: Gavarni's work was diffused by instalments, in the same way as the popular novels of Balzac and Dickens – which also took urban life as a central theme. Gavarni's publisher Léon Curmer set out to present the French with an 'encyclopaedia of nineteenth century manners' categorized into 423 types, of which over half were Parisian.

This project can be compared in some ways to Balzac's *comédie humaine* (and indeed Balzac was one of Gavarni's early supporters). It was also typical of the broader preoccupations of nineteenth-century Europeans with the documentation of the uncharted territory of the big city on the one hand, and the construction of taxonomies for all areas of experience on the other. Half a century later, Hans Ostwald set out to map the social contours of the new Berlin, brash latecomer among the *Weltstädte* of Europe. Ostwald's project was a response to urban introspection and spoke to a readership similar to that which was addressed by the local interest items in mass-circulation newspapers.[4] Peter Fritzsche's discussion of the Berlin press at the turn of the century in Chapter 5 is concerned with this phenomenon. Berliners were fascinated by Berlin, but found it incomprehensible. The press reassured them by making sense of it and guiding them through it – not least by providing practical information. But newspapers were not merely a means of communicating the mundane and the routine; journalists, like Ostwald's documenters of the city, collected what Fritzsche calls the 'debris of the city', to compose entertaining 'snapshots', 'sketches' and 'one-act dramas'. Newspapers not only provided guides to urban culture in the form of concert and theatre listings, and news and reviews of cultural events, but also – arguably – provided something of that culture themselves.

The commercialization of literature, which had begun during the eighteenth century, had led to the testing of the boundaries of 'good taste'. Among the niche markets that were exploited by the printing and publishing business

---

[4] See Peter Fritzsche, 'Vagabond in the Fugitive City: Hans Ostwald, Imperial Berlin and the Grossstadtdokumente', *Journal of Contemporary History*, 29, 1994, pp. 385–402.

in the nineteenth century were those which wanted entertainment, sensation, titillation – '*Schmutz und Schund*' (dirt and trash) as it was known among Germans anxious about the state of their culture. In Chapter 4 Sarah Leonard explores the response of the authorities in Berlin and other German cities to the proliferation of popular reading that was deemed dangerously immoral. The courts and the 'morality police' constituted an apparatus of censorship and control which sought to assuage bourgeois anxieties about the 'filth' that seemed to threaten the 'respectable' citizen and the established social order. Dirty books were equated with contagion and disease, a predictable enough nineteenth-century metaphor, but one which nevertheless mobilized a second powerful urban anxiety and suggested a clinical solution. In practice, however, the boundaries of decency and good taste were negotiable, and the police and the courts were forced to take a pragmatic approach to the issue, seeking to control the 'poison' of immoral publications, rather than eradicate it altogether.

The operation of censorship and control is a constant theme in the history of print culture. Both Mellot and Varry remind us that this was the case from the very beginning of the print revolution. In early modern Europe any book that was not authorized was deemed illicit, a principle asserted with the establishment of the Index by the Catholic church in 1564. Their studies also remind us that dealing in forbidden books – whether heretical, immoral or simply unlicensed – could be a lucrative business. Smuggling was an important element in the economics of the Lyons printing trade throughout the era of the *ancien régime*; and at the end of the seventeenth century some 40 per cent of publications in Rouen were illegal. Printers and booksellers were defying the royal authorities (with the connivance of the local elite). The black market was encouraged by the enthusiasm with which the authorities, ecclesiastical and secular alike, sought to regulate publication, whether for ideological or commercial reasons. With the Enlightenment the balance altered: where a text was once deemed illegal until it was licensed, it became possible in the course of the eighteenth and nineteenth centuries to presume to some extent that publication was generally permissible unless the authorities intervened to prevent it. The French Revolution had declared the principle of the freedom of the press, and although this freedom was then swiftly curtailed by ensuing regimes, it was finally, triumphantly and durably, reinstated by the Third Republic in 1881.[5] By the eve of the First World War freedom of expression could be taken as the norm in many parts of Europe, and this had a powerful stimulus on the newspaper industry.

The press came to be a power in the land, a 'fourth estate', an institution that was central to the political life of the nation. Political ideas had been

---

[5] See, Marc Martin, *Médias et Journalistes de la République*, Paris: Odile Jacob, 1997, pp. 52–9.

tested, debated and promoted in the press from the time of the eighteenth-century coffee house, but with the emergence of popular politics and the increases in literacy at the end of the nineteenth century its power was reinforced, as was the range of ideas that it catered for and promoted. In the two decades before the outbreak of the First World War the European press became a vehicle for the increasingly open nationalistic hostilities of the time. In France the extremist views of Charles Maurras and Léon Daudet, articulated in their journal *L'Action française*, found echoes in the anti-German positions developed in mainstream newspapers such as *Le Matin*. Fay Brauer's contribution to this volume (Chapter 6) explores the ways in which attitudes towards art were affected by the xenophobia that was increasingly articulated in public life through the press. Even Socialist politicians framed their critique of modernism in nationalistic terms. The 'invasion' of the salons by foreign artists was represented as yet another example of '*pénétration pacifique*', and one that struck at the very heart of French pride: if France was a world leader in any field it was surely in fine art.

When war finally broke out, the press was one of the most important media through which governments sought to shape and manipulate public opinion. In France and Germany its significance led to tighter controls. In neutral Switzerland the press freedom enshrined in the constitution continued to be guaranteed and, as Debbie Lewer shows in Chapter 7, the columns of newspapers became a natural outlet for freedom of expression of opinion about the war from supporters of all sides. Tensions between the French and German communities within Switzerland were articulated in the press in ways which made the authorities increasingly nervous. Moreover, Swiss cities became both a haven for exiled revolutionaries and a hunting-ground for spies – and their activities exacerbated the situation. Above all, the belligerent governments were engaged in the waging of a propaganda war by proxy and the public prints of Zurich and Geneva were one of a number of ways in which their message could be reiterated. A scandal broke out in 1916 when it transpired that a controversial pamphlet castigating the pro-French sympathies of Swiss in the western cantons had been paid for by the German foreign office.

The use of print as vehicle for propaganda is, of course, as old as the medium itself. Flysheets, pamphlets and posters paid for by sectarian interests figured prominently in the religious and political struggles in France and Britain in the sixteenth and seventeenth centuries. Here, as elsewhere, however, industrialization and 'modernity' brought changes of scale and scope. The 'totalitarian' ambitions of Communist and Fascist regimes of the twentieth century required greater control of the new mass media. These now included radio and film, but print remained fundamental to the guidance and formation of public opinion. The circumstances of the Second World War also led to the more explicit engagement of democratic regimes with propaganda both at home and abroad. During the war, for example, the British government sought to subvert Nazi control of the press on the Continent by dropping propaganda flysheets from the air over Germany and occupied Europe. Valerie Holman's contribution here (Chapter 9) examines the ways in which the RAF targeted audiences in France, adjusting the message according to whether leaflets were destined for people in the countryside or for the more receptive workers and intellectuals in the towns.

Pictures have been used in propaganda since printing was invented. The combination of image and text on a large scale, however, long posed a major technical problem that was only resolved in the nineteenth century through the use of wood-engraving, as David Gray points out in Chapter 3. The development of photogravure at the end of the century had repercussions for both the elite and the popular press. Specialist periodicals such as those discussed by Malcolm Gee were able to illustrate art works properly for the first time, while newspapers such as *L'Excelsior* in Paris and the *Berliner Illustrirte Zeitung* could provide 'authentic' news images with a new level of immediacy.

Changes in print culture have usually been driven by technical innovation. The Gutenbergian revolution was of course technological – the invention of a mechanical means of producing text. In this system the typographer carried out the essential task of transforming the written word into a reproducible, metallic, construct, the *forme*. The print shop became the unavoidable staging post for the transmission of text from its creator to the consumer. It was a long-standing aspiration to find a way of actually writing mechanically which would permit the author to produce his or her own printed text, and the invention of the typewriter made this possible for the first time. It created a whole new kind of printed matter, produced in offices by new types of workers, almost exclusively female. As Catherine Viollet points out in her contribution on the impact of the typewriter in this collection (Chapter 10), it transformed the relationship between writer and text, not least because it produces an apparently definitive version almost at the moment of composition. Many (but not all) creative writers in the twentieth century have written directly on the machine: Viollet explores the many forms that their relationship with the typewriter has taken.

Viollet begins her essay by suggesting that the computer has made the typewriter a redundant curiosity after only a century, but the implications of the new technology are much more far-reaching. Within a decade computerized typesetting, desk-top publishing and electronic publishing alone have already transformed printing and publishing beyond recognition. We are undoubtedly faced by a 'third' print revolution that is having a profound impact on the ways in which text and image are made, assembled, diffused and consumed. Theoretically, in the global world of communication, the dense urban networks that have been fundamental to print culture since its inception are no longer necessary, not least as the city itself changes, and urban occupations are carried out from remote terminals in the suburbs and the countryside. And yet the cultural connection, the existential link, between the city and print still seems as strong now as it was for the Viennese feuilletonist Anton Kuh in the strike-bound, newspaperless Vienna of January 1918: 'The city lives only when it reads itself in print'.[6]

---

[6] 'Wien ohne Zeitung'. *Prager Tagblatt*, 20 Jan. 1918, p. 2; cited in Anton Kuh, *Zeitgeist im Literatur-Café. Feuilletons, Essays und Publizistik: neue Sammlung*, edited by Ulrike Lehner, Vienna: Löcker, 1985, pp. 26–9. Also excerpted and translated in Harold B. Segel (ed.), *The Vienna Coffeehouse Wits 1890–1938*, West Lafayette, IN: Purdue University Press, 1995, pp. 306–8.

CHAPTER ONE

Rouen and its printers from the fifteenth to the nineteenth century

Jean-Dominique Mellot

From the fifteenth to the nineteenth century, between the end of the Middle Ages and the industrial revolution, printing, publishing and book-related trades occupied a not insignificant place in the urban geography of Rouen and indeed in its identity. In fact, publishing output contributed quantitatively and qualitatively to the influence of the city, of the province of Normandy of which it was the capital until the Revolution, and even of French culture within a national space in the process of unification, and beyond. Throughout most of this long period the Norman city was either the third or second largest city in France, notably from the mid-sixteenth to the mid-seventeenth century,[1] only losing this position comparatively recently (fifth after Paris, Bordeaux, Lyons and Marseilles around 1800, eleventh in 1914). Seat of an archbishop, capital of a rich and strategically important province, attached to the royal domain of the Capetians since the beginning of the thirteenth century, Rouen had established itself in the Middle Ages as a key centre of economic activity at the heart of the kingdom. As an inland seaport and outport of Paris (some 120 kilometres distant), the city developed a kind of complementarity with the capital, to which the interaction of the Rouennais and Parisian merchant elites at the end of the Middle Ages bears witness. However, while this early-cultivated 'Parisian tropism' proved itself to be an undeniable factor of maturity and emulation, it also contributed to putting Rouen in a position of dutiful dependence vis-à-vis a central authority that became increasingly demanding and exclusive. Indeed, after the Harelle de Rouen (1382), municipal autonomy was suspended indefinitely to the benefit of Royal officials; the city remained without its mayor until 1692.[2]

The English occupation of Normandy during the first half of the fifteenth century (1419–49) posed the problem of the ambiguous status of Rouen particularly acutely. On one hand, emphasizing its role as capital of the ancient duchy arguably encouraged the latter's autonomy, and the threat of a centrifugal tendency, even eventually a break of allegiance to the crown. On

---

[1] See J.-P. Bardet, *Rouen aux XVIIe et XVIIIe siècles: les mutations d'un espace social*, Paris: SEDES, 1983, 2 vols.

[2] See M. Mollat (ed.), *Histoire de Rouen*, Toulouse: Privat, 1979.

the other, limiting the city to a single, exclusive function as a link with Paris could, by the same token, be seen as reducing its influence within a wealthy, ancient province, an influence that was necessary to the prosperity and stability of the kingdom itself. The history of the book trades in Rouen needs to be understood in the context of this enduring problematic of the city and its elites. Locus of a 'Norman pride' that was never abandoned, despite the proximity of Paris, Rouen also tried to assert itself as this ambiguous focus of prosperity and legitimacy, simultaneously promoted and curbed by the centralizing process.

At the end of the Middle Ages, in an epoch when book production depended almost exclusively on the presence of wealthy patrons, either individuals or institutions, the establishment of Rouen booksellers,[3] and also the achievements of local book craftsmen (such as illuminators, calligraphers, copyists and bookbinders) are evidence of privileged relations with both the municipal bourgeoisie[4] – who established the work of the illuminator known as the Master of the Rouen *Échevinage*[5] in the years 1450–1480, and later ordered the sumptuous *Livre des Fontaines* by Jacques Le Lieur (*c.* 1525) – and the archbishop and canons. Thus most of the bookshops were situated at the Booksellers' Portal (*atrium Librariorum*) of the cathedral. However, because there was no university and the judicial elites were relatively small, the book business in Rouen, though occasionally brilliant, as for example during the period of patronage of cardinal Georges d'Amboise I, still basically corresponded to a local and discontinuous demand. Even its regional role hardly bears examination.

The fifteenth and sixteenth centuries: the printed book trade in search of firm foundations

The coming of the printed book was to transform the structure of the book trade and its public, bringing about a set of new relationships between book and city. The logic of serial production, which gradually imposed itself, quickly forced a development beyond the stage of personal relations between patrons and book craftsmen. It was no longer a question of working to

---

[3] See notably, M.-T. Gousset, 'Parcheminiers et libraires rouennais à la fin du XIVe siècle d'après un document judiciaire', *Viator*, 24, 1993, pp. 233–47.

[4] See C.-V.-L. Richard, *Notice sur l'ancienne bibliothèque des échevins de la ville de Rouen*, Rouen: impr. A. Péron, 1845.

[5] G. Ritter and J. Lafond, *Manuscrits à peintures de l'école de Rouen: livres d'heures Normands* ... , Rouen: A. Lestringant, 1913; C. Rabel, 'Artiste et clientèle à la fin du Moyen Âge: les manuscrits profanes du Maître de l'Échevinage de Rouen', *Revue de l'art*, 84, 1989, pp. 48–60; F. Avril and N. Reynaud, *Les Manuscrits à peintures en France, 1440–1520*, Paris: Bibliothèque nationale/Flammarion, 1993.

individual order; producers needed to sell their output outside the almost feudal circle of the local patrons. The market dictated its rules, submitting the book to the constraints of financing and exportation, demanding the seeking out of an increasingly distant and anonymous public, and consolidating the role of major bookseller investors, without whom no publishing venture was possible. This first age of the printed book was that of commercial metropolises, crossroads often distinguished by their cosmopolitan character (Venice, Lyons, the German fairs, later Antwerp), where the book, an elite if not always luxury item of export, was taken up by a trading dynamic that functioned apparently independently of the local potential for consumption. In this new context, the key factors were the presence of trade fairs, capital, a banking and maritime transport infrastructure, the possibility of attracting skilled labour and expertise, and finally the existence of extended distribution networks whose principal focal points were constituted by the humanist and university centres of Europe.

This convergence of interests between international trade and the humanist movement formed the basis of the success of the Renaissance printed book. But by no means all European cities fully benefited from this. In France, Paris – a political capital whose star was in the ascendant and the 'mother' of university studies – combined prestigious offer(s) and demands(s); it dominated the publishing scene in the kingdom from the installation of the first printing press in the Sorbonne in 1470. The parallel success of Lyons was based on its European rather than its provincial position; it represented the establishment of an international model of merchant capitalism. The city also profited from the 'Italian mirage' that caused the centre of gravity of royal policy to shift south-eastwards.

Rouen had no such advantages. Certainly all sectors of its economy demonstrated renewed vitality after a long period marked by wars, plagues and tribulations. Once the city had been freed from the English occupation in 1449, and particularly after 1480, the upturn was equally evident in shipping, the cloth and wool trade, and minting. The population began to increase steadily, reaching a first high point, of 70 000 inhabitants, around 1560. But this dynamism initially only partly affected the Rouen book trades. The potential urban market had grown thanks to increased numbers of solvent clients. Yet, despite the encouragement of the cathedral chapter, which as early as July 1483 invited the *venditores librorum impressorum* to set up under its protection, the latter generally avoided the Booksellers' Portal and the vicinity of the archbishop's palace. Were they discouraged from doing so by the jealous conservatism of the manuscript trade? Possibly, although the chapter for its part was well disposed towards the printing press and its products.[6] Whatever the reason,

---

[6] See L. de Laborde, *Étude sur la bibliothèque de la cathédrale de Rouen, le portail des Libraires, les commencements de l'imprimerie à Rouen* ... , Paris: H. Leclerc, 1919.

when he established his workshop in 1485 the Norman Guillaume Le Talleur, the 'prototypographer' of Rouen, chose the Saint-Lô district, near the future Palace of the *parlement*, and his successor Martin Morin did the same.[7] After this, while the de facto monopoly of the Booksellers' Portal disintegrated, it seems that no specific district superseded it. Successive waves of bookmen set up in such diverse parishes as Saint-Jean and Saint-Michel near the Place du Vieux-Marché, Saint-Godard and Saint-Laurent to the north east of Saint-Lô, Notre-Dame-de-la-Ronde close to the famous Great Clock, Saint-Martin-du-Pont near the banks of the Seine, and so on. In Rouen, unlike Paris (the University precinct), Lyons (the peninsula between the Rhône and the Saône), and most major European cities, no district was specifically identified with the book trades. This dispersion meant that the Norman capital became, in due course, one of the rare European 'complete cities' in terms of the book, but in the immediate term the settlement of the profession was hesitant.

Up to the end of the sixteenth century the Rouen book trade was also seeking its way in relation to several important and interdependent factors: that of protection and legal status; that of dominant influences; and that of the market and stock. In the last century of the Middle Ages, the presence of active lay and ecclesiastical patrons compensated for the absence in Rouen of a university and its *communitas* of professors, students and stationers. During the early days of the printed book, this established clientele appears to have acted as a restraining influence, encouraging the medieval town to turn in on itself. In effect, the Rouen *Échevinage* and the cardinal archbishops Georges d'Amboise I (1494–1510) and II (his nephew, 1510–50), more attached to works of art *ad unicum* (as exemplified by the illustrated manuscript), seem to have made virtually no effort to encourage or organize the development of the printing trades. Dispersed through the city according to their resources, in search of collective standing, financial backing and an unlikely powerful protection, the first typographers and dealers in printed books were from the start under Parisian influence. Whatever the area – training, fonts and typographical materials, even binding[8] – Rouen tradesmen were indebted to Paris, even though they drew their workforce from the local population. Moreover, in contrast to Lyons, the merchant elite in Rouen seems to have put little money into books. In consequence the book trades apparently turned their

---

[7] See É.-B. Frère, *De l'imprimerie et de la librairie à Rouen dans les XVe et XVIe siècles, et de Martin Morin ...* , Rouen: A. Le Brument, 1843; and P. Le Verdier, *L'Atelier de Guillaume Le Talleur, premier imprimeur rouennais: histoire et bibliographie*, Rouen: A. Lainé, 1916.

[8] A bailiwick decree from Rouen, dated 10 December 1588, still noted: 'Usually one has to send as far as Paris to have books fully bound, due to the too great ignorance of most of the masters of this city ... Only with great difficulty can you find five or six who know how to bind properly' (Departmental Archives of Seine-Maritime 5 E 488); cited by G. Lepreux, *Gallia typographica ou Répertoire biographique et chronologique de tous les imprimeurs de France ... Province de Normandie ...* , Paris: H. Champion, 1912, p. 97.

back on a commercial and municipal bourgeoisie that was too taken up with
running local affairs and by the concerns of river and maritime traffic to pay
much attention to a sector that was still marginal and that was marked by its
artisanal character. This relative mutual indifference may explain the early
domination of the book trade in the Norman city by important Parisian
booksellers like Jean Petit. Identified as the outport of the capital, Rouen
seems to have opted to complement Paris rather than to seek out a hypotheti-
cal role for itself as provincial centre, for which no definite structure fitted it
as yet.

Thus already from the age of the incunabula on,[9] the published output of
Rouen was limited to the 'crumbs from the table' of the humanist and university market: Norman or Anglo-Norman customary law, the liturgy of the
nearest bishoprics (in Normandy or England), text books for the nearby
Universities of Caen and Angers produced in conjunction with local booksellers. None of this threatened the supremacy of the Parisian and Lyonnais
presses in the most valuable fields of the period: theological editions, Roman
and canon law, learned and scholarly works – large format publications in
Latin. The Rouen trade was not on the same level quantitatively either: it
produced a mere 51 incunabula between 1485 and 1500, compared to 2850 in
Paris (1470–1500) and 1140 in Lyons (1473–1500). The gap closed somewhat in the sixteenth century: 2 569 publications appeared in Rouen between
1501 and 1600, against more than 15 000 in Lyons and around 25 000 in the
capital. Rouen was far more active than other printing centres in the provinces such as Toulouse and Caen, but could not compete with Paris or Lyons
either in terms of workforce (five times smaller than the Parisian and three
times that of Lyons throughout the sixteenth century) or through its major
personalities. Men such as Jacques Le Forestier, Laurent Hostingue and
Pierre Olivier – and, later, the Du Gord, Le Mesgissier, Loyselet and other
families – were eclipsed at the time, as they have been since, by stars in Paris
and Lyons like the Estienne and the de Tournes families.[10]

Despite this, changing conditions from the mid-sixteenth century onwards
led in due course to an improvement in Rouen's position. The humanist Europe
of the first republic of letters now became fragmented as a result of political
and religious division, and this brought about a decline in the influence of the
major publishing centres which had relied on an elite but dispersed clientele

---

[9] See A.-R. Girard, 'Les incunables rouennais: imprimerie et culture au XVe siècle', *Revue
française d'histoire du livre*, 53, Oct.–Dec. 1986, pp. 463–525.

[10] On the printing production of Rouen in the sixteenth century, see P. Aquilon, *Bibliographie
Normande. Bibliographie des ouvrages imprimés à Caen et à Rouen au XVIe siècle*, Baden-
Baden: Koerner, 1968– , issues 8, 14, 22, 27 and 5, 6, 7, special issues of the *Bibliotheca
bibliographica Aureliana. Répertoire bibliographique des livres imprimés en France au XVIe
siècle*; also his 'Les réalités provinciales', in *Histoire de l'édition française*, Paris: Promodis,
1983, vol. 1, pp. 351–63.

of latinist scholars. Markets became compartmentalized into national sectors, dealing a serious blow to the Renaissance book economy with its key centres (such as Lyons, Venice, Basle), its networks and fairs. Together with the restructuring of commercial axes in Europe in favour of the North West, these developments helped to make Rouen's situation more favourable.

In addition, the institutional framework in the city itself was evolving. The construction of the Palace of the Exchequer in Rouen in 1499, which became the *parlement* after the splitting up of the Parisian *parlement*'s jurisdiction in 1515, was a turning point in the city's history.[11] In addition to the influx of the new elites attached to the sovereign courts (*parlement, chambre des comptes, cour des aides*, the last two having been established since the fifteenth century), the Norman capital won a 'territorial legitimacy' and a new glamour from this development. The metamorphosis of the medieval *bonne ville*, still entrenched behind the ramparts that protected it from the flat lands beyond and freed it from feudal control, now accelerated. By becoming the unquestioned sovereign outpost of royal justice, the city now established itself finally as the centre of a province of key importance in the realm through its population, prosperity, distinctiveness and proximity to Paris. The Rouen Palace of Justice – the largest, most sumptuous and busiest civic building in the city – in this context now also became the legitimate heart of Normandy. This new urban regime, steadily eclipsing the town hall, suited the book trades very well. Throughout the sixteenth century they can be observed gravitating to the neighbourhood of the Palace, as the authority of the Normandy *parlement* became established and the province became identified with the city and the city with the *parlement*. 'To judge is to govern', went the medieval saying. Booksellers and printers understood this; abandoning their reticence, it was now to these magistrates, the key figures in the city – who, after all, took pride of place in the annual procession at the feast of the Assumption – that they looked for the protection and influence that they still lacked.

However, this process was interrupted by the troubles associated with the Wars of Religion. During this period in which the Queen Mother, Catherine de Medicis, declared that the Rouennais were 'the most difficult inhabitants of the kingdom', two arduous sieges (1562 and 1591–92), the Saint Bartholomew's Day massacre (September 1572), six months of Protestant power (1562) and six years of League domination (1588–94), left the city debilitated. Its population had dropped to 60 000 souls by 1600. But these

---

[11] On the history of the Rouen *parlement*, we can cite two recent publications marking its fifth centenary: É. Caude, *Le Parlement de Normandie, 1499–1999: Ve centenaire du palais de justice de Rouen,* [Rouen-Paris: Ministry of Justice; Évreux: Hérissey, 1999]; and N. Plantrou (ed.), *Du parlement de Normandie à la cour d'appel de Rouen, 1499–1999,* Rouen: Association du palais du parlement de Normandie; Paris: Imprimerie nationale, 1999.

trials reinforced the position of the *parlement*, that had managed to navigate through these times of crisis and preserve the town from the worst. When Rouen finally opened its gates to Henri IV on 30 March 1594, he had grasped the situation: no need here to limit further the administration of already malleable councillor-aldermen. On the other hand, with the growth of hereditary office followed soon after by the spread of the sale of posts, the Rouen *parlement* became more autonomous, and 'Normanized.' It already dominated local society, now it saw itself increasingly as the key representative of the province, given the weakness of the provincial Estates, that were debilitated before their disappearance in 1655. The absolute monarchy was now going to have to deal with this 'grenadier among *parlement*s', as it was soon nicknamed, and with its protégés, the printers and booksellers of Rouen.

The seventeenth and eighteenth centuries: a paradoxical success?[12]

The brief golden age of Rouen publishing (c. 1600–1670)

The final years of the sixteenth century saw the emergence of a period of growth that in the century that followed was to put Rouen in second place behind Paris among French publishing centres, with some 5700 recorded editions, excluding pamphlets and short texts (as against around 17 500 in Paris).[13] The community of printers, booksellers and bookbinders in Rouen (regulated by a series of *arrêts* of the Normandy *parlement* in 1579) grew in spectacular fashion, from 71 to 173 masters between 1600 and 1670; real professional dynasties established themselves; about 60 printing presses were in operation in the middle of the century (Paris had more than 180 at the same epoch). At the same time, the bookselling and binding trade infiltrated the urban fabric of Rouen, penetrating all the districts of this 'complete' city of the book (see Figure 1.1), at precisely the moment when 'jobbing printing' was becoming general. But it was in the precincts and stairwells of the Palace, and along the adjacent streets, that the vital elements of Rouen publishing were concentrated: around 30 per cent of booksellers from 1600 and as many as 38 per cent in 1670 (see Figures 1.1 and 1.2).[14] The great local names of the trade, too, were based there: Raphaël Du Petit Val,

---

[12] See J.-D. Mellot, *L'Édition rouennaise et ses marchés (vers 1600–vers 1730): dynamisme provincial et centralisme parisien*, Paris: École des chartes; distributed by H. Champion, Paris: Droz, Geneva, 1998.

[13] See J.-D. Mellot, 'Clés pour un essor provincial: le petit siècle d'or de l'édition rouennaise (vers 1600–vers 1670)', *Annales de Normandie*, **45** (3), September 1995, pp. 265–300.

[14] See J.-D. Mellot, 'Le parlement et la librairie', in Plantrou, *Du parlement de Normandie à la cour d'appel de Rouen, 1499–1999*, pp. 222–42.

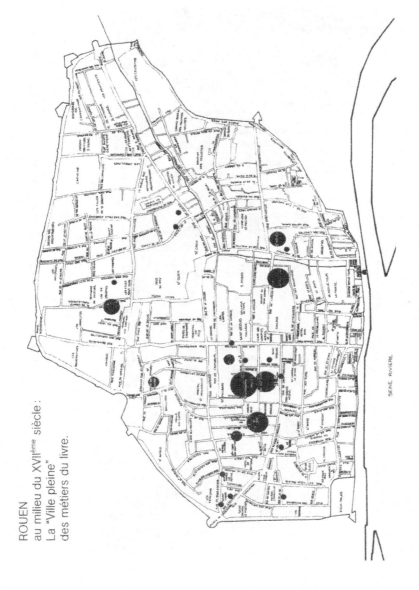

ROUEN
au milieu du XVIIème siècle :
La "Ville pleine"
des métiers du livre.

SEINE RIVIÈRE.

1.1   Plan of Rouen in the mid-seventeenth century: 'La "Ville pleine" des métiers du livre' (J.-D. Mellot).

1.2   *La cour du Palais de Justice, haut lieu de l'édition rouennaise.* Engraving by Garneray Sr., c.1791 (private collection).

bookseller and printer to the King, then his son David and sons-in-law Jean I Berthelin (a Calvinist) and Jacques I Besongne (a Catholic); the printer and poet David II Ferrand, author of the dialectical and satirical *Muse Normande*; Laurent II Maurry, printer to the archbishopric and the local stars Pierre and Thomas Corneille; Jean III Viret, another prominent printer to the King; also Jacques Cailloué, the active Huguenot bookseller, and so on. Meanwhile nearby, a little to the north, the exceptional success of the Jesuit college (which had around 2000 pupils up till its suppression in 1762) gave rise to another cluster of printers and booksellers, dominated by the respected Lallemant and Le Boullenger families.

This dynamism of the early seventeenth century may appear surprising at a time when Lyons, Antwerp and, to a lesser extent, Paris were stagnating. The general circumstances did indeed seem unfavourable; against a background of first undeclared and then open war, an economic slowdown developed. In addition, the fiscal pressure exerted by a state bent on authoritarian centralization gave rise to growing discontent and sometimes violent reactions. In Rouen, with the more or less open backing of the *parlement*, this situation led to revolt and to the severe repression of 1639–41. The episode ended with, amongst other consequences, the dissolution and exile of the sovereign courts and the creation of new posts, called 'semesters', that were awarded largely to men from outside Normandy. In 1649, when the passage of troops and anti-tax agitation was intensifying, the Fronde of the Norman *parlement* showed another eruption of provincial resistance to the *commissaires* sent from Paris.

However, none of this seems to have held back the expansion of the Rouen book trade. Contradicting the widespread view that 'from the end of the XVIth century, there was no publishing industry [in France] outside Paris',[15] the book trades in Rouen evidently continued to flourish until the beginning of Louis XIV's personal rule. Linked to the local and provincial State legal elites (bailiwicks, sovereign courts), the printers and booksellers of Rouen enjoyed a corporate autonomy that mirrored that of their protectors. The publishing professions were free to organize themselves as they wished, provided that their practices and customs were approved by a parliamentary *arrêt* or bailiwick judgement – even if that contradicted the legislation on privileges laboriously put in place by the central power in 1566 (edict of Moulins). For example, the Rouen practice of 'community registration', a sort of prolongation of the 'copyright' recognized by two *arrêts* of the Normandy *parlement* in 1609 and 1644, went directly against the 'continuation of privileges' that the Great Chancellery was seeking to generalize in the sole interests of Parisian publishers. In the same spirit the *parlement* issued privi-

---

[15] P. Chauvet, *Les Ouvriers du livre en France des origines à la Révolution ...*, Paris: Presses Universitaires de France, 1959, p. 205.

leges or permissions to booksellers and authors in its jurisdiction, ignoring the theoretical exclusive privilege of the Great Seal to do this.

The reason for this seems to be that, whereas a less enlightened body would have used its position mainly as an instrument of surveillance, censure and repression of the book trade, the members of the Normandy *parlement* apparently looked above all to the advantages that could accrue from having an active commerce in books on their doorstep. These included ready provision of books, easy publishing (including material in the interest of the parliamentary *fronde*), profitable use of the premises (in the most 'noble' areas of the Palace, the precincts and stairwells, approximately 50 per cent of the stalls and workspaces were let to booksellers) and, above all, the economic and cultural promotion of the province, that redounded to the credit of the magistrates in charge of its destiny. This without even mentioning the personal ties that existed between these great officers, who were often authors themselves, and the most eminent booksellers around them: Raphaël and David Du Petit Val, Jean III Viret, David II Ferrand, and later Claude II Jore and François III Vaultier. Far from restricting the activities of the book trade through detailed supervision, the Norman parliamentarians happily applied to it their rather advanced notions of commercial freedom. *'Est res inaestimabilis libertas'*, they proclaimed as a body from the beginning of the sixteenth century, echoing the city's merchants. Consequently their supervision of the book trades appears rather similar to that undertaken several centuries later by our contemporary local and regional public authorities – combining concerns for identity, economic dynamism, and cultural values. It would be wrong to see this attitude as a manifestation of selfish anti-centrism or feudal sympathies. On the contrary, it derived from a sense of provincial responsibility that was capable of opposing when necessary the monopolistic excesses of a centralizing monarchy. So, in 1659, it was in the defence of the economic interests of all the provinces of the kingdom that the Norman *parlement* took umbrage at the confiscation of re-editions, that benefited Parisians exclusively: 'If we accepted these privileges obtained so easily in Paris, the printers of Rouen and all those elsewhere would have nothing left to print!'

In the light of this protection, it is understandable that the printers and booksellers of Rouen chose the *parlement* and its palace as the focal point of book trades activity. In its dealings with the councillors and municipal bourgeoisie, on the other hand, the bookmen's corporate 'little republic', full of pride (amongst these 'men of their word', even though they were printers, wasn't the law 'inkless', as David Ferrand amusingly recalls in his *Muse?*), solidarity and patriarchal traditions, generally seems to have demonstrated an indifference that came close to contempt.

The population of Rouen continued to grow up to the 1640s, reaching around 90 000 inhabitants, its high point under the *ancien régime*. With its large elites – around 1000 salaried officials and their families, 2000 school students, 2000 clerics and members of religious orders, the high level of literacy amongst its inhabitants – 66 per cent of men and 41 per cent of women were able to sign their names in 1670,[16] the striking percentage of book owners – between 38 per cent and 46 per cent from the last quarter of the seventeenth century,[17] a well developed level of education in the surrounding countryside, and its numerous and highly thought of libraries,[18] the Norman city comes over as an ideal centre of consumption for the local publishing trade. However, while the city and its region certainly accounted for a fair proportion of Rouen's publishing output, these were not the key factors in its expansion.

In fact, the rise of Rouen, the 'outsider' on the scene of French and European publishing, cannot be explained purely in terms of the success of provincial production opposed to a homogenizing cultural enterprise undertaken by and in the capital. Rather it was part of a broader process: the 'nationalization of culture' and the integration of the market, that was taking place in Europe at the level of each major state. In France, because of the size of the territory needing cultural 'irrigation', and the network of provincial capitals that constituted its legitimate (post-feudal) backbone, this process of nationalization, of progressive liberation from European humanist models, could not be carried out by Paris alone. An active part was played by the output of provincial publishers that diffused at a lower cost works usually legitimized in the capital: whether it was royal acts, secular literary hits (these played a major role in the process in the classical era), works intended for the Jesuit colleges, or religious literature inspired by the remarkable thrust of the Counter-Reformation, adjusted for the Gallican market. By decisively playing the card of Parisian leadership, publishers in the large provincial cities – particularly those in Rouen, helped as they were by their closeness to Paris and by the success *there* of their own authors – were able to target a far broader public than just the Parisian one. Through books that the capital had approved, they could cater to a demand emanating from all the significant publics of the kingdom.

---

[16] J.-P. Bardet, *Rouen aux XVIIe et XVIIIe siècles* , table p. 103.

[17] J.-D. Mellot, *L 'Édition rouennaise*, p. 419.

[18] See J.-D. Mellot, 'Rouen au XVIIe siècle', *Histoire des bibliothèques françaises. Vol. II: Les bibliothèques sous l'Ancien Régime, 1530–1789*, Paris: Promodis-Editions du Cercle de la librairie, 1988, pp. 454–65; also 'Au cœur de la vie (érudite) du livre: Émery Bigot (1626–1689) et la *Bibliotheca Bigotiana*', *Sources – travaux historiques*, special number *Les Usages des bibliothèques*, 41–2, 1997, pp. 65–78.

Legitimate but inadmissible? The prosperity of a provincial publishing centre during the final century of the Ancien Régime (late seventeenth to late eighteenth century)

At first, the crown did not look askance on this expansion of provincial publishing, because it aided the political and religious unification of the kingdom and contributed to its grandeur. It only began to be alarmed by it from the onset of Louis XIV's personal reign, when the operational autonomy enjoyed by the book trades in the provinces, particularly in Rouen thanks to the active support of the *parlement*, seemed increasingly inadmissible. These political concerns coincided with matters of private interest – that of Parisian publishers who were increasingly disinclined to tolerate competition from provincial printing centres able to cut prices and move in on Paris' local market. As a result, the authorities conceived the idea of applying the principle of deliberate centralization to the book trades, as a way of satisfying both the 'law of order' dear to the absolute monarchy and the monopolistic ambitions of the Parisian book trade. From the end of the 1660s, initiated by Jean-Baptiste Colbert,[19] a process of 'de-legitimization' of provincial publishing dynamism, and then provincial publishing itself, was undertaken. Between the end of the seventeenth century and the middle of the eighteenth, the entire publishing system was autocratically restructured in several stages, to the advantage of the business in Paris. The renewal of re-editing privileges in Paris was made general; then, in 1667, the admittance of printers was suspended throughout the country. In 1678 the obtaining of publishing privileges from *parlements* was prohibited and it was required that they be sought from the Great Chancellery; in 1699 a *Direction de la librairie* for the kingdom was created; in 1701 the system of privileges and censorship was extended to all publishing activity including re-editions; in 1704, 1739 and 1759 increasingly draconian measures were taken to restrict printing positions throughout the kingdom; professional associations (*chambres syndicales*) on the Parisian model were set up in the provinces as a means of curbing any tendencies towards corporate autonomy; finally, in 1744 the Parisian publishing regulations of 1723 were extended to the provinces. If we add to these measures the establishment of a real 'book police' whose job was to enforce them, backed up in the provinces primarily by the intendants of the *généralités*, then by book trade inspectors, it is evident that, under the guise of instituting a national standard, in a very short space of time a control apparatus of unprecedented rigour had been imposed on the book trades. Unable to satisfy the new demands of the regime, provincial printing seemed to be condemned to either die or allow itself to become a mere instrument, its output limited to

---

[19] See H.-J. Martin, *Livre, pouvoirs et société à Paris au XVIIe siècle (1598–1701)*, Geneva: Droz, 1969, 2 vols.

specific orders from the authorities or individuals. This was in fact why the network of towns of secondary importance was relatively untouched by the successive 'dirty blows' of the eighteenth century, unlike those publishing centres capable of competing with Paris that these restrictions were specifically aimed at.[20] The number of printing workshops in Rouen and Lyons dropped from 28 and 30 in 1700 to 10 in 1759 under the impact of the *numerus clausus*.[21]

In order for these kinds of constraints to function without problems, they needed to reflect the realities of economic development; but this was not the case. First, because the Parisian trade, as a result of its limited productive capacity and the high prices it charged, did not have the means to replace the provincial centres 'brought into line'; and second because, as a consequence of, among other factors, the educational efforts undertaken by the Church and parishes before, and especially after the Revocation of the Edict of Nantes (1685), demand for books increased and spread continuously in both town and countryside.[22] This contradictory state of affairs did not go unnoticed in the provinces, and certainly not by the lieutenant general of the police in Rouen, Pierre Le Pesant de Boisguilbert (1646–1714), a pioneer of economic thought. Taking over, after his own fashion, the role of the provisionally stifled Normandy *parlement*, this enterprising magistrate took the Rouen book trades under his protection and encouraged their dynamism by preaching the maxims of 'economic disobedience', and granting printing licences in excess of his authority. This was so effective that, with the complicity of the local and provincial elites, bookselling and printing in Rouen was discreetly put back on course after a phase of crisis and difficult adaptation. During the most intense period of absolutist rigour, between 1690 and 1715, production of illegal editions of all kinds reached an astonishing level in Rouen – more than 40 per cent of the whole. This was all the more remarkable in that they were perpetrated by 'good men', artisans traditionally bound by ties of family and corporation. No fewer than 12 imprisonments of Rouen printers in the Bastille between 1710 and 1725, increased severity of censorship, an impres-

---

[20] Presaging this development, a memorandum on printing from the beginning of the eighteenth century had no compunction in stating: 'There are perhaps fewer than four cities in France where works of any significance are printed; printers in provincial centres [*capitales des généralités*] are provided with enough to keep them busy by the intendancies and general tax departments and receivers [*Fermes*] ... A single printer is more than adequate for other towns.' (Bibliothèque nationale de France, ms. fr. 22128, fol. 397).

[21] See J. Quéniart, *L'Imprimerie et la librairie à Rouen au XVIIIe siècle*, Paris: Klinksieck, 1969, esp. pp. 48–9.

[22] On this contradiction, characteristic of the late eighteenth century, see J.-D. Mellot, 'Entre "librairie française" et marché du livre au XVIIIe siècle: repères pour un paysage éditorial', *Le Livre et l'historien. Études offertes en l'honneur du professeur Henri-Jean Martin* ... , Geneva: Droz, 1997, pp. 493–517.

sive series of prosecutions, raids, police and customs seizures – nothing seemed to be able to curb Rouen's pugnacity. Chancellor Pontchartrain might well remonstrate furiously with the Rouen intendant in April 1703: 'From the information reaching us from all places, there are no other locations in the kingdom where printing is carried out … with more licence than in Rouen'. One thing was clear: this widespread fraud was not the work of poor or marginal desperados. It was in fact inspired by what the Chancellor himself called the *'maxime de police* of this city, which consists in protecting freedom of trade at all costs and the encouragement of all means of attracting money there.'

In this context, the recall and exile of the lieutenant of police Boisguilbert to Brive-la-Gaillarde in March 1707 hardly deterred the Rouen printers from continuing to produce – behind a slim official facade of school books, Church books, legal and administrative publications – a mass of pirate editions of Parisian books, of new prohibited works, and of colportage booklets falling outside the regulated system. Behind these so-called 'pirates', these 'crooked Masters' (*dixit* Voltaire), these 'thieves from Rouen' (*dixit* the Parisian engraver Cochin le jeune), was an entire city, an entire province, that, via its judicial elites, asserted the claim of its publishing vitality and demanded its rightful share in the dissemination of national culture. In 1714–15, the Rouen printer Claude II Jore, held in the Bastille for having published prohibited Jansenist books, went so far as to declare that his fraud was patriotic on grounds of economic realism: 'If it is objected that I issued books without a licence, my response is that it was *tolerated* and … after I had let it be known that *we would give our people work and destroy the Dutchmen's business.'* Because these attacks on provincial dynamism favoured that of foreign and peripheral printers that could not be controlled, the royal *Direction de la Librairie* was soon obliged to adjust the publishing regime in favour of provincial presses. In Rouen, the bastion that had inspired provincial resistance, the Abbé Bignon, first Director of the book trade, inaugurated the system of *tacit authorization* in 1709, that made possible the control of the least conformist publications without approving their content.

However, it took some years before this discreet organization, in fact a renunciation of the determined policy of centralization conducted thitherto, became really effective in the provinces. Around 1728 Chancellor d'Aguesseau decided to put M. Camus de Pontcarré, the senior president of the Normandy *parlement*, in charge of the book trade within his area of jurisdiction. From then onwards, until the end of the *ancien régime*, the senior presidents were active, now officially, in promoting the interests of those under their jurisdiction, their neighbours the printers and publishers of Rouen. Their 'tolerances', their tacit authorizations, their 'local laws' (as the Rouen printer Jacques-Nicolas Besongne called them in 1758) erected a screen of protection around the publishing activity of Rouen that matched the popularity of the *parlement* in the province.[23] These protections were all the more irremovable in that they were intended to counter the arbitrary weight of the Parisian monopolies: 'The ease with which the printers of Paris increase their privileges', the senior president of the *parlement* wrote bluntly to the Director of the book trade, 'and the exorbitant prices that they charge for their books ... have more or less forced provincial publishers ... to pirate [Parisian editions]'.[24]

Rouen, the 'bad conscience' of centralizing absolutism, Rouen, 'suburb of French publishing', in this way enjoyed a kind of unofficial privilege in escaping from the official ones. It had, indeed, lost status but, contrary to the conclusions of J. Quéniart, it had not lost 'during the eighteenth century two major struggles already underway in 1700 against the royal power and against the Parisian publishing trade.'[25] In many respects it was the opposite which had occurred. Rouen remained, until the eve of the Revolution, the capital of a province that was simultaneously distinctive and close to Paris, capable of autonomy and at the same time ready to take advantage of the concentration of stakes in the capital: able to tap into the Paris of consumption while defeating the ambitious constructions of the Paris of centralization.

The revolution and the nineteenth century: watershed and change of scale

By breaking, throughout the eighteenth century, the monopolies granted to Parisian publishers, by short-circuiting censorship procedures that were as pernickety as they were unrealistic, by defying the protectionist and corporatist constraints weighing on the Parisian market, the printers and booksellers of Rouen had in fact survived and prospered through implementing an early version of the freedom of the press. It seems, however, that they were not fully aware of this. At any rate, in Normandy the books of grievances of the Third Estate rarely refer explicitly to the achievement of this freedom.[26] It should be noted that, thanks to the initiative of the keeper of the seals Arman-Thomas Hue de Miromesnil (who, it is no surprise to discover, was a former senior president of the Normandy *parlement*), a total review of the French publishing regime had been undertaken in August 1777, to the explicit ben-

---

[23] This popularity only declined on the eve of the Revolution. It was still spectacularly in evidence in 1771–74 during the episode of the suppression of the court at the moment of the 'Maupeou revolution'.

[24] Cited by G. de Beaurepaire, *Le Contrôle de la librairie à Rouen à la fin du XVIIIe siècle*, Rouen: A. Lainé, 1929.

[25] J. Quéniart, *Imprimerie et la librairie*, p. 78.

[26] See É. Wauters, *Une presse de province pendant la Révolution française: journaux et journalistes Normands (1785–1800)*, Paris: Editions du CTHS, 1993, esp. p.30. Only four *cahiers* from the bailiwick of Rouen demanded this freedom in 1789.

efit of the provincial presses. Legalization of the enormous stocks of provincial piracies,[27] 'thaw' of the public domain through the discontinuation of Parisian privileges, the creation of 'simple permission' for reprints: all these measures indicated an admirable concern for rebalance between Paris and the provinces, and were indeed celebrated by memorable festivities in Rouen. In the years that followed, Rouen businesses took considerable advantage of these new conditions, to the extent of capturing almost a quarter of the total 'simple permissions' granted to provincial printers.[28]

The change of scenario was therefore all the more brutal at the Revolution. In a few months, the proclamation of the freedom of the press (26 August 1789), the abolition of publishing privileges, the proliferation of improvised printing shops, the flourishing of periodical sheets and the focalization on political events, brought about the concentration in Paris of all the critical issues of the nation. From one day to the next deliberate centralization and its paradoxical concessions to provincial activity gave way to a 'spontaneous' centralization, in the service of national mobilization, that was a far greater threat to provincial publishing. Now, under the pressure of unrestricted competition, prices in Paris began to go down as fast as it became the site of all the most recent news worthy of interest. With the disappearance of the provinces, of the *parlements* (1790) and corporations (1791) of the *ancien régime*, there was soon no structure in place capable of acting as a counterweight to the hypertrophy of the role of the capital. All the more so since book production itself collapsed under the impact of periodical publications and political brochures. Severely hit by the reorganization of civil and ecclesiastical institutions, some of the hitherto most solid publishing businesses foundered – including, in Rouen, that of the printer to the king, Richard-Gontran Lallemant, recently ennobled and now forced into emigration. As the book trade lost virtually all autonomy and the last of the Palace boutiques shut or were dispersed through the city, established families of printers, such as the Oursels, the Le Boullengers, and the Behourts, sought with varying degrees of success to put themselves at the service of the new administrations. Even then the increased rights of the royal, and latterly national, Print Office in Paris deprived them of re-editions of major interest.

The takeoff of the local press, significant at the provincial level, with several major publications (particularly the *Journal de Rouen* and the

---

[27] See A. Boës and R. L. Dawson, 'The legitimation of *contrefaçons* and the Police Stamp Act of 1777', *Studies on Voltaire and the eighteenth century*, 230, 1985, pp. 461–84; J.-D. Mellot and É. Queval, 'Pour un repérage des contrefaçons portant l'estampille de 1777 au département des Livres imprimés', in B. Blasselle and L. Portes (eds), *Mélanges autour de l'histoire des livres imprimés et périodiques*, Paris: Bibliothèque nationale de France, 1998, pp. 178–94.

[28] See M.-T. Bouyssy and J. Brancolini, 'La vie provinciale du livre à la fin de l'Ancien Régime', in F. Furet (ed.), *Livre et société dans la France du XVIIIe siècle*, Paris-The Hague: Mouton, 1970, vol. II, pp. 3–37.

Chronique nationale et étrangère) did provide work for some typographers both newly arrived (S.-J.-B. Nöel de La Morinière, Jacques Duval, François Mari, Pierre Périaux) and not (Jacques and Pierre Ferrand). But while it is true that the proximity of the capital and revolutionary 'Paris-centrism' did not snuff out a nascent Rouen press, and that a truly local demand allowed this to survive, at least until the restrictive measures imposed under the Consulate in 1800–1802, Norman newspapers and journalists were initially only the reflection of their Parisian models. Revolutionary decisions and events were mainly seen through the prism of debates in successive assemblies and the capital's news-sheets.[29] Ultimately, this output, despite its qualitative importance – as the royalist Rouen journalist Magloire Robert declared in his *Observateur*: 'We are representatives of opinion' – never counted for much in the face of the mass of periodical media in Paris, where nearly 200 titles appeared in the single year 1789. Above all, the production and distribution of these sheets never claimed to compensate for the decline of a flourishing publishing centre that, in the French second rank, had managed to counterbalance with discreet efficiency the theoretical exclusivity of the privileged Parisian booksellers. The disappearance of the great families of Rouen printer-publishers (Besongne, Dumesnil, Lallemant, Machuel, Viret) from the beginning of the Revolution bears witness to this rupture with an illustrious past. Moreover, the licensing regime (*régime du brevet*)[30] managed to remove the traces of it: the number of printers in Rouen was limited to 9 in 1811 (against 80 in Paris), and to 11 in 1843, at a time when the population of the city was nearing 100 000.

At the end of this period of change, then, Rouen returned to the ranks. The *chef-lieu* of the department of the *Seine-Inférieure* (1790) sank now into the anonymity of the 'provinces', that 'desert' outside Paris, when it had earlier shone, through its *parlement*, on a province that was one of the proudest of the old France. Certainly, for the first time since the Middle Ages, the municipality gained something in terms of economic, police and requisitioning powers. But this new significance did not correspond to autonomy. Extended to all municipalities, it led, on the contrary, to fragmentation, to a 'localism' in which petty local pride played a role; thus the smallest 'district' in the new department (for example, Montivilliers, Gournay, Neufchâtel, Saint-Valery) insisted on having a printer, without taking any account of the viability of their establishment.

At the political level as in publishing, Rouen was now relegated, like the other regional centres of the country, to the role of more or less a passive

---

[29] É. Wauters, *Une presse de province.*

[30] See G. Dubois, *La Réglementation de l'imprimerie, de la librairie et de la presse à Rouen sous le Consulat et l'Empire*, Rouen: A. Lainé, 1938; L. Andrieu, 'Les brevets d'imprimeurs et libraires en Seine-Inférieure', *Actes du 105e congrès national des sociétés savantes. Caen, 1980, section d'histoire moderne et contemporaine*, Paris, 1984, vol. II, pp. 133–45.

transmitter of Parisian influence. To depart from this line by appealing to provincialism, federalism or royalism, was seen as playing into the hands of the counter-revolution and exposed one to severe reprisals, as in the case of the young Rouen journalist and printer Jacques Leclerc who was summoned before the Revolutionary Tribunal and guillotined on 6 September 1793 after the failure of the Rougemare royalist uprising of January 1793. Hence the generally moderate position of the municipal bourgeoisie, too accustomed to the changeability and excesses of the capital to slavishly follow it, and also too prudent to draw down on itself the wrath of the 'Parisian ogre'. This formula of 'neither one nor the other' was perpetuated after the Revolution and characterized the political behaviour of the city in the modern period. It allowed Rouen to avoid excessive turbulence but at the same time did not enable the city to emerge from its eclipse.

For a long period in the nineteenth century the fifth city of France, Rouen sank into a state of nostaligic decline that was not without its charm. 'Athens in the gothic mode', a centrepiece in Baron Taylor's *Voyages pittoresques*, it already exerted an appeal to the masters of romanticism such as Hugo and Stendhal, to painters, draughtsmen and lithographers, and to the pioneers of cultural tourism (see Figure 1.3). And this new interest helped to generate business for the best local printers – the Brière father and son; the Périaux; H. Boissel; Espérance Cagniard up to 1895 and his successor to 1912 Léon Gy, then Albert Lainé; Julien Lecerf and his descendants from 1866 to the present – as well as for the most eminent bookseller-publishers – Édouard-Benjamin Frère from 1827 to 1842; Auguste Le Brument to 1876; Auguste Lestringant father and son from 1890 to the 1980s.[31] Indeed, their output often records the vitality of learned societies (such as the *Académie de Rouen*, the *Société de l'histoire de Normandie*, the *Société des bibliophiles normands*, the *Société d'émulation libre de la Seine-Inférieure* and the *Société rouennaise de bibliophiles*), the quality of erudite journals, and the appearance of regionalist sentiment based primarily on archaeology and history. It is at this point that a type of self-consciously regional production emerged on a scale never known under the *ancien régime* – then the major publishing field had been that of the nationalization of culture, now it had been largely taken over by triumphant centralism.

However, this evolution was accompanied by a provincial complex that was more and more pronounced. Not only had the city been deprived of most of its leadership functions, it was now permanently limited to the role of a district within the context of a regimented department. With the constitution of year VIII, an omnipotent prefect and a State administration seen as out-

---

[31] I am indebted to G. Pessiot, of Editions du P'tit Normand, Rouen, for this information, drawn from an ongoing study of the main Rouen publishers of the nineteenth and twentieth centuries.

1.3 R. P. Bonington, *Rouen Palais de Justice: Entrée de la salle des pas perdus*, lithograph by Feillot, 1824 (Bibliothèque nationale de France, Paris). A reconstruction of the ambience of the Palais during the mid-seventeeth century. One of the numerous booksellers' stalls can be seen on the right.

siders, the removal of local elites from public life seemed evident. Even the radical achievements of nineteenth-century urbanism seemed inspired by a highly provincial desire to 'catch up'. Although Gustave Flaubert sent his Emma Bovary to the bookshops of Rouen to look for novels that would fill out her country isolation (*Madame Bovary*, 1857), the cultural life of nineteenth-century provincial cities was considered to bore or embarrass those who were condemned to live it, more particularly after 1843 when the railway rendered the capital and its lights so accessible. Hence the symptomatic attitude of major figures in cultural and economic life who could not admit to either the retrograde character of certain very local choices (for example the prioritization of the cotton industry after the crisis of 1845–50) or the phenomenon of forced dependence on the Parisian sphere of influence – a dependence symbolized by the activity of the port whose prosperity revived at the very end of the nineteenth century (when Rouen regained its position as the second port in France) as a result of a fuller adaptation to the growing needs of the Parisian conglomeration.

As far as publishing went, the success of the Mégard publishing house in the nineteenth century (Sébastien Mégard, initially in partnership with Thomas Lecrêne-Labbey, then his son Sébastien Mégard and his heirs)[32] also seemed to rely largely on a model drawn from the past: the family business that combined printing and bookselling, the partial exploitation of existing stocks of the Norman *Bibliothèque bleue*,[33] the production of almanacs, distribution supported by a pre-existing network of colportage. That said, the long career of the Mégard family was also supported by new conditions: the expansion of literacy, the development of Catholic private education, the takeoff of moralizing literature aimed at youth, the fashion for book prizes and awards, the taste for coloured covers, technical efficiency, and so on. This kind of specialization, together with the effort to keep prices low, made Mégard one of the few provincial publishing houses (with Mame in Tours, Lefort in Lille, Ardant and Barbou in Limoges) that were able to wrest a part of market share on the national level from the all powerful publishing trade in Paris. However, failure to foresee the evolution of this complementary relationship vis-à-vis the output of the capital meant the end of this long lasting 'provincial exception' in 1908.

Up to the end of the twentieth century, printing workshops, bookshops and even publishing houses, have continued to contribute book and printed matters to the animation of Rouen's streets and alleys. But their presence, however dynamic and typical it sometimes is, does not bear comparison with the resplendent 'beehive' of booksellers that the Palace of Justice was during the golden age of Rouen publishing. On the other hand, the final chapter on the history of books and printing in Rouen is not yet written.[34] Who knows, perhaps we can expect a revival of the sector and its new media in the city from the promises of the future and the lessons of the past. In other words, what constitutes the specificity of Rouen's history. Exploiting its position, as not only close to Paris but also the capital of a province – Normandy, never forgotten even at the height of Jacobinism and today partially revived by the existence of two regions (High and Low Normandy) and their universities – Rouen has managed at certain privileged moments of its history, such as the

---

[32] See M. Manson, *Rouen, le livre et l'enfant de 1700 à 1900. La production rouennaise de manuels et de livres pour l'enfance et la jeunesse* (exhibition, Musée national de l'education), Paris: Institut national de la recherche pédagogique, 1993; also his, 'Continuités et ruptures dans l'édition du livre pour la jeunesse à Rouen de 1700 à 1900', *Revue française d'histoire du livre*, 82–3 1st and 2nd quarters 1994, pp. 93–125.

[33] See R. Hélot, *La Bibliothèque bleue en Normandie*, Rouen: A. Lainé, 1928.

[34] See G. Pessiot, 'Cinq siècles d'édition rouennaise face au centralisme parisien', *Précis des travaux de l'Académie des sciences, belles-lettres et arts de Rouen*, Rouen: 1996, pp. 129–65.

seventeenth and eighteenth centuries, to base its success on this apparently unmanageable combination. It remains to be seen whether this city of the book, a city in the provinces but not a provincial one, can regain this subtle equilibrium, without sacrificing its dynamism in the process, or allowing its identity to be swallowed up by either provincial anonymity or the insidious suburbanization of the Lower Seine.

Further reading

General

M. Mollat (ed.), *Histoire de Rouen*, Toulouse: Privat, 1979.
J.-P. Bardet, *Rouen aux XVIIe et XVIIIe siècles: les mutations d'un espace social*, Paris: SEDES, 1983, 2 vols.

Monographs on printing and publishing (by period)

G. Lepreux, *Gallia typographica ou Répertoire biographique et chronologique de tous les imprimeurs de France ... Province de Normandie*, Paris: libr. H. Champion, 1912.
É.-B. Frère, *De l'imprimerie et de la librairie à Rouen dans les XVe et XVIe siècles, et de Martin Morin ...* , Rouen: A. Le Brument, 1843.
A.-R. Girard, 'Les incunables rouennais: imprimerie et culture au XVe siècle', *Revue française d'histoire du livre*, 53, Oct.–Dec. 1986, pp. 463–525.
P. Aquilon, *Bibliographie Normande. Bibliographie des ouvrages imprimés à Caen et à Rouen au XVIe siècle*, Baden-Baden: Koerner, 1968– , issues 8, 14, 22, 27 and 5, 6, 7, special issues of the *Bibliotheca bibliographica Aureliana. Répertoire bibliographique des livres imprimés en France au XVIe siècle*.
J.-D. Mellot, *L'Édition rouennaise et ses marchés (vers 1600–vers 1730): dynamisme provincial et centralisme parisien*, Paris: École des chartes; distributed by H. Champion, Paris; Droz, Geneva, 1998.
J. Quéniart, *L'Imprimerie et la librairie à Rouen au XVIIIe siècle*, Paris: Klinksieck, 1969.
É. Wauters, *Une presse de province pendant la Révolution française: journaux et journalistes Normands (1785–1800)*, Paris: éd. du CTHS, 1993.
M. Manson, *Rouen, le livre et l'enfant de 1700 à 1900. La production rouennaise de manuels et de livres pour l'enfance et la jeunesse* (exhibition, Musée national de l'education), Paris: Institut national de la recherche pédagogique, 1993.

CHAPTER TWO

Lyons' printers and booksellers from the fifteenth to the nineteenth century

Dominique Varry

Over a period of many years French historians have presented a number of important theses on national urban history in the form of monographs on individual cities. Among them are Goubert's study of seventeenth-century Beauvais, Perrot's Caen and Garden's Lyons in the eighteenth century.[1] This trend culminated, in the early 1980s, in the publication of a monumental *Histoire de la France urbaine*, edited by Georges Duby in five volumes.[2]

Surprisingly, however, even when these urban studies have dealt specifically with printers and booksellers, the links binding them to the cities where they lived and worked have not really been explored. Over the same period, a number of major academic works have been published on the history of the book, especially Henri-Jean Martin's *Livre, pouvoirs et société à Paris* which deals with seventeenth-century Paris, the works of Jean Quéniart on Rouen and the towns of western France in the eighteenth century, and René Moulinas' study of Avignon in the same period.[3] These books generally ignore the inscription of such an activity in the local urban landscape.

Moreover, there has been little work on the impact of these occupations on the urban economy and urban space, nor their effect on the development and reputation of the city. The first attempt to undertake a reflection on such matters was contained in two papers given by Henri-Jean Martin and Frédéric Barbier at a conference in Strasbourg in 1981: *Pouvoir, ville et société en*

---

[1] P. Goubert, *Beauvais et le Beauvaisis de 1600 à 1730. Contribution à l'histoire sociale de la France du XVIIe siècle*, Paris: SEVPEN, 1960; J.-C. Perrot, *Genèse d'une ville moderne Caen au XVIIIe siècle*, Paris The Hague: Mouton, 1975; M. Garden, *Lyon et les lyonnais au XVIIIe siècle*, Paris: Les Belles Lettres, 1970. See also: B. Lepetit, 'La ville moderne en France. Essai d'histoire immédiate', in J.-L. Biget and J.-C. Hervé (eds), *Panoramas urbains. Situation de l'histoire des villes*, Fontenay-aux-Roses, E.N.S. éditions Fontenay/Saint-Cloud, 1995, pp. 173–207.

[2] G. Duby (ed.), *Histoire de la France urbaine*, Paris: Le Seuil, 1980–85, 5 vols.

[3] H.-J. Martin, *Livre, pouvoirs et société à Paris au XVIIe siècle, 1598–1701*, Paris and Geneva: Droz, 1969 (English translation: *Print, Power and People ...*, London: Methuen, 1993); J. Quéniart, *L'Imprimerie et la librairie à Rouen au XVIIIe siècle*, Paris: Klincksieck, 1969, and *Culture et société urbaines dans la France de l'Ouest au XVIIIe siècle*, Paris: Klincksieck, 1978; R. Moulinas, *L'Imprimerie, la librairie et la presse à Avignon au XVIIIe siècle*, Grenoble: PUG, 1974.

Europe 1650–1750.[4] At around the same time two conferences were held in Paris, unfortunately unpublished, on the theme of '*Les espaces du livre*'. Here, some speakers, for the first time, looked at the organization of workshops and bookshops within urban space. The source material for this subject is difficult in a number of respects. It generally derives from inventories following death or bankruptcy, and is very variable in terms of quality and precision. My own work owes a great deal to the paper given by Jacques Rychner and Anne Sauvy at that conference: 'Espaces de l'atelier d'imprimerie au XVIIIe siècle', which has recently appeared in a book in honour of Henri-Jean Martin.[5] The present essay offers some considerations and reflections on the case of Lyons, building on a more specialised project of the Lyons book trade in the eighteenth century, a study based on biographical information on more than 700 persons involved in the authorized and prohibited book trade during that period.[6]

Printing and publishing: a secondary industry in an ancient city

Lyons is an old city, founded as a Roman colony in 43 BC. The Emperors Claudius and Caracalla were both born in the city, and since the days of the Roman empire it has been an important crossroads between southern Europe (Italy and Spain) and northern Europe (Flanders and the Rhineland). Capital of the Gauls in Roman times, it remains the second French city after Paris. It was always an important economic centre, and achieved greater economic significance with the development of fairs from the fifteenth century and the arrival of Italian bankers.[7] The seventeenth and eighteenth centuries saw the expansion of the silk industry, which had been introduced in 1536 and is still active today. In the middle of the eighteenth century, the city had about 3300

---

[4] H-J. Martin, 'Lecture et société dans la ville française, 1650–1789', in G. Livet and B. Vogler (eds), *Pouvoir, ville et société en Europe 1650–1750*, Paris: Ophrys, 1983, pp. 241–50; F. Barbier, 'Le pouvoir et la géographie du livre en France au XVIIIe siècle', in ibid., pp. 251–63.

[5] J. Rychner and A. Sauvy, 'Espaces de l'atelier d'imprimerie au XVIIIe siècle', in F. Barbier, A. Parent-Charon, F. Dupuigrenet Desroussilles, C. Jolly and D. Varry (eds), *Le Livre et l'historien. Etudes offertes en l'honneur du Professeur Henri-Jean Martin*, Geneva: Droz, 1997, pp. 291–318.

[6] *Les gens du livre à Lyon au XVIIIe siècle*, a project supported by the CNRS. See also: D. Varry, 'Round about the Rue Mercière: The 18th Century Lyon Bookfolk', SHARP conference, Cambridge, 3–8 July 1997, readable on: www.enssib.fr.; and *idem*, 'L'imprimerie et la librairie à Lyon au XIXe siècle', in J.-Y. Mollier (ed.), *Le Commerce de la librairie en France au XIXe siècle 1789–1914*, Paris: IMEC Editions and Editions de la Maison des sciences de l'Homme, 1997, pp. 61–9.

[7] R. Gascon, *Grand commerce et vie urbaine au XVIe siècle, environs de 1520–environs de 1580. Lyon et ses marchands*, Paris: SEVPEN, 1971.

silk-mercer masters. Both the French Revolution and the industrial revolution had negative effects on the silk industry in Lyons. Indeed, the French Revolution was an important step in the history of the city as a whole. The revolt of 1793 against the Convention and the republican government ended in destruction, bloodshed and executions.[8] The industrial revolution ruined many craftsmen, and the industry's problems during the nineteenth century led to the proletarian revolts of the 'Canuts', the silk workmen, in 1831 and 1834.

Lyons had around 20 000 inhabitants at the beginning of the sixteenth century, about 150 000 in 1789, 256 000 in 1851, 350 000 in 1871 and 558 000 in 1911. The town developed at the confluence of two rivers, the Saône and the Rhône. The hill of Fourvières constitutes its western boundary, and is the site of ruined Roman monuments and numerous monasteries. Lyons is bounded in the north by the hill of Croix-Rousse, which was only incorporated into the city in the middle of the nineteenth century. The Croix-Rousse hill was densely settled by silk-workers. Today, as in the past, Fourvières is known as the 'praying hill', and La Croix-Rousse as the 'working hill'. The city grew up first on the Fourvières hill and at its foot, on the right bank of the Saône river where the cathedral had been built. Then it spread into the peninsula formed by the junction of the two rivers. It spilled over onto the left bank of the Rhône only in the nineteenth century, and the suburbs of La Croix-Rousse, Vaise, Les Brotteaux and La Guillotière were incorporated into the city only in 1852. At the end of the eighteenth century that part of the left bank of the Rhône known as Les Brotteaux was a swampy empty place where the revolutionary army shot hundreds of Lyons inhabitants after the revolt of 1793.

The first printing press appeared in Lyons in 1473, three years after its introduction in Paris. From then until the end of the *ancien régime*, Lyons was the second most important centre of printing and publishing in France, after Paris and ahead of Rouen. Its most famous period was the sixteenth century, which is associated with the names of Etienne Dolet, Sébastien Gryphe, Jean de Tournes, and many others. After this period of splendour, printing in Lyons is generally held to have experienced a long-term decline up until the nineteenth century. This was a real decline, which was brought about by the constraints imposed by royal legislation and the part played by Paris printers, who reserved novelties and the works of fashionable authors for themselves. Nevertheless Lyons remained an important centre of the

---

[8] W. D. Edmonds, *Jacobinism and the Revolt of Lyon 1789–1793*, Oxford: Clarendon Press, 1990. The repercussions of this tragic event are still present in Lyons' identity and role in contemporary French political, economical and social life. This struggle has not yet been forgiven! See B. Benoit, *L'Identité politique de Lyon. Entre violences collectives et mémoire des élites 1786–1905*, Paris and Montreal: L'Harmattan, 1999.

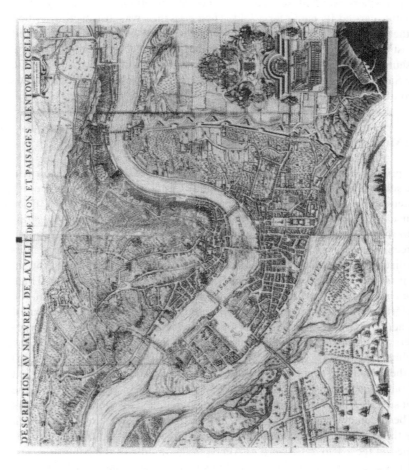

DESCRIPTION AV NATVREL DE LA VILLE DE LYON ET PAISAGES ALENTOVR DICELLE

2.1 Plan of Lyons, 1659, by Maupin (photo Bibliothèque municipale de Lyons).

printing and publishing industries throughout this period. Although printers and publishers were of secondary economic importance to the city, their activities carried its name far afield. Their presence was also well inscribed on the urban landscape. Today, printers and publishers have disappeared almost entirely from Lyons. The memory of their trade is kept alive by the Museum of Printing and Banking, which is situated in the heart of the city, near Saint-Nizier the printers' parish, and is the most important French museum of this kind.

Rue Mercière and the urban landscape

The printers' and booksellers' homes and places of work were inscribed precisely in Lyons' urban space. From the fifteenth to the nineteenth century printers and booksellers lived in the parish of Saint-Nizier, at the heart of the peninsula. Their workshops were in the rue Mercière, a street running parallel to the Saône. There is evidence of the existence of this street from the thirteenth century, and in the Middle Ages it was the most important commercial district in the town. A few decades ago it was abandoned to prostitution, but it is now a pedestrian area, lined with cosmopolitan restaurants. There were also printers' workshops on the neighbouring streets: the rue Tupin, rue Confort, rue Ferrandière, rue Saint Dominique, and rue de la Grenette. Out of 394 addresses of eighteenth-century printers, booksellers, binders and typesetters, 100 were located in the rue Mercière, and 125 were housed in the neighbouring streets, between the monasteries of the Jacobin (Dominican) and the Franciscan friars. Other addresses are scattered throughout the present first and second districts of the city, which are also at the heart of the peninsula. By the nineteenth century this geographical distribution of printers had been somewhat modified. In 1823, three printers settled in St Jean ward, near the cathedral, at the foot of the hill of Fourvières, and two bookshops opened in the aristocratic ward of Ainay, in the middle of the peninsula. The first bookshops to be established in the suburbs opened later: in 1838 at La Guillotière, in 1840 at Vaise, and in 1841 at the Croix-Rousse. But all these implantations remained isolated.

For some five centuries the rue Mercière and the other streets around it constituted a sort of 'village of the book' in the heart of the city. The bookshops themselves generally opened on the ground floors of buildings, while the printing workshops tended to be upstairs. We have few details about the internal organization of the bookshops, except that they were usually divided into two parts by a wooden counter. The bookshelves were usually behind the counter, while in front of it there was generally a large table and benches where customers could sit down to have a look at the books, and chat. We know, for example, that in 1730 Barthélémy Martin's bookshop in the Grande rue Mercière contained 'a walnut bank counter with two drawers, a walnut bench, a chair, a walnut coffer, a fir-wood writing desk'.[9] A large number of the printing workshops were located on the upper floors of the same buildings: often on the second or third floor, and sometimes even higher, on the fifth or sixth, and in the attics under the roofs – which is not the best place for heavy machines such as printing presses, especially in the confined spaces such as these small rooms in narrow apartments. In 1701, for example, Rolin Glaize's workshop was located on the fourth floor of a house in the Buisson, while Jean Goy's was in a similar sixth-floor room in rue Grolée. In 1702 César Chappuis owned two printing presses on the third floor of a house located in the rue Bellecordière; and in 1741, the workshop belonging to the widow of Nicolas Barret was located in the rue 'Thomassin, at the Fat Capon, house belonging to Lallemant, on the fifth floor'. Most of the binders had their workshops in their own lodgings, again generally on the upper floors. They were known as 'garret craftsmen', who were said to work 'en chambre'. Similar arrangements were to be found in Paris and the same was probably true of the bookbinding trade in other French cities.

One of the principal problems of all these workers, then, was the lack of space. Many of them had their bookshop in one house, their workshop located on one of the upper floors of another one, and their lodgings in a third. In addition, many of them moved frequently from one place to another, and sometimes did so several times during the space of a single career. Moreover, they also needed space to store their books and printed sheets before they were put on sale, and they often took advantage of the hospitality of the neighbouring monasteries, which were willing to rent out some of their buildings as warehouses. (As we shall see, these monasteries were often used to hide pirated or prohibited books.) Finally, the buildings of the rue Mercière also housed the large number of journeymen employed by the master printers. Clearly, the book trades were well inscribed in the urban space. They lived and worked around the rue Mercière, and they were parishioners of St Nizier. The booksellers' and book-binders' brotherhood was at the Jacobin (Dominican) monastery, and that of the printers was at the Carmelite monastery. These two monasteries, along with that of the Franciscan friars, marked the boundaries of the 'book district'.

This official and visible geography concealed another more secret one, that of the prohibited book. It is well known that, in order to survive, Lyons printers had to print pirated and prohibited books, which were published under false addresses.[10] Moreover, Lyons was also an important crossroads

---

[9] Rhône departemental Archives: BP 2121, after death inventory, 6th September 1730.

[10] D. Varry: 'La diffusion sous le manteau: la Société typographique de Neuchâtel et les Lyonnais', in F. Barbier, S. Juratic and D. Varry (eds), *L'Europe et le livre. Réseaux et pratiques du négoce de librairie XVIe–XIXe siècles*, Paris: Klincksieck, 1996, pp. 309–32; 'Voltaire et les

for prohibited books coming from Avignon and for publications which had been smuggled into the country from Switzerland (Geneva and Neuchâtel) despite the vigilance of the police. Pirated and prohibited books that had been printed in Lyons were often hidden in the monasteries. We know, from the evidence of numerous house searches for such contraband conducted during the seventeenth and eighteenth centuries at the request of Paris booksellers whose goods had been pirated, that these were also very secure hiding places, as the police were reluctant to enter monasteries. When the authorities did decide to undertake such searches, the superior of the house was generally absent, the brothers themselves did not know anything, it took a long time to get from room to room, the keys to rooms were frequently lost, and so on. All these delays gave the monks time to hide the contraband elsewhere, often in imaginative places. In 1694, for example, they used the coffin in a chapel burial vault to hide such books.

For smaller quantities of prohibited books, the printers often used the services of friends or neighbours, who would take them home or store them in their cellars. Who would think, for example, of looking for banned books on the premises of a butcher or a baker? Although we know that such hiding places were used, however, we only know about those cases that are revealed to us from the files of the police, and nothing of the scale and frequency of the practice. In the case of illegal printed material that was being imported into Lyons from outside, the main difficulty was to avoid being stopped by the customs officials on the routes into the city. Pirated material from Avignon that was ultimately destined for Paris tended to arrive by road via the small town of Vienne, to the south of Lyons. There it was received by the Sisters of Mercy, or by an innkeeper, divided into smaller parcels, and taken by boat on the regular Rhône river service to Givors or Lyons, which meant that the true origins of the material could not be detected. In a 1763 report to Paris, Bourgelat, the inspector of the book trade in Lyons, wrote:

> Skilful at evading my scrutiny, they take advantage of the facilities offered by the Rhône. Their bales are not brought as far as the city, but are unloaded at Givors or in some other neighbouring place. From there, they cross to the Forez, from the Forez to Roanne, and from Roanne to their destination.[11]

---

imprimeurs-libraires lyonnais', in U. Kölving and C. Mervaud (eds), *Voltaire et ses combats. Actes du colloque international Oxford Paris 1994*, Oxford: The Voltaire Foundation, 1997, vol. 1, pp. 483–507; 'De la Bastille à Bellecour: une "canaille littéraire", Taupin Dorval', in Barbier et al., *Le Livre et l'historien*, pp. 571–82; and 'Le livre clandestin à Lyon au XVIIIe siècle, in *La Lettre clandestine*, no. 6, 1997, pp. 243–52.

[11] L. Moulé, 'Rapport de Cl. Bourgelat sur le commerce de la librairie et de l'imprimerie à Lyon en 1763', in *Revue d'histoire de Lyon*, 1914, vol. 13, pp. 51–65, Bibliothèque nationale de France: manuscrit français 22128, f° 291–302.

The Lyons suburbs were used to evade the city customs and police. Books destined for Paris had to pass through La Croix-Rousse, Vaise, or Saint-Clair to the north of the city, while on the left bank of the Rhône material destined for the south of France, especially Protestant prints, passed through La Guillotière. In 1778, Revol, a forwarding agent wrote to the Neuchâtel Typographical Society:

> ... those [bales] for Paris must be unloaded at the Croix-Rousse, and from there they will be transported via Châlon avoiding Lyons ... those for southern France will have to cross half a league outside Lyons where Mr Révolle will have them taken and sent on to their addresses.[12]

It was in suburban inns that deals were made and prohibited material was passed on. All kinds of discreet rendezvous were arranged in such places, between people involved in all manner of smuggling activity. In August 1747, for example, three women were arrested on the Guillotière bridge as they attempted to smuggle in prohibited books hidden under their skirts.[13] The books had been printed in Avignon, and the three women had obtained them in the Guillotière suburb, in an inn called 'Le Logis de la table ronde'. In his correspondence with the Neuchâtel Typographical Society,[14] Revol referred to bales of books arriving from Switzerland that were to be stored by a certain Boutary, innkeeper at Saint-Clair, and later by his successor, a man by the name of Mottet. This geography of illicit practices was as important as the visible and official geography of the printing trades.[15] The situation was similar in the suburbs of Paris and Versailles, although it has not yet really been studied. Indeed, in urban history generally, the part played by the suburb has too often been underestimated.

Printers and booksellers as cultural and social mediators

By producing books and thereby providing reading matter, printers and book-sellers were, of course, mediators of culture between authors and their readers. But this cultural role extended beyond their commercial activity. Several of them also participated in the city's cultural life in other more formal ways. For instance, the printers Aimé Delaroche and Jean-Marie Bruyset belonged to Lyons Academy, which was founded in the eighteenth century. (Indeed, the

---

[12] Neuchâtel public and university Library, mss. 1059, J.F. Favarger's journey notebook.

[13] Rhône departemental Archives: 1C 251. On this particular case, see: D. Varry, 'Women in the 18th Century Lyons Booktrade', paper presented at the SHARP conference held at the Simon Fraser University, Vancouver, 15–22 July 1998, readable on: <http://www.enssib.fr>.

[14] Neuchâtel public and university Library, mss. 1205: 3 May 1778, 29 March 1779.

[15] I have developed this question in 'Une géographie de l'illicite: les espaces du livre à Lyons au temps des Lumières', La Lettre clandestine, no. 8, 1999, pp. 113–33.

latter was also a member of the Berlin Academy.) Others were freemasons. We know of seven masons among the most famous of the eighteenth century printers: Jean-Marie Bruyset (1749–1817), his brother Pierre-Marie Bruyset (born 1745, executed 1793), Aimé Delaroche (1715–1801), his son-in-law Jacques-Julien Vatar (1727–77) and his grandson Aimé Vatar-Delaroche (executed 1793), Claude-André Faucheux (born 1741, executed 1793), Jean-André Périsse-Duluc (1738–1800). Two of the newcomers who settled in Lyons during the Revolution were also freemasons at the beginning of the nineteenth century: Michel-Alexandre Pelzin (1751–1828), and Jean-Baptiste Kindelem. The number of freemasons in the profession during the nineteenth century has not yet been established but may well have been higher. Membership was often a family matter: as, for example, in the case of the brothers Jean-Marie and Pierre-Marie Bruyset; or that of Aimé Delaroche, his son-in-law Jacques-Julien Vatar and his grandson Aimé Vatar-Delaroche. The Bruysets and the printers' syndic Périsse-Duluc were very close to Jean-Baptiste Willermoz, founder of the sect of the 'Illuminés martinistes', who made Lyons a European capital of freemasonry.[16]

An important social function was fulfilled by the *cabinets de lecture* (reading rooms), which sprang up in the second half of the eighteenth century. The first one in France opened in Lyons in 1759, and a second followed in 1764. Neither of them survived for longer than a few years. Two new reading-rooms were active about 1770, and a third opened at the beginning of the Revolution. Their number increased in the nineteenth century, to reach a maximum of 34 in 1899. There were still 11 in use in 1950.[17] Readers who used the *cabinets de lecture* would not only read the current newspapers and the most recently published best-sellers (which were available to borrow); they also stayed to chat. These *cabinets* appear to have been an important conduit of information of all kinds, including the politically subversive. The owner of one of the reading rooms, Pierre Cellier, was executed in 1793, accused of having organized counter-revolutionary lectures in his shop, under the guise of public readings.

Another way in which booksellers were important in the diffusion of information was in their role in the distribution of national and international newspapers. This function took on a new dimension when Aimé Delaroche published the first French local paper, a weekly, in 1750: the *Affiches de Lyon, annonces et avis divers*. This was an advertising paper for people who were looking, for example, for a seat on a coach, or for work and accommodation; and for those who had something to sell. This exchange of information

---

[16] A. Joly, *Un Mystique lyonnais et les secrets de la Franc-Maçonnerie. Jean-Baptiste Willermoz 1730–1824*, Paris: Demeter, 1986.

[17] L. Pabot, 'Le Temps des Nouveautés. Une librairie sur la place lyonnaise de 1888 à nos jours', MA thesis, Université de Lyon 2 1994, p. 62.

passed through the special office which Delaroche opened in the city. He is today considered to have been the creator of the French local periodical press.[18] Reading these *Affiches* gives us important information about the part that printers and booksellers played in the different events of daily life in the city. This role had always existed, of course, but the existence of the publication gives us a better sense of how it worked in practice. Not least, booksellers themselves used the *Affiches* to advertise their own professional activities. In 1760, for example, Los Rios advertised newspapers from France and Bern along with the *Mercure de France* for 18 livres per year. But we also learn from such adverts of the more unusual activities of the printers:

> Mr de Los Rios sells engravings, cuttings, geographical maps, and large and small sizes of wall-paper, which he will undertake to hang for private customers. He offers copy writing services for the public and will even write letters for those who do not know how to write. For the convenience of the public, he is authorized to receive advertisements and to give out addresses to those who do not want to take the trouble of going up to the advertising office.

Booksellers were sometimes used as intermediaries for people who wanted to sell their own books:

> A private owner would like to divest himself of the large Moreri *Dictionary* in ten volumes. Those wishing to see it should contact Mr Réguilliat ... where they will be able to inspect the first and last volumes. They will be given the name of the person who owns this book. (1763)

Moreover booksellers were sometimes used as middlemen for products outside their professional field. In 1763, Miss Ollier, a bookseller, announced that she sold a printed remedy against rabies. In the same year, another bookseller offered to obtain each week for customers a special pomade against haemorrhoids from Saint André en Dauphiné. Some journeymen did not hesitate to give their employer's address for their own independent commercial activities. For example, the following short advertisement appeared in 1760: 'Mr Courcelles, typographer with the printer and bookseller Mr Réguilliat of rue Raisin at the sign of the two vipers, is authorized to distribute Mr Pitra's patent ointment for women.'

Like other tradesmen, the booksellers were also used to provide various services for people in the neighbourhood. For example, the keys of flats which were for sale or to let were often left at the nearest bookshop, where visitors could pick them up. An advertisement of 1763, for instance, tells us

---

[18] M. Gasc, *La Naissance de la presse périodique locale à Lyon 'les Affiches de Lyon, annonces et avis divers'*, Villeurbanne, mémoire ENSB, 1977; N. Dumont, *Aimé Delaroche, imprimeur lyonnais du XVIIIème siècle et la presse locale*, Villeurbanne, Mémoire ENSB, 1982.

that the keys to a flat in a house in the rue Mercière could be obtained either at the house itself from Miss Vaguet, or from Mr Jacquenot *fils*, the bookseller opposite, or from Mr Bruyset-Ponthus, another bookseller in rue Saint Dominique.[19]

Such snippets of information are of course of very little importance in themselves, but given the frequency with which they occur they constitute a source of great value to the historian, even for the period before the emergence of the local press when the situation was probably the same. They remind us that a bookshop was not only a place for trade, but also a place of conviviality, where everyone could enter to see and buy books, to meet other people and chat about things, to hear the latest news, to negotiate private business, or even to buy an old wives' remedy. Perhaps even more than in other places used for commercial activity, bookshops were important sites of sociability at the heart of a busy and populous city.

Political and municipal involvement

The history of France in the sixteenth century had been marked by bloody religious conflicts, and those printers who had chosen Protestantism had been forced to flee. Such was the case of the De Tournes for example, who settled in Geneva and were not allowed to come back to Lyons until the eighteenth century, and then on condition that they agreed to sell only Latin and other classical texts. Others had chosen the Roman Catholic camp, and become involved in the *Ligue*, in which they played an important part, as is evident from their printed production.[20] The Revolution, too, marked a bloody rupture with grave consequences in the history of Lyons.[21] Workers and journeymen of all professions, including those in the book trade, joined the movement led by Chalier and took vengeance on their former masters. One of the best known of them is Jean-Joseph Destéfanis, a Piedmontese who denounced his employer, Charles-François Millanois in 1793 as a troop commander in the siege of Lyons. A judgement of the temporary Commission of 13 December 1793 awarded him Millanois' printing shop, which he ran for a year, signing his production 'Destéfanis-le-sans-culotte', before returning home to practise

---

[19] Lyons public library: *Affiches de Lyon, annonces et avis divers*. Examples taken from the years 1760–63.

[20] H. Baudrier (ed.), *Bibliographie lyonnaise. Recherches sur les imprimeurs, libraires, relieurs et fondeurs de lettres de Lyon au XVIe siècle. Première série*, reprinted Paris: F. De Nobele, 1964, 12 vols.

[21] W. D. Edmonds, *Jacobinism and the revolt of Lyon 1789–1793*; E. Gourvitch, 'Les Imprimeurs-libraires lyonnais et la Révolution française', MA thesis, Université de Lyon 2, 1995. For a comparison, see C. Hesse, *Publishing and Cultural Politics in Revolutionary Paris 1789–1810*, Berkeley, CA: University of California Press, 1991.

his trade in Milan. The 1793 siege was accompanied by numerous acts of destruction, including that of the Delamollière printing works. It was also followed by many executions. Among the 1684 victims there were seven printers and booksellers, which amounted to a quarter of all the masters, and around 15 binding and papermaking journeymen and print workers.

In the nineteenth century, the political involvement of Lyons printers was marked mainly by the part they played as the publishers of political newspapers. This was especially the case of Chanoine, who founded *Le Progrès* in 1859, a local daily newspaper which is still published today. Under the *Ancien Régime*, a certain number of important printers and booksellers were involved in local government. From the beginning of the sixteenth century, the city had been divided into 36 wards called '*Pennons*'. Their number was reduced to 28 in 1746. Many printers and booksellers paid to hold the functions of lieutenant, captain or colonel of St Nizier *Pennon*, and to command 100 men in the city militia. This was expensive, because they had to buy their own arms and equipment, but it gave them the opportunity of being known both by the people of the city and by the municipal and royal magistrates. After the 1793 revolt against the republican government, about half a dozen printers were executed for having held such military positions.

This was the first step of a *cursus honorum* towards municipal responsibilities. The second step could either be the position of 'syndic' of the printers, or that of rector of one of the two city hospitals. Here again, the leading printers and booksellers were keen to be elected to such offices. This was certainly the case of seven of them during the seventeenth century.[22] In fact, only very few, the richest, could enter the *Consulat*, the town council. Municipal responsibilities brought with them, for the office-holders and their heirs, entry to the ranks of the nobility albeit at the lowest rank, which was known derisively as the '*noblesse de cloches*' – but it was membership of the nobility nevertheless. The first bookseller entered the *Consulat* in 1610. Of the 200 municipal magistrates of the seventeenth century, only six were booksellers. In the eighteenth century, there were only three out of 182 magistrates.[23] This is very few, given that we know of some 700 people in the book trade during this period; and it shows how closed this elite was. After their term of office these men generally gave up work and lived on their rural estates. This was true of the Cardons, for example, perhaps the most famous Lyons printers of the seventeenth century. Among the ennobled Lyons booksellers, we should also mention the Anisson family, whose members left the city to become the directors of the *Imprimerie royale* in Paris at the beginning of the eighteenth century.

---

[22] S. Legay, 'Un milieu socio-professionnel: les libraires lyonnais au XVIIe siècle', PhD thesis, Université de Lyon 2, 1995, p. 443.

[23] M. Garden, *Lyon et les lyonnais au XVIIIe siècle*, pp. 501–2.

Finally, a special place must be assigned to the printer-cum-bookseller André Périsse-Duluc.[24] Son and brother of some of the most important booksellers in the city, he was born in 1738 and died in 1800. He opened his bookshop in 1760, bought a printing workshop in 1766, was assistant to the syndical chamber in 1774 and 1775, and had been syndic from 1776 to 1790. He was a freemason, close to Willermoz with whom he was in correspondence while sitting on the National Assembly in 1789; he had been administrator of the Charity hospital, and was well on his way to joining the *Consulat* when the Revolution broke out. He was then elected second of the eight deputies of the Third Estate of Lyons to the Estates General. His political career ended in 1791, when he returned home. He was designated a counsellor to the Rhône *Préfecture* a few months before he died in 1800.

As we can see, the richest and most famous printers and booksellers took their place in municipal affairs, along with their fellow-citizens and representatives of the other trades in the city, throughout the centuries. This was, of course, proof of their involvement in the daily life of the city. It was also a real opportunity for some of them to climb the social ladder and to enter the hereditary nobility, which was an aspiration shared by all ambitious commoners.

The transformations of the nineteenth century

The nineteenth century is still a little-known period in the history of the book in Lyons.[25] The Revolution constituted a profound rupture with the period of the *ancien régime* and its organization in corporations. In 1789 Lyons had 13 printing works and 14 bookshops. Although it is difficult to follow the developments, because of the non appearance of the *Almanach de Lyon* between 1792 and 1796, the period was characterized by a major renewal in the

---

[24] E. H. Lemay, *Dictionnaire des constituants 1789–1791*, Paris: Universitas 1991, vol. 2, p. 743; T. Tackett, *Becoming a Revolutionary. The Deputies of the French national Assembly and the Emergence of a revolutionary Culture 1789–1790*, Princeton, NJ: Princeton University Press, 1996 (French translation: *Par la volonté du Peuple. Comment les députés de 1789 sont devenus révolutionnaires*, Paris: Albin Michel, 1997).

[25] D. Varry, 'L'imprimerie et la librairie à Lyon au XIXe siècle'; L. Pabot, 'Le passage de la librairie "contrôlée" à la librairie "libérée" à Lyon 1870–1900, in J.-Y. Mollier (ed.), *Le Commerce de la librairie en France au XIXe siècle 1789–1914*, Paris: IMEC Editions and Editions de la Maison des sciences de l'Homme, 1997, pp. 71–80; B. Béguet, *L'Imprimerie et la librairie à Lyon, 1800–1850*, Villeurbanne, mémoire ENSB, 1986; L. Guillo, *Louis-Benoît Perrin et Alfred-Louis Perrin, imprimeurs à Lyon, 1823–1865–1883*, Villeurbanne, mémoire ENSB, 1986; M. Audin, *Somme typographique, sixième volume. L'imprimerie à Lyon aux XVIIIe et XIXe siècles*, forthcoming edition at Lyons Printing Museum, by A. Marshall; A. Vingtrinier, *Histoire de l'imprimerie à Lyon de l'origine jusqu'à nos jours*, Lyons, Vingtrinier, 1894, though obsolescent, remains useful.

ownership of printing works and bookselling establishments. Numerous new-comers seized the opportunity to set up in the city, often for only a short period of activity. Of the 15 print shops established after 1790, six rapidly disappeared. The same was true of four of the 12 new bookshops. No doubt the siege had something to do with this phenomenon.

Amongst the newcomers, four of the 15 printers and three of the 12 booksellers had been in business elsewhere before. Mistral had been a printer in Montélimar, Kindelem in Bellay, Lambert-Gentot in Vienne. Robert and Gauthier had been book- and paper-sellers in Bourg-en-Bresse, and opened a shop in Belfort in 1781. Destéfanis had been a journeyman with Delaroche-Millanois (before denouncing the latter). Jean-Théophile Reymann had served his bookselling apprenticeship in Leipzig and worked as a journeyman in Nuremberg and then Lyons, where he had lived for 12 years before opening his business in 1792.

In 1800 Lyons had 16 printing works and 10 bookshops. A decade later the introduction of the *brevet* system in France altered this situation. The geo-graphical concentration of printing and bookselling remained firmly between Bellecour and les Terreaux, and in particular on the rue Mercière. However, in 1823 there were three printing works in St Jean and one other on the right bank of the Rhône. The d'Ainay district had two bookshops. This trade was absent from the right bank of the Rhône and the slopes of the Croix-Rousse. In 1842 there were only two printers in St Jean. The others, like the booksell-ers, were based in the traditional districts of the peninsula. The first establishment of bookselling in the *faubourgs* was relatively late: 1838 in La Guillotière, 1840 in Vaise, 1841 in the Croix-Rousse.

In 1810 the city had 19 active printers: seven 'hereditary printers' dating from the *ancien régime* (Ballanche, Barret, Bruyset, Cutty, Leroy, Tournachon-Mollin, Périsse); eight printing works set up during the Revolutionary period (Esnault, Kindelem, Lambert-Gentot, Maillet, Mistral, Roger, Rolland, Rusand[26]); and four created after 1800 (Boget, Boursy, Brunet, Pelzin). These workshops had 96 printing presses and employed 176 workers of whom 76 were typographers; 18 of these were authorised and received a *brevet* on 9 July 1811. A distinction was made between 'maintained printers' and 'toler-ated printers', whose works were to close at their death. The aim of this policy was to reduce the number of establishments to 12, the *ancien régime* level. A delay and compensation terms were envisaged to allow the heirs of 'tolerated' printers to find another profession. These were the poorest busi-nesses: Boget, Rolland, Esnault (closed by 1812), Boursy, Brunet, Mistral.

Of the 44 printers' *brevets* delivered between 1812 and 1849, all but four were not the renewal of an existing one. Two of these new authorizations

---

[26] Rusand's father was only a bookseller in 1789.

concerned the *faubourgs*: Bajat in La Guillotière (1831), Lepagnez in La Croix-Rousse (1839). The two others met resistance from those already in place and were granted only as a result of political circumstances. Chanoine, in 1846, was backed by a conservative lobby: he set up the newspaper *Le Progrès* in 1859. The second, Joseph Rey, in February 1848, was being rewarded for his support of the February government. Over the same period two *brevets* were withdrawn, also for highly political reasons: that of the liberal Mistral in 1823 and that of the widow Madame Ayné in 1850, whose workshop had been used by ultra progressive republicans in 1848 and 1849.

It is also worth noting the case of two lithographic printers who obtained *brevets* as typographers after several years of activity. The reverse also occurred, as eight typographers also took on a lithographic *brevet* between 1820 and 1849.

The number of bookshops, for its part, was increasing. The *Almanach de Lyon* listed 29 bookshops in 1815. At the beginning of the 1830s there were 46 in the city, well above the national average: 1 for every 4000 inhabitants as against 1 for every 18 000 nationally. A watershed seems to have been reached in 1850, when 22 *brevets* expired and 27 new ones were created. The *brevet* system was also progressively imposed on reading rooms (three in 1789, 26 in 1813, 29 in 1842) although there were still resisters (nine in 1842) who refused to accept it. (As the period between 1850 and 1870 has not yet been researched, one cannot yet go beyond this observation.)

These developments also had a social dimension. Between 1811 and 1849, 63 typographers' *brevets* and 155 booksellers' *brevets* (32 to printers) were issued to 180 individuals (63 printers and printer-booksellers, 123 booksellers). Almost half of these were not originally from Lyons but from neighbouring *départements*: Loire, Isère, Drôme, Ain, Hautes-Alpes. Bruno Béguet has established the social origins of 47 printers and 85 booksellers:[27] 30 per cent of printers and 10 per cent of booksellers were born into the business; 33 per cent of printers and 17 per cent of booksellers were the sons of manufacturers or wealthy traders; 7 per cent of printers and 39 per cent of booksellers came from an artisan or shopkeeping background; and 10 per cent of printers and 15 per cent of booksellers were sons of peasants (labourers and manual workers). However, 64 per cent of printers and 15 per cent of booksellers had already worked in the book trades before obtaining their *brevet* and setting up on their own. As was the case under the *ancien régime*, we see several cases of entry into the book milieu through marriage. The most notable example is undoubtedly that of Louis Babeuf, Gracchus' grandson, who married the daughter of the bookseller Jacques Régnier and carried on the business from 1826 to 1835 before setting up in Paris.

---

[27] B. Béguet, *L'Imprimerie et la librairie à Lyon*, p. 18

The pull of the capital at a time when the modern figure of the publisher was about to emerge no doubt contributed to the decline of book production in Lyons. The biggest and most dynamic of the Lyons printers and booksellers opened branches in Paris. This was true of Rusand, Périsse, Pélagaud, Bohaire and Babeuf. The Périsses opened a Paris branch as early as 1812:[28] it moved several times, had various directors and experienced mixed fortunes before being taken over by Mignard in 1913. Pélagaud, Rusand's successor since 1835, opened a Paris branch in 1854, first in the rue St Pères, then rue Tournon until its closure around 1880. In 1883 the Pélagaud business was bought up by the company Vitte and Perrussel. The history of the relations between the Paris branches and their head offices in Lyons has yet to be written. It is a difficult task because most of the relevant archives have disappeared. The shift of interests to Paris is worth noting however. To maintain their position these big Lyons printer-booksellers found themselves obliged to establish a presence in Paris. They had made religious books their speciality.[29] In this field the old businesses dating from the *ancien régime* dominated, with Périsse and Rusand-Pélagaud. The output of these two houses, published by Claude Savart, shows that they were national leaders in the field of religious books.[30]

The most important print workshop of the period was undoubtedly Rusand: it had seven presses in 1810, 19 in 1814 and 27 in 1824. Taken over by Pélagaud in 1835 it boasted '20 presses in operation, sometimes 25, as well as two mechanical presses'. Pélagaud was one of the main producers of the *Annales de le propagation de la foi*, a bi-monthly publication of 60–80 pages in octavo, published from 1822 to 1933. This journal had several foreign-language editions and circulated throughout Catholic Europe.[31] Other printers in Lyons were reduced to an output of local and regional interest. At the middle of the century the printing trade employed just under 200 persons and operated 83 presses, of which only 12 were mechanical. The suppression of *brevets*, by a decree of 10 September 1870, brought about new opportunities. Nathalie Lacroix has shown that in the period between 1870 and 1900 the number of printers in Lyons grew dramatically.[32] Lithographers remained important, and their number increased from 44 to 64. The number of typographic printers doubled, from 20 in 1869 to 39 in 1880 (the date when the occupation of printer-bookseller disappeared from the *annuaires*). The pass-

---

[28] Etienne Périsse until 1834, then André Périsse until 1860 owned a *brevet* for Paris.

[29] C. Savart, *Les Catholiques en France au XIXe siècle. Le témoignage du livre religieux*, Paris: Beauchesne, 1985.

[30] *Idem*, pp. 117–23.

[31] D. Varry, 'Les éditeurs lyonnais, les Jésuites et la connaissance de l'Asie à l'époque moderne et contemporaine', in *Cahiers d'histoire*, **XL** (3–4), 1995, pp. 211–27.

[32] N. Lacroix, *Les Imprimeurs lyonnais 1870–1900*, Villeurbanne, DEA ENSB, 1991.

ing of liberal legislation in 1881 brought about a new increase in the number of typographic workshops, which reached a total of 80 in 1900. Some workshops handled lithography, typography and etching. However, this fragmentation is indicative of the fragility of these businesses, only 13 of which were active throughout the period from 1870 to 1900. Mostly they were limited to local jobs, posters, small brochures, and local and religious periodicals. Apart from Joseph de Maistre no major author was now published in Lyons. The most important printers of this period included *L'Imprimerie catholique* also known as *Oeuvre de Saint Paul*, founded in 1872, which had the unusual distinction of employing young women; *L'Association typographique lyonnaise*, founded in 1866, which became a workers' co-operative in 1930, and still exists today; and the *Imprimerie Rey*, that celebrated its bicentenary in 1991.[33] This firm is the old Barret business of the *ancien régime*, that passed to François Pitrat in 1866 and then in 1891 to Alexandre Rey. In 1868 Pitrat launched a new publication of the Office for Propagation of the Faith: *Les Missions catholiques*, an illustrated weeky in quarto, that was published into the twentieth century. His workshop was one of the two most important of the period.

These few success stories should not disguise the deep and irreversible decline into which printing in Lyons had fallen. The sixteenth century was undoubtedly its golden age. From then onwards observations by members of the profession continually regret its decline. This decline has to be seen as relative in the seventeenth and eighteenth centuries when, in addition to production for local consumption, Lyons was responsible for a large number of forgeries and 'sensitive material', published under false addresses, only a small number of which can be identified. In contrast, the nineteenth century, when the largest establishments moved to Paris and the fragmented network of miniscule workshops no longer printed important works, saw the final bursts of publishing activity in the city.

Spreading the city's name far and wide

Despite its five centuries of tradition, Lyons is no longer an important centre of printing. Today the rue Mercière is full of restaurants, but it is still haunted by the memories of the men and women who lived and worked there. As in the case of Paris, and perhaps Rouen – certainly more than for other French cities where their number was smaller – the printers and booksellers of

---

[33] N. Lacroix, ibid., Lyons municipal Archives: 300 957, *Historique de la fondation de l'Imprimerie catholique*, Lyons, 1878; Lyons municipal Archives: 701 200, *Association typographique lyonnaise 1866–1966*; and J. Etevenaux, *1791–1991 Bicentenaire des établissements A. Rey éditeur imprimeur*, Lyons: Rey, 1991.

Lyons, along with the city's bankers, silk-workers and other craftsmen, spread the name of the city abroad, throughout Europe and beyond to South America and to the far East. They left their mark on the urban space and the city landscape. The geography of printing in Lyons was complex, from the peninsula to the suburbs, from the heart of the city to the rest of the world, from the lawful to the illicit. The cultural role of the printers was important, of course, but so was their function as social mediators and providers of everyday information and services. Although the nineteenth century saw the end of their secular activity, and with that the conclusion of a golden age, the representation of their story as one of long decline from the sixteenth century onwards is open to question. After all, the best of these printers and booksellers, albeit a very small minority, played their part in the running of the city, served their fellow citizens and rose to the nobility. As a profession they constituted a small group in a populous, dynamic and expanding city, but over the centuries they left their imprint on the city's destiny. And their names, whether still famous or almost forgotten, printed on the title-pages of books that can be seen in libraries throughout the world, remain bound to the city they served.

Further reading

F. Barbier, S. Juratic and D. Varry (eds), *L'Europe et le livre. Réseaux et pratiques du négoce de librairie XVIe–XIXe siècles*, Paris: Klincksieck, 1996.

B. Benoit, *L'Identité politique de Lyon. Entre violences collectives et mémoire des élites 1786–1905*, Paris and Montreal: L'Harmattan, 1999.

M. Garden, *Lyon et les lyonnais au XVIIIe siècle*, Paris: Les Belles Lettres, 1970.

C. Hesse, *Publishing and Cultural Politics in Revolutionary Paris 1789–1810*, Berkeley, CA: University of California Press, 1991.

G. Livet and B. Vogler (eds), *Pouvoir, ville et société en Europe 1650–1750*, Paris: Ophrys, 1983.

J.-Y. Mollier (ed.), *Le Commerce de la librairie en France au XIXe siècle 1789–1914*, Paris: IMEC Editions and Editions de la Maison des sciences de l'Homme, 1997, pp. 61–9.

CHAPTER THREE

Gavarni's Parisian population reproduced

David W. S. Gray

A diary entry made by Gavarni in 1828, at the age of 24, reads: 'Every time I come back from travelling around Paris I am persuaded that it has yet to be described, and tormented by the desire to try doing it.' This comment is an index of his life's work graphically recording the life of the city.[1] By his death nearly 40 years later, Gavarni had produced and published something in the order of 10 000 pictures, almost all of them being pictures of social types from every Parisian milieu.[2] During his lifetime he was often compared to his friend Balzac, though one critic pointed out later that Gavarni's work constituted rather more a *comédie Parisienne* than a *comédie humaine*.[3] He was usually bracketed with Daumier as one of the most important producers of social imagery in the middle years of the century, from 1830 to 1860. He was avidly collected by artists, such as Degas, who had more than 2000 of his lithographs. Much of his work was first published in lithographic form, though some substantial sequences consisted of drawings made specifically to be engraved on wood by craftsmen engravers. This essay will show how

---

[1] Edmond and Jules de Goncourt, *Gavarni, L'homme et l'œuvre, Postface de M. Gustave Geffroy*, Paris: Flammarion, with Pasquelle, Edition définitive publiée sous la direction de l'Académie Goncourt, 19 (first published 1873) 1925, p. 57. At another point, Gavarni writes of his aim using an interesting neologism: 'Je veux tachygraphier' ('I want to draw and record with speed.') (p. 56).

[2] There has been no systematic attempt to republish all this work in the twentieth century, though parts of it have appeared in various collected and selected editions. One was by Nancy Olson, *Gavarni: the Carnival Lithographs* (New Haven, CT: Yale University Art Gallery, 1979), a relatively small selection based on a collection of over 4000 prints bequeathed in 1955 by Frank Altschul; another was by Gerhard Schack, *Paul Gavarni, 1804–1866, Aquarelle, Handzeichnungen und Lithographien, Horst Janssen, Handzeichnungen und Radierungen nach Gavarni*, Hamburg, 1971 (republished in book form in 1980). Both Schack's catalogue and his book feature the name of 'Paul Gavarni' in the title, and perhaps the warranty for the Christian name derives from the great Thieme-Becker lexicon, though the name does not appear in the Goncourt account or indeed on any publication produced in Gavarni's lifetime. I have found this name used only in German sources and without any kind of argument or authority.

[3] André Warnod, *Gavarni*, in the series 'Maîtres de l'art moderne,' Paris: F. Rieder et Cie., 1926, p. 8. This essay is rather typical of twentieth-century treatments, being a 52-page critical essay accompanied by 40 selected plates of Gavarni's lithographs, drawings and watercolours.

much of the lithographic work was also converted to wood-engraving to reach even wider audiences, a practice raising issues of authorship which may help to account for the partial eclipse which his reputation has suffered. The only *catalogue raisonné* for Gavarni was produced in 1873 by Armelhaut and Bocher and was limited to the lithographs, drawings and watercolours.[4] It omits the wood-engraved material central to my argument, for reasons of authorial ambivalence. This essay aims to consider the medium and the general message of the œuvre, rather than specific images, though special attention will be given to two major compilations, while some examples may help to establish the ways in which technical matters in the history of printing affect the meanings of the images reproduced.

The secondary literature on Gavarni is not profuse and has not generally helped to keep him in the prominent place in the cultural history of nineteenth-century France which contemporary comments in his own lifetime accorded and celebrated. In the twentieth century, the most substantial treatment was published in the 1920s by Paul-André Lemoisne in two volumes. Gavarni appears to have dropped out of sight so far that the most recent notable works in the area of French book and periodical illustration scarcely mention him. For almost a century there seem to have been no issues of current concern to art historians that have led them to study Gavarni's work. The mildly dismissive note with which art historians sometimes refer to illustrators may have something to do with this; perhaps we just need to adjust our mental perspectives to see the real achievement of his work in printed images in the context of the cultural history of printing in the last 200 years. This essay aims to take a step toward such readjustment.

Modern cultural theory offers many radical conceptual perspectives by means of which we might approach the problems of Gavarni's work, its meanings and values. Roland Barthes's notion of the seme, or myth, as a second-level cultural sign connecting rhetoric and ideology, has helped to formulate the hypothesis of the project of which this essay forms a part. The large question for consideration is whether and how we should see printed illustrations of social types as mythic semes which establish social identities in a familiar communicational rhetoric. Following Barthes, we do not use the word 'myth' to identify a *false* statement or story, but simply as a unit of rhetoric, whether visual or verbal, whether true or false. These identities are the clichés of a culture, a kind of map of social reality, which may indeed come to supersede the reality when we fail in our critical vigilance. In French the term 'cliché' is primarily a technical term in printing and photography, meaning 'stereotype plate' or 'printing plate'; only secondarily does it mean

---

[4] J. Armelhaut and E. Bocher (eds), *L'Euvre de Gavarni. Catalogue raisonné des Lithographes, etc.*, Paris, 1873. (This is sometimes cited as Mahérault and Bocher; it appears that Armelhaut was a pseudonym.)

a fixed pattern of words or fixed method of representation repeated until it becomes worn through use like an old coin. The cliché is thus the key to understanding the relation of rhetoric to ideology. In rhetoric it is the device or technique of representation, the physical aspect of the seme, while in ideology it is the product of the device, or mental aspect of the seme. We may conceive that such semes are especially interesting in any culture undergoing rapid social, economic and technical change. The focus in this essay is on a function operating in the cradle of modern mass communications, but with an emphasis on the production side rather than reception and with an emphasis on the visual rather than the literary component.[5] We need to examine how the concept of the 'type' emerged in the publishing trade in Paris between 1835 and 1845, with Gavarni playing a central role in establishing it, interacting with three publishers. This was occurring at a moment of significant change in the printing and publishing of pictures. There had in fact been two separate innovations in printing at the end of the eighteenth century which had ushered in the new era of illustration. Lithography and wood-engraving were to develop in parallel during the nineteenth century and the relationship between them is both particularly crucial and pointedly confusing in the study of Gavarni's work.

The confusion might perhaps best be cleared up with reference to another piece of theoretical writing, Walter Benjamin's essay 'The Work of Art in the Age of its Technical Reproducibility.'[6] Benjamin offers us the distinction between cult value and exhibition value and a theory of collecting, both of which are clearly relevant to printed images. Cult value is that appropriate to unique, or near-unique, works of art to which we have access only through a form of hierarchized mediation because the objects are collected, located and cherished in a protective cocoon of private or public ownership. Exhibition value is that belonging to reproduced works – and here Benjamin was mainly interested in photography and film – which are by definition not unique, but which acquire through the very power of reproducibility a resonance deriving from their 'exhibition' or showing. In some ways this is to be understood on a banal, commercial level, such as the number of people who see a film, the number of copies in circulation, and so on. In other ways which shall be a key

---

[5] The literary angle has at least been treated, though with a characteristic rejection of the visual contribution to the practice. See C. Aziza, C. Oliviéri and R. Sctrick, *Dictionnaire des types et caractères littéraires*, Paris: Nathan, 1978. This essay returns the compliment.

[6] First published in French in 1935, in German in 1955, and in English in 1968, and still in print, this essay is better known to English speakers under the misleading title given it by Harry Zohn for its publication in the collection of Benjamin essays, *Illuminations* – 'The Work of Art in the Age of Mechanical Reproduction.' This mistranslation was brought about by the influence of the French translation made by Pierre Klossowski in 1935, because it was known that Benjamin had approved of the translation of *technische Reproduzierbarkeit* into French as *réproduction mécanique*.

focus of this essay, this very exhibition value should perhaps be understood as a publishing value. The contrast between cult and exhibition may even be reduced, or perhaps heightened, to the contrast between quality and quantity. Such a perspective helps us to see the relevance of this theoretical distinction to the complete corpus of Gavarni's work. The exclusion of the wood-engraved work from Armelhaut and Bocher's catalogue is surely exemplary here: because Gavarni did not actually cut his own wood-engravings, they were not conceived as his work. Degas's collecting of Gavarni lithographs is evidence of a cult value (as indeed is all collecting), while the republication of Gavarni in wood-engraved copies is clear evidence of the exhibition value of the 'same' images. Let us consider why this should be so, why it is interesting to notice it – and why we might need to modify this view.

Lithography was a new process invented in Germany in 1798 and patented in England shortly after. In this process the artist draws freehand with a greasy crayon or ink directly onto a specially prepared stone surface. This stone can then be used to pull large numbers of copies without any signs of wear, so that several thousand good copies can be produced. The essential point of this method of printing is that it is autographic, in that artists directly draw onto the stone with their own hands. The resulting print has much of the appearance and quality of a drawing. It does not seem mechanical in any of the senses of the word, although as a means of reproducing images it is, strictly speaking, a mechanical method. It is considerably easier and faster (and therefore cheaper) than etching or other types of intaglio engraving, which are very slow, finicky techniques. Stone printing began to be exploited by artists in France during the Restoration period after the fall of Napoleon. Commentators of the time remarked on the speed and immediacy of its productions – Adolphe Thiers, for example, as a young journalist writing in 1824, waxed lyrical on the rapidity with which the artist-lithographer was able to capture his most fleeting impressions. He also saw that this would encourage the artists to extend and expand their repertoires, and that in turn this would expand the taste and demand for pictorial information.[7] The very promptitude of response led to a new use for the medium that Thiers had not foreseen, and one that he was himself to become victim of, in his second career as a politician. After the fall of the restored Bourbons (caused in 1830 by their attempt to bring in censorship laws) lithography was used by a number of artists to produce political caricature of biting immediacy and power, so much so that the new regime of Louis-Philippe brought back

---

[7] Adolphe Thiers, 'De la lithographie et de ses progrès,' in *La Pandore*, no. 259, 30 mars 1824; reproduced in W. McAllister Johnson, *French Lithography, The Restoration Salons 1817–1824*, Kingston, Ontario: Agnes Etherington Art Centre, 1977, pp. 46–8. We should note that Thiers twice uses the notion 'prompt' to emphasize the special characteristic of the medium.

censorship in 1835. The new censorship was in fact to lead to one of the most powerful cultural developments of the period. We will see how, with political caricature aimed at the government banned, a *social* caricature was to develop which was from many points of view even more truly political purely because it satirized impersonally the new ruling class of the time, the bourgeoisie. Before exploring this dimension, however, we must notice a feature – perhaps a value – of the new medium commented on by Thiers, namely that it had inspired artists to be more original and more true than on many canvases classed as high art in the salons: 'Lithography has stimulated the verve of our draughtsmen, they have shown more originality, more truthfulness on the stone than can be found in many 'noble', and richly rewarded, canvases.'[8] The point is significant because this is the value that made an artist as demanding as Degas cherish and collect lithographs. This is cult value despite being in a medium of reproduction.

At the same time that lithography was creating a powerful medium of caricature, French publishing was beginning to exploit the possibilities of the new wood-engraving techniques developed in Bewick's workshop in Newcastle and already revolutionising book and periodical production in London.[9] Using a new end-grain technique on boxwood (instead of the old cross-grain technique on pear or apple wood), new levels of accuracy and artistic expression could be reproduced cheaply in large print runs. This produced a phenomenon which came to be called 'illustration' in England around 1815, and the French borrowed this new term with the new process, around 1830.[10] By the 1840s the notion had become central to many great and long-lasting publishing initiatives, such as *The Illustrated London News* and *L'Illustration*.

The great disadvantage of lithography was that it could not be combined with letter-press printing on the new Stanhope printing presses. It required its own kind of press, using a roller under great pressure. Another important disadvantage was that the size, weight and cost of the lithographic stone meant that once the print run was completed, it would normally be cleaned down and prepared for re-use. For practical and economic reasons it could not be kept or stored, which meant that the original autographic image was lost –

---

[8] Ibid., p. 47. He goes on to claim that Charlet's lithographs (of everyday scenes in Paris) are worth more than many of the great history paintings of the day.

[9] For an excellent short account of these developments, see Ségolène Le Men, 'Book Illustration', in Peter Collier and Robert Lethbridge (eds), *Artistic Relations. Literature and the Visual Arts in Nineteenth Century France*, London and New York: Yale University Press, 1994, ch. 6.

[10] A useful collection of quotations from contemporary sources showing early uses of the words 'illustration' and 'illustrer' is given in Philippe Kaenel, *Le métier d'illustrateur 1830–1880, Rodolphe Töpffer, J.-J. Grandville, Gustave Doré*, Paris: Editions Messene, 1996, Annexe 1, pp. 357–9. His introduction 'Pour une histoire sociale de l'illustration' and Part 1 'La naissance d'un métier' are important contributions to our knowledge of the birth of modern illustration.

a feature that was to play a fateful role in what follows. Engraved woodblocks, on the other hand, could be easily fitted into the letter-press *forme* with blocks of type and used on an ordinary printing press. This was the vignette. Furthermore, and crucially unlike the bulky stones, the woodblocks could be stored for later re-use, perhaps more than once; *and* they could be copied by mould in metal: the original stereotype. In consequence, a new kind of printed page became popular, mixing words and images in a variety of inventive ways which appealed enormously to an expanding reading public. There is reason to think that wood-engraving in particular appreciably helped to expand the demand for printed material by providing attractive texts which could be easily approached by people unaccustomed to reading for pleasure. With more than half the population illiterate at the time and with the growing influx of a largely illiterate rural population to the cities, especially Paris, it would seem clear that the new, moderately-priced illustrated book production could help motivate and familiarize those trying to adapt to the new lifestyle of the metropolitan city.

In 1840 Paris was the second biggest city in the Western world – second only to London. Its population was less than half that of London, but at around 1 million it had doubled since the Revolution and in the decade between 1830 and 1840 it had grown by nearly a third. London had already become, and Paris was in process of becoming, bigger than any known city in history. The metropolitan masses that were coming into being were finding new patterns of life and new social attitudes. Traditional ways of depicting human beings in printed images were out of tune with the developing culture, with its capacity for dynamic, even volatile change. What was coming into being was a community of strangers, in a strange new environment, behaving in strangely unpredictable ways. Both the idealizing imagery of refined culture in expensive intaglio engravings and the condescending imagery of popular culture found, for example, in 'street cries', *images d'Épinal*, had been created within habits of technical practice and social attitude which were essentially static, far removed from the social realities of Louis-Philippe's July monarchy.[11] It may not be surprising that in these circumstances, and with the new techniques of printing available as described, new kinds of publication should develop to exploit new markets for images and assist in the creation of new cultural forms. Nor is it surprising that the political establishment should view the potential for dynamic change with suspicion, to say the least. As already noted, the new political censorship of 1835 had an interesting effect on the market for images: by forbidding political caricature

[11] See Petra Ten-Doesschate Chu and Gabriel P. Weisberg (eds), *The Popularization of Images: Visual Culture under the July Monarchy*, Princeton, NJ: Princeton University Press, 1994. This collection offers some very interesting material and honours Gavarni with two references in the index.

lampooning the prominent personalities of the establishment, it turned the attention of the key publishers of lithographic caricature away from political satire to social satire. Spells in prison for both publishers and artists gave them time to think of new ways to deploy their skills. The most important publishers of caricature were Aubert et Cie. in the Galerie Véro-Dodat, and especially Charles Philipon the dominant partner in that company, who was also active as a caricaturist. At the suggestion and under the direction of Philipon, a change of emphasis led to the specific creation by Daumier of the *Robert Macaire* series of 99 lithographs, published in Philipon's periodical *Le Charivari* in twos and threes over two years. This series was based on a figure in the popular theatre of the day, acted by Frédéric Lemaître.[12]

Daumier had made his debut in Philipon's stable of artists as a political caricaturist. On Balzac's recommendation, Philipon also took Gavarni on, but Gavarni had no interest in governmental politics and never saw himself as a caricaturist.[13] He was best known at this early period as a fashion illustrator, which had been the medium through which Balzac, with his consuming obsession with fashion, had discovered and befriended him. In fact, much of his work throughout his life shows a high level of interest in clothes as a major index of the character depicted. His best known self-portrait, a lithograph of 1845, shows a dandyish figure in a relaxed, informal posture (see Figure 3.1). Philippe Kaenel has pointed out[14] how deliberately Gavarni has posed with a cigarette in his hand rather than an artist's brush or crayon: his self-image was not at all that of an artist or illustrator. According to the Goncourt brothers,[15] Philipon asked Gavarni to work on a female version of Robert Macaire. Gavarni argued that a female version would just be Robert Macaire in skirts, and would not be interesting. He offered instead to do a series entitled *Les Fourberies de femmes en matière de sentiment*,[16] and with this series, begun in 1837 and continued for three years, he embarked on his own views of life in contemporary Paris.

Unsurprisingly for a fashion illustrator, he was already known for his focus on women. *Les Fourberies* showed two things which rapidly became Gavarni's hallmark. First, the kind of wit, humour and irony in the legends placed under

---

[12] The mixed origin of the figure of Robert Macaire, his development by Philipon and Daumier, and his resonance in the culture of the late 1830s, would together suggest that he ought to be considered as an archetype rather than a mere type. Distinctions between archetype, stereotype and type deserve more analysis than is appropriate in the present study.

[13] According to the Goncourts: 'Gavarni est un portraitiste de types ... On conçoit alors que le mot caricature n'a rien à faire avec ses lithographies, et qu'il trouvait même assez plaisant qu'on lui donnât le titre de caricaturiste' (*Gavarni L'homme et l'œuvre*, p. 127). (In this context 'plaisant' means 'funny' or 'ridiculous'.)

[14] Kaenel. *Le métier d'illustrateur*, p. 104.

[15] Ibid., pp. 125–6.

[16] 'Women's little deceits in matters of feeling'.

L'HOMME A LA CIGARETTE

3.1 Gavarni, *L'homme à la cigarette* (self-portrait), lithograph, 1842.

the images were often made piquant by the colloquialisms which are notoriously difficult to translate, and this literary skill was to remain a defining feature of his work despite other fundamental changes in later phases of his career. (This contrasted with Daumier, who never wrote his own legends, which were supplied instead by Philipon.) Second, it became clear that Gavarni was less of a caricaturist and more of a social documentarist, albeit with a satirical angle to his observation. After *Les Fourberies* he went on to produce a number of lithographed series which identified specific kinds of social types in Paris. At this juncture he was mainly interested in the younger generation at leisure and pleasure, such as the Students of Paris (essentially in medicine, law or art); or situations such as the fancy dress balls of Carnival, the period between Twelfth Night and Ash Wednesday, where he acquired fame as an inventor of costumes, particularly that of the unisex *débardeur* (stevedore or docker; see Figure 3.2). The carnival tradition of *travesti*, called 'fancy dress' in English, had been built on a basic codebook of types from the Italian comedy (such as Pierrot the lovelorn youth), most of which had achieved the status of archetypes, or universal human characters found in every culture. The carnival environment coupled with his experience of fashion stimulated Gavarni to identify new types, partly defined by their clothes, but also by characteristic behaviour or 'manners' (in the old sense of the word, where it may be the closest rendering in English of what is meant by *mœurs*). His *Les Lorettes* identified a new type of immoral, demure, domestic, self-possessed, calculating, kept woman – kept, that is, by several men. Quite a few of the lithographs in this sequence focus on the arrival of one of the gentlemen while another has not yet left. Although the idea (and the name) of the *lorette* had been the invention of a journalist (Nestor Roqueplan), it was Gavarni's images of the type which established it as part of the language and gave it the resonance of a seme. A sequence of images would be assembled cataloguing characteristic situations with a short comment or piece of dialogue: the whole set formed a kind of codebook establishing the dimensions and meanings of the type (or semé). At this stage, both Gavarni and Daumier were producing lithographic series of this kind, exploring newly prominent character types in the culture of Paris under the July monarchy. Daumier's work was predominantly caricatural, Gavarni's mainly satirical.

Philipon published these series by instalment in his periodical *Le Charivari*. He is an extremely interesting producer figure, selecting, promoting and directing artists and writers in what might be seen almost as industrialized production.[17] The role of publisher had not yet really settled into a recognizable form, and many individuals were attempting to exploit the fluid situation

---

[17] James Cuno has helped us see more clearly how Philipon was functioning at this period. 'The Business and Politics of Caricature: Charles Philipon and La Maison Aubert' in *Gazette des Beaux Arts*, vol. 106, October 1985, pp. 95–112.

LES DÉBARDEURS.

— ... Et si Cornélie ne trouvait pas de voiture ? — Nous irions à pied ! — Merci ! Je serai
canaille tant qu'on voudra, mais mauvais genre, jamais !

3.2   Gavarni, '... And if Cornélie can't find a cab? – We'd walk! – Thanks! I'll go as
low as you want, but common, never!' Lithograph from *Les Débardeurs,* 1840
(author's collection).

of new markets for printed material. Balzac himself, and Gavarni also, made their own attempts in the commercial field, though both failed and suffered chronic financial problems as a result. (Gavarni actually spent nine months in the debtors' prison in rue de Clichy – an experience he converted into a series of mordant lithographs.) Balzac's novel *Les Illusions perdues* (*Lost Illusions*) gives a detailed account of the printing and publishing world in both Paris and the provinces. The novel exemplifies five kinds of publishers,[18] each representing very real experiences where Balzac had fallen foul of the emerging system. It is useful to remember Lukacs's summary of this novel as being about 'the transformation of literature into a commodity';[19] this is, after all, the publisher's function. We may find reason to extend this idea to see wood-engraved copies of lithographs as the commodification of art.

However, two real publishers of the period deserve particular attention, both of whom were well known to Balzac and to Gavarni: Léon Curmer and P. J. Hetzel. They both exploited the possibilities of instalment publication to produce two of the most interesting illustrated books of the era. Both publishers recognised that Gavarni was special in the sense that, exceptionally, they gave him complete freedom to draw what he wanted.[20] Curmer published *Les Français peints par eux-mêmes* (or 'The French depicted by themselves') from 1840 to 1842 and Hetzel published *Le Diable à Paris* (*The Devil in Paris*) in 1845–46. Gavarni and Balzac were key contributors to both works, which were first published in weekly or twice-weekly fascicles. Both works used many contributors, though Gavarni was clearly the dominant visual artist in both. Only when the market confirmed the initiative by buying the fascicles in sufficient quantity was there a commitment to republish in bound form. *Les Français* ended up as nine fat volumes, each item presented as a chapter in the form of an eight-page disquisition on a character or type to be seen in contemporary Paris or France, with a full-page illustration, called a 'portrait' or 'type' at the front.[21] This is clearly different in kind to the

---

[18] In the Penguin Classic translation, where chapters are numbered (unlike some French editions): Part 2, Chapter 3 'Two varieties of publishers' (Vidal et Porcheron and Doguereau); Chapter 10 'A third variety of publisher' (Barbet); Chapter 13 'A fourth variety of publisher' (Dauriat); Chapter 33 'A fifth variety of publisher' (Fendant et Cavalier) (*Lost Illusions*, Harmondsworth: Penguin, 1971). Together with other chapters focusing on the printing and publishing trades, these present vivid and pointed insights into the literary business of the time.

[19] Georg Lukács, *Studies in European Realism*, London: Merlin, 1972, p. 49.

[20] This point was argued by Paul-André Lemoisne in *Gavarni, Peintre et Lithographe*, Paris, 1924, 2 vols (vol. I, pp. 169, 174).

[21] This publication is also interesting because of its international resonance. There was an English edition in one volume, published by William Orr of Paternoster Row in 1840: it contained 43 of the types. The pictures are clearly printed from the same blocks as those used for the French edition. They have been printed separately on laid paper and pasted onto blank header sheets for each chapter. Another English edition was published a year later by Thomas

lithographed series we have referred to. In all, Curmer collected 423 'types' into these volumes, five of which were devoted to Paris, three to the provinces, and one is a supplement. The subtitle of this compilation was 'Encyclopedia of Nineteenth-Century Manners'.[22] Gavarni designed 84 of the types published, about one-fifth of the total; no legends were required or offered. These works were not lithographed at any stage;[23] they were submitted as drawings and converted to wood-engraving by one of the many staff engravers at the printers; or they were drawn 'on the wood' by Gavarni and then cut by the engraver.[24] Some original drawings have survived, but the wood-engraved print is mostly the only evidence of Gavarni's conception. The poignancy of this is underlined by a remark that Curmer makes about Gavarni in his epilogue to the whole work, where he singles him out as the most refined and profound talent of his time because of his ability to draw without any preliminary studies or sketches, and from memory.[25]

Hetzel's *Le Diable à Paris* is a very different work, though many of the same people were involved and the same methods of publication were adopted. This was a smaller project than *Les Français*, being only two volumes, at any rate in this first edition. The title derives from the literary conceit of the Prologue, written by Hetzel himself under his pseudonym of P. J. Stahl. Satan is bored and sends one of his underlings to visit Paris to find out what is going on there. He is to appear there disguised as a dandy of the boulevards, collect information and send it back to Hell. This provides the rationale for a variety of contributions by writers and artists, including among the writers George Sand, Gérard de Nerval, Charles Nodier, Honoré de Balzac, Arsène Houssaye, Théophile Gautier, Alfred de Musset; and among the artists and illustrators,

---

Tegg of Cheapside; the 22 types included here do not repeat any of those in the other edition; the full-page portraits here are also clearly from the same blocks, but they were not printed in the same way. There was a second French edition of *Les Français* produced in two volumes in 1853. I have not yet been able to see a copy of this edition to see how a nine-volume work has been reduced to two volumes. A further edition, abridged with no indication of the omitted material, was published by J. Philippart in four volumes, 1877–78.

[22] For an excellent treatment, see Ségolène Le Men in the series 'Les Dossiers du Musée d'Orsay', *Les Français peints par eux-mêmes, Panorama social du XIXe siècle*, Paris: Réunion des musées nationaux, 1993.

[23] None of this work by Gavarni is so much as mentioned by the Goncourt brothers, perhaps because they were only interested in the autographic work, mainly the lithographs, of which they themselves had a very substantial collection of more than 2000.

[24] See Paul-André Lemoisne, *Gavarni, Peintre et Lithographe*, Paris: H. Floury, 2 vols, 1924, vol. I, p. 171.

[25] *Les Français peints par eux-mêmes*, vol. 8, p. 459: 'Gavarni, modèle d'élégance et de distinction, spirituel entre tous, trace sans étude, et de mémoire, ses plus frappants portraits, privilège merveilleux du talent le plus délicat et le plus profond de ce temps-ci.' Curmer saw Gavarni as the most important of his illustrators and gave him an exceptional degree of freedom to decide what to illustrate for this series. (See also Lemoisne, *Gavarni, peintre et lithographe*, Vol I, p. 167.)

Bertall, Champin and most prominently Gavarni. Gavarni's contribution is mainly a vast sequence of full-page images of urban 'types' or portraits of characters to be seen in the expanding, bustling, heaving swarms of humanity now thronging the streets. The whole sequence contains 204 images, under the general title of *Les Gens de Paris* ('The People of Paris'); they are subdivided into 38 sets, some with only a few images, others with 10–15 examples.[26] These do have brief legends in the characteristic Gavarni mode. The titles of these subsets, which might be seen as captions, often fix on a social environment – funerals, theatres, boudoirs, prisons, bars, social introductions, carnival, or just the suburbs; some on activities, such as small trade; some are ironic labels such as '*Loyal et vautour*' ('[Both] Upright and Vulture' – *vulture* was a slang term for a pitiless landlord, and property-owners have traditionally been seen as the upright backbone of decent society; see Figure 3.3). The legends are subordinate to the captions, just as the type here is established by the set rather than by individual image. In one of the few recent appreciations of Gavarni's work, the American art historian Aaron Sheon[27] has shown how mistaken it was to see Gavarni's work as lacking political meaning. *Les Gens de Paris* shows a new trend in his work, a more pessimistic view of human nature than had been evident in his earlier work, which had been devoted to the younger generations gallivanting in carnival dances, disguised in fancy dress, and so on. These images focus in the main on the poor, the old, the victims of the new economy, or on the agents of repression such as court bailiffs or the self-satisfied petit-bourgeois or pretentious nouveau-riche bourgeois, whom Gavarni detested. They are surely an indictment of the new social system – and as such, make a political statement. Sheon's interpretation is cast in the light of the last contribution to the compilation, an analysis of Parisian statistics made by Alfred Legoyt, a well-known authority on the subject. He shows that Gavarni enjoyed a very sophisticated understanding of statistical matters, particularly of the feature known as statistical determinism, which gives the lie to so much political posturing. Sheon's article seemed to presage a new approach to Gavarni, suggesting points of contact with the Realism of the era, especially in so far as this was the first treatment to focus on this wood-engraved imagery.[28]

---

[26] It is notable that Judith Wechsler's account of this book, in her influential study *A Human Comedy. Physiognomy and Caricature in 19th Century Paris* (London: Thames and Hudson, 1982, p. 38), skips over Gavarni's contribution, mentioning a few only of the titles to his subsections. This may be because Gavarni's work is not a good example of her thesis about the significance of physiognomic theory in this field.

[27] A. Sheon, 'Parisian Social Statistics: Gavarni, "Le Diable à Paris", and Early Realism', *Art Journal*, Summer 1984, pp. 139–48.

[28] In 1988, however, Raymond Grew, only devoted one paragraph to Gavarni, seeing his 'cartoons' as lacking in sympathy for his material: 'Picturing the People: Images of the Lower Orders in Nineteenth Century French Art', in Robert I. Rotberg and Theodore K. Rabb (eds), *Art and History. Images and Their Meaning*, Cambridge: Cambridge University Press, 1988.

3.3 Gavarni, *Loyal et Vautour-3*: 'On the 30th April next you will please pay to his order the sum of one thousand écus that you haven't got.' Wood-engraving from *Les Gens de Paris*, 1845 (author's collection).

The series *Les Gens de Paris* did not only appear in *Le Diable à Paris*.[29] Many of them were to reappear six years later in Edmond Texier's

---

[29] The second volume of *Le Diable à Paris* seems to have been pirated at some date in the late 1840s, appearing again under the title of *Le Tiroir du Diable*. The original publisher's name on the title-page has become 'Chez les principaux Libraires' (At the principal bookshops). This kind of piratical reproduction adds an incalculably piquant dimension to the significance of the work. Although all the literary material is included most of the visual material is omitted – of Gavarni's 204 plates, only 14 are given. The pagination remains identical, because the Gavarni plates had been bound into the original in between signatures and not numbered or paginated. The name of the printer given on the fly is different from the original, though the colophon is identical. This would suggest that the original stereotype plates were being reused for this edition.

LES ETUDIANTS DE PARIS.

— Tu ne la reconnais pas, Eugénie ? l'ancienne à Badinguet ? une belle blonde... qui aimait les meringues et qui faisait tant sa tête... Oui ! Badinguet l'a fait monter pour 36 francs... — Si c'est vrai ! — Non, va ! c'est un tambour de la garde nationale... bête ! Tu vois donc pas que c'est un homme ?

3.4   Gavarni, 'Don't you recognize her, Eugénie? Badinguet's old woman? A beautiful blonde ... who loved meringues and was always doing her hair ... yes, Badinguet had her mounted for 36 francs ... yes it's true! No, come on, it's a drummer from the National Guard ... silly! Can't you see it's a man?' Lithograph from *Les Étudiants de Paris*, 1839-40 (author's collection).

ŒUVRES DE GAVARNI.   Les Étudiants de Paris.

Tu ne la reconnais pas, Eugénie, l'ancienne à Badinguet? une belle blonde... qui aimait tant les meringues et qui faisait tant sa tête... Oui, Badinguet l'a fait monter pour 36 francs...

— Si c'est vrai!

— Non, vas! c'est un tembour de la garde nationale... bête! tu ne vois donc pas que c'est un homme?

Par Gavarni.   Gravé par Rouget.

3.5 Gavarni, (same legend). Wood-engraving from *Les Étudiants de Paris*, 1846, cut by Rouget (author's collection).

Chambre garnie.

3.6   Gavarni, Wood engraving, from *Tableau de Paris par Edmond Texier, Ouvrage illustré de quinze cents gravures*, 1852, p. 95 (author's collection).

Tableau de Paris, another two-volume survey of Paris, published by Paulin and Lechevalier in 1852 with 1500 wood-engravings. Many of these are topographical views of Paris, or buildings and street scenes of various kinds, commissioned for this new work. However, a large number of *Les Gens de Paris* of Gavarni are here reused, clearly from the original blocks, or perhaps more likely, from metal stereotype copies of the blocks – though with all the original legends and classifications or set-identities deleted and with new textual additions which might really be called captions rather than legends. In many instances the image is showing signs of deterioration. They now illustrate a narrative description. As an example of this process of republication we can look at three versions of the same image. Firstly, an original lithograph from *Les Etudiants de Paris*, published in 1839–40: it shows a young man in dressing gown and slippers, standing in front of a skeleton which hangs from a hook on the wall (see Figure 3.4). His female companion is cowering behind him, looking with wide, fearful eyes over his shoulder at the skeleton. She is wearing some kind of apron over her dress. The angle of a beam in the background suggests that this is an attic room, appropriate for a student, who must be a medical student. The girl's appearance and demeanour fit the well-known stereotype of the period, the *grisette* – an unsophisticated young woman, most probably from a rustic background, living and working in Paris at a quasi-menial level. She is in some kind of intimate relation with the sophisticated medical student from a bourgeois background, and he cannot forbear poking some gentle fun at her naïveté. The legend provides a monologue interspersed with pauses or silences:

> Don't you recognize her, Eugénie? Badinguet's old woman? A beautiful blonde ... who loved meringues and was always doing her hair ... yes, Badinguet had her mounted for 36 francs ... yes it's true! No, come on, it's a drummer from the National Guard ... silly! Can't you see it's a man?

Secondly, just over six years later, this image was copied onto wood by Rouget and republished as a wood-engraving in 1846 by Jules Hetzel in the *Œuvres choisies de Gavarni, Revues, corrigées et nouvellement classées par l'Auteur*, with the subtitle *Études de mœurs contemporaines* on the title-page (see Figure 3.5). Like all the engravings, the image has been reversed, since the easiest method of copying by hand was simply to redraw the image, either directly onto the surface of the wood, or onto the specially whitened wood, or onto thin paper pasted onto the wood; after which it would be cut with the burin and other tools to produce a positive copy of the lithograph in wood. When used to print from, the impression would be reversed. If a stereotype were made, by whatever process, the metal block would be identical to the wooden block, so would also produce the negative impression. This sometimes has a strange effect, such as when showing two men shaking hands; since even left-handed men shake hands with the right hand, it looks decidedly odd when they shake by the left (see Figure 3.6). But normally, there are no indications other than mild oddities of compositional balance. In the case of the medical student and his skeleton, the differences are rather subtle changes of emphasis, which in view of the editorial claim that Gavarni has himself had the oversight of the work are not of any real significance. The same legend is offered as before, and the impact of the work is close to the original even if one may lament the loss of autographic subtlety. The most telling issue in respect of the publishing value ('exhibition value') of the work is that it was marketed as Gavarni's, not that of the engravers. It is true, of course, that the engraver usually signed his work in addition to transcribing the artist's signature; but that was clearly not an authorial claim as such. Publisher, engraver and purchaser were all acknowledging the authorial value of an artist we might call the 'designer'.

Thirdly, and later again by another six years or so, the first volume of Texier's new *Tableau de Paris* republished this same image in the way referred to above, from the same stereotype block, but with a new and much shorter legend: 'Furnished room.' (see Figure 3.7). It appears in the chapter 'The School of Medicine', among 10 engravings, of which four originated from Gavarni. This is still only 12 years since their original publication. The original legend has become less comprehensible, or perhaps just less appropriate to Texier's purposes. The meaning of the image is completely changed by the change of context. What had originally shown insight into the relations between student and *grisette*, with social and psychological resonances still perceptible at the end of the twentieth century, had become a rather flat joke. The new caption – it can scarcely be called a legend – is a droll witticism about student rooms saying nothing at all about the relationship between the two types, student and *grisette*. Was it social change that had made the figure of the *grisette* less comprehensible, or was it perhaps an ideological change? It is suggested here that the need to change the legend to make it fit into the new book is a very precise indicator of ideological change, as noted either by Texier or his editor-publisher (or indeed, all together). They, after all, knew something it is very difficult for us to know: the temper of their audience or readership. They would soon spot it if something seemed outdated and old-fashioned.

What is more, it seems that there was another edition of *Le Diable à Paris* produced in 1868–69, more than 20 years after the original and two years after Gavarni's death. This edition is remarkably different from the first in that it entirely omits all the literary contributions, the descriptive chapters on the history and geography of Paris, as well as the statistical chapter by Alfred Legoyt. The publishers can only have thought that the literary material was too dated for repetition, but that the visual material could still find a market. This second edition at the end of the Second Empire contains only the pictures of the first edition, but includes a large amount of visual material not in the first edition. On top of the 204 original plates, there are in this edition another 380 full-page plates by Gavarni, making 584 plates by him, with further wood-engraved material by other artists such as Bertall, Grandville and Champin – 185 plates, to a grand

Adieu, mon bon homme! je te laisse ma pipe et ma femme; .. t'auras bien soin
de ma pipe!

3.7 Gavarni, 'Goodbye, old fellow! I am leaving you my pipe and my woman; take good care of my pipe!...' Wood-engraving from *Les Étudiants de Paris*, 1846, cut by Bisson.

total of 769 plates.[30] The point to emphasize is that all the extra Gavarni material in this edition had been published originally in lithographic format in the late 1830s and early 1840s, firstly by Philipon and *Le Charivari*, and later republished by Hetzel in wood-engraved versions in 1846–47 copied from the lithographs by a number of wood-engravers. This is its fourth outing. It is clear that the original blocks have been reused for this second edition of *Le Diable à Paris*, though now printed on both sides of a much cheaper paper, with a fair amount of print-through showing, especially with the solid blacks. This time the original legends are reproduced, but with new letterpress indices on each plate, establishing its address in the new text while acknowledging their source in a series with such famous titles as *Les Lorettes*, *Les Étudiants de Paris*, *Les Enfants terribles*, *Les Artistes*, *Les Débardeurs*.

These titles of Gavarni's series had rapidly become part of the language in the 1840s. Their phrases and images entered the communicational rhetoric of the day and were inscribed in contemporary consciousness, that is to say as ideology. They had become 'essential' components of the myth of Paris. This claim is supported by, for example, citing the terms used by the artist-illustrator Constantin Guys, who had been instrumental in cajoling Gavarni to come to London to work for *The Illustrated London News* in December 1847, specifically to bring to that paper 'types from French society ... such as would avoid awaking the stupid prejudices of the English ... who take far too seriously the bad things we say about ourselves. ... Disabuse them ... one drawing by you, with that stamp of nature that everyone recognises immediately, is worth more than any written statement.'[31] These words from the man later celebrated by Baudelaire as 'the painter of modern life' show clearly how Gavarni was appreciated for his social types. But recirculated 30 years later they no longer offered insights into current social reality. Paris and its people had moved on. Like old maps, Gavarni's wood-engraved types remain as evidence of a specific culture in Paris at the end of Louis-Philippe's regime. But by the end of Napoleon III's regime his visual rhetoric was out of date; indeed, Gavarni abandoned illustration after 1859. By 1869, he was dead, and his myth, once true, had become untrue.

But the woodblocks and stereotypes remained, with publishers ready to reprint, and markets for their sale. Printers, publishers and booksellers had an old but fecund commodity on their hands which could be resold to a new

---

[30] The copy to hand at the time of writing has neither title-page, imprint information, nor any other index of content or purpose of publication. Both Gavarni and Grandville were recently dead, but Bertall was still very much alive. Hetzel himself was still a very active publisher, though it is not yet possible to ascertain the extent of his involvement in this second edition.

[31] Letter to Gavarni, early 1847, cited in Lemoisne, *Gavarni, peintre et Lithographe*, vol. 2, pp. 4–5.

generation of purchasers. This leaves us to sort out the meaning and value of the prints struck and restruck from the blocks, and to ponder the transition from true to false consciousness. The types still have a certain currency 150 years after their creation, though now somewhat attenuated, and perhaps mainly of interest to the cultural historian. We should, however, recognize a clear difference in value between those which are copies of lithographs, where we have an extant original in the lithograph itself, and those which have no extant original referent because the original was drawn on the woodblock by the artist and destroyed in the act of cutting by the engraver. This applies to all the types contributed to *Les Français* and to all of *Les Gens de Paris* published in the first edition of *Le Diable à Paris*. It is obvious that a collector of prints would always prefer the lithograph to the wood-engraved copy of it; perhaps not so obvious, but still true, that the types in this latter category have a special resonance beyond those which might be called epilithographs. Gavarni remains the greatest typologist of his age, an artist unsurpassed in the two most prolific and far-reaching techniques of visual communication of his time. He has been ignored for long enough. As a key creator of the *comédie parisienne*, one of the most powerful myths of Western civilization, his work deserves much closer attention than it has received to date. The next step in studying this material will need to consider more closely the physical realities and studio practices of engraving and stereotyping in nineteenth-century print technology. We have not begun to consider the engravers, such as Lavieille, who translated Gavarni's drawings and lithographs into the new medium. It is surely beyond doubt that we need to understand the process of creating, establishing and circulating those fixed reproductions of humankind which are the basic currency of the mass media of communication and entertainment: what we think of as 'types' or 'stereotypes', and what we might with greater accuracy call 'typological semes'. The dissemination and currency of such typological semes are crucial functions in modern culture, and we should develop distinctions and discriminations to refine our understanding of the grammar of such visual rhetoric. The study of Gavarni's wood-engraved œuvre offers us perhaps one of the clearest and most interesting paths towards this end.

Further reading

Peter Collier and Robert Lethbridge, *Artistic Relations. Literature and the Visual Arts in Nineteenth Century France*, New Haven and London: Yale University Press, 1994.

Edmond and Jules Goncourt, *Gavarni, l'homme et l'œuvre*, Paris: Flammarion, Postface de M. Gustave Geoffroy 1925.

Philippe Kaenel, *Le métier d'illustrateur 1830–1880: Rodolphe Töpffer, J.-J. Grandville, Gustave Doré*, Paris: Éditions Messene, 1996.

Ségolène Le Men, *Les Français peints par eux-mêmes, Panorama social du XIXe siècle* (Les Dossiers du Musée d'Orsay), Paris: Réunion des musées nationaux, 1993.

Paul-André Lemoisne, *Gavarni, Peintre et Lithographe*, Paris: H. Floury, 2 vols, 1924.

Aaron Sheon, 'Parisian Social Statistics: Gavarni, "Le Diable à Paris," and Early Realism,' *Art Journal*, Summer 1984, pp.139–48.

Petra Ten Doesschate Chu and Gabriel P. Weisberg, *The Popularization of Images: Visual Culture under the July Monarchy*, Princeton, NJ: Princeton University Press, 1994.

CHAPTER FOUR

The literary dangers of the city: policing 'immoral books' in Berlin, 1850–80*

Sarah L. Leonard

During the 1860s and 1870s, residents of Berlin complained that they could not walk down city streets without being accosted by the shouts of book peddlers selling their 'filthy wares'. An anonymous letter to the justice minister pointed to the shameful state of the city streets: 'In the boxes of various itinerant booksellers we continue to find the disgusting novels of the Marquis de Sade, which belong to the most scandalous works of worldly literature.'[1] Further, these books were 'displayed in store windows and likewise sold publicly, without shame, by peddlers'. In 1872, a Pastor Quistorp wrote to complain that 'itinerant booksellers spread poison ... and licentiousness in mass quantities.'[2] What troubled the authors of these letters – and the many others who addressed complaints to city officials – was the visibility of the illicit book trade. They described a city that was disorienting, filled with hidden spaces, unsavoury elements and opportunities for illegal transactions. As Berlin expanded to accommodate hundreds of thousands of migrants from rural areas, contemporaries described unfamiliar city streets. These urban dangers crystallized around the image of the book peddler offering illicit, sensational or obscene writings to innocents.[3]

The idea that books could be morally dangerous was certainly not invented during the decades of reaction following 1848. As early as the seventeenth

* I would like to thank V.R. Berghahn, Mary Gluck and Mark Meyers, who read earlier versions of this article and offered helpful suggestions. Research for this article was funded by an Annual Grant from the German Academic Exchange Service and a travel fellowship from Brown University.

[1] Geheimes Staatsarchiv Preußischer Kulturbesitz (hereafter GStA), HA I. 77. 380. 7. Bd. 2., p. 43, Berlin, 16 September 1878, Anonymous letter to the State and Justice Minister Dr Leonhard.

[2] By and large, booksellers and itinerant peddlers were resourceful and continued to sell illicit literature in spite of bans, confiscations and the requirement that they submit a list of the works they carried to the police.

[3] In almost every discussion of 'immoral writings' readers are cast as victims, not co-conspirators.

century, German theologians and pedagogues had warned readers that excessive novel-reading could lead to seduction, superstition and fanaticism. Prescriptive literature urged literate women to confine their reading to devotional literature and household books.[4] What had changed by 1850 was the scope and meaning of 'immoral writings', an elastic category that left room for many varieties of popular print. One interpretation of this category was provided by the police in Berlin; modelled on an article from the French *Code Pénal*, a police rescript from 1819 excluded writings that 'offended against religion, morality and *bürgerliche Ordnung* [bourgeois or civil order].'[5] Not surprisingly, the police had no difficulty producing long lists consistent with these criteria. On these lists, the *Memoirs of a Berlin Night Watchman* occupied the same pages as *New Letters from Heaven*, or *Open Letter from the First Democrat Jesus Christ to his Brothers on Earth*. Accounts of revolution in France were squeezed in beside popular medical tracts, and novels, particularly those of Victor Hugo and Eugène Sue, joined German translations of Thomas Paine and French materialist philosophy.[6]

While these lists speak to the many critical voices circulating at mid-century, they also reveal the difficulty of carving out a concise definition of 'immoral writings'. What was the meaning of this term, and who had the authority to decide which books occupied it? Whose standards should inform the decision to remove ideas, narratives and stories from public circulation? Answers were particularly difficult to generate in the years following the Revolution, as assumptions about authority and order were temporarily thrown into question. A few resourceful members of the book trade used the brief suspension of censorship laws after 1848 as an opportunity to print new editions of illegal books. In 1850, for instance, a publisher from Berlin published all 12 volumes of the *Memoirs of Casanova von Seingalt*, a work that had been banned in the early decades of the nineteenth century.[7] Though the police did not ignore the new edition of *Casanova*, or the reprints that followed, they evoked the authority of a rescript that had lapsed in 1848.

Though the revolution ended the existing system of preventative censorship, it did not result in the freedom of citizens to read and write what they wished. Instead, censorship was recast in terms consistent with new expectations of limited government. Protecting the interests of the church or state no

---

[4] For more on these early debates about novel-reading in Germany, see S. L. Leonard, 'Poison of the Soul and Mind: Readers, Peddlers and Police in Germany, 1848–1890', PhD thesis, Brown University, 2000.

[5] 'Die Beaufsichtigung der Leihbibliotheken', *Berliner Gerichts-Zeitung*, 8, 1859.

[6] For more on these lists, see my discussion below and footnote 10.

[7] In 1850 Gustave Hempel published *The Memoirs of Casanova* in Berlin. The police confiscated Hempel's publication, appealing to a rescript no longer valid after 1848. *Casanova's Memoirs* were originally published by F.A. Brockhaus, who purchased the original French manuscripts and brought them out in German translation.

longer justified constant, unchecked supervision of print. This meant that a case had to be made that the exclusion of ideas, stories and representations was beneficial to society and the private individual. This essay will explore how new ideas of moral censorship – and with them, authority – were carved out in the post-revolutionary period. We will also consider how the authority of the police and courts was permeable from below.

New laws, new questions

In Berlin, the police shared the role of interpreters of texts and laws with the courts. The detailed records they kept of their campaign to 'suppress indecent writings' reveal a world of illicit books and print that circulated within the city, and from urban centres to smaller towns. As part of the campaign to trace the routes of illicit books, the police and the interior minister in Berlin solicited reports from local governments in other Prussian cities. They kept meticulous records of laws, court decisions, confiscations, anonymous denunciations and appeals from religious authorities. Through careful accumulation of detail, they documented a world that took great pains to conceal itself. In the process, the police also managed to document their own, often confused, relationship to print culture and the laws that governed it.

The Prussian penal code of 1851 introduced a new law concerning 'immoral writings', or *unzüchtige Schriften*. The law read: 'He who sells, distributes or otherwise disseminates immoral writings, or who otherwise displays or attaches [such writings] in areas accessible to the public will be punished with a fine of ten to one hundred *Thaler*, or a jail sentence of fourteen days to six months.'[8] The meaning of the central legal term, 'immoral writings', was to be carved out by the interpretive efforts of the police and courts. Following closely on the heels of the Revolution, the legal language appealed to the interests of the public; what exactly was meant by this 'public' was yet to be defined.[9]

---

[8] Strafgesetzbuch für die preuß. Staaten vom 14. April 1851, as cited in R. Schauer, *Zum Begriff der unzüchtigen Schrift, Ein beitrag zur Erläuterung des §184 R.St.G.B.*, Roßberg'schen Buchhandlung, 1893. The law also specified that the court's report must identify the confiscated work. All translations are mine.

[9] Very little historical work has been done on the policing of 'immoral and obscene writings' in nineteenth-century Germany. See G. Stark, 'Pornography, Society, and the Law in Imperial Germany', *Central European History*, 3, 1981, pp. 200–229; and P. Englisch, *Irrgarten der Erotik: Eine Sittengeschichte über das gesamte Gebiet der Welt-Pornographie*, Leipzig: Lykeion, 1931. Stark's article treats late nineteenth- and early twentieth-century Germany. There has been a good deal of work on the historical meaning of obscenity in other national contexts. On France, see R. Darnton, *The Forbidden Best-Sellers of Pre-Revolutionary France*, New York: Norton, 1996; C. J. Dean, 'Pornography, Literature, and the Redemption of Virility in France,

As the law did not initially clarify what was meant by 'immoral writings', interpretive differences arose. Confessional and regional particularities, for example, found expression in correspondence between Berlin and local governments. In one case, the authorities in the Catholic city of Münster discovered a bookseller distributing five books offering advice on marriage and reproduction.[10] The bookseller in question, Wundermann, protested the confiscation of his wares in a letter to the authorities in Protestant Berlin. The confiscated books were sold all over Germany, he wrote, and attracted little attention; Münster's Catholic authorities were persecuting him because of his Protestant beliefs. In response, police headquarters in Berlin offered its own evaluation: 'Works of this kind have been published in large numbers under various titles. He who simply judges these books by their more or less seductive titles easily concludes that they excite the senses. This is not by extension true of the content.'[11] Münster's authorities disagreed; while popular medical books of this kind were unexceptional in a big city, they stood out on the streets of a small, Catholic city. Religious and regional differences underscore just how awkward and contentious the definition of 'immoral writings' could be.

Within the larger structure of Berlin's police department, the *Sittenpolizei* (literally the police of morals or customs) were responsible for maintaining the moral order of public spaces. In other cities in Germany, this branch of the police was called the *Zuchtpolizei*, or *Zuchtherren*, referring to the *Zuchtordnungen* (discipline ordinances) codified in the wake of the Reformation. Originally, the definition of *Zucht* (discipline), pursued by the police included public manners and morals, sumptuary laws, displays of luxury and public gatherings. Historian Isabel V. Hull explains that during the seventeenth and eighteenth centuries *Sittlichkeit* 'had a wide, inclusive meaning, encompassing Christian tenets of behaviour and religious observance as well as a broad range of social customs. Sexual conduct was merely a subcategory of *Sittlichkeit*, in both religious and secular senses.'[12] Mark Raeff, who stud-

---

1880–1930', *Differences*, 5, 1993, pp. 62–91; L. Hunt (ed.), *The Invention of Pornography: Obscenity and the Origins of Modernity, 1500–1800*, New York: Zone, 1993; and A. Stora-Lamarre, *L'enfer de la IIIe Republique: Censeurs et Pornographes 1880–1914*, Paris: Imago, 1990. On the origins of obscenity law in England, see C. Manchester, 'A History of the Crime of Obscene Libel', *Journal of Legal History*, 12, 1991, pp. 26–57.

[10] Münster was a Catholic city in the predominantly Protestant state of Prussia. In this case, the bookseller in question appealed to the authorities in Berlin on the grounds that he was persecuted for his Protestant beliefs. In court, he was acquitted of selling indecent writings, but convicted of harassing government employees while conducting their jobs.

[11] GStA, I. 77. 380. 7. Bd. 1, p. 108, Berlin, June 13, 1868. Report from the Chief of Police to the Interior Minister regarding the complaints of the bookseller Wundermann from Munster. In Berlin, the police found one of the confiscated books, *A Gift for those Engaged to be Married*, by 'Dr Brandt' on Friedrichstraße.

[12] For more on the history of the police in Germany, see I.V. Hull, *Sexuality, State and Civil Society, 1700–1815*, Ithaca, NY: Cornell University Press, 1996, esp. chs 1 and 3; M. Raeff,

ied the ordinances of the German police explains that one of the goals of the police in the early modern period was to discipline society by eliminating the '"superfluous", purposeless, unrestructured and fickle elements of society'.[13] The desire of the police to order public spaces also animated their efforts to monitor bookstores, peddlers, and the print that occupied city streets.

By the middle of the nineteenth century, concerns about luxury and custom had given way to a more circumscribed definition of *Sittlichkeit*, and this specialized body of the police were no longer attentive to displays of dress and luxury. Their authority was whittled down to two tasks: regulating prostitution, and enforcing the laws related to obscene writings. Though their official duties had changed, the *Sittenpolizei* continued to focus on disciplining city streets, marketplaces and other public spaces. They were responsible for knowing how books passed into the city, where they originated, which booksellers sold them. In addition, they patrolled the streets for phrases, words or images – for example, a book cover or an advertisement – that might fall under the law. Their knowledge of the illicit book trade was accumulated in bits and pieces, and their growing collection of confiscated books, pamphlets and images was carefully catalogued and stored. By the beginning of the twentieth century, the number of confiscated books housed in Berlin's police headquarters filled six large double cabinets; they amassed a collection of 'immoral writings' that rivalled any in Germany.[14]

The importance of metaphor in obscenity law

To understand the history of a law, we have to consider how ideas of authority, society and the individual animate legal language. How did obscenity law acquire meaning and legitimacy during the second half of the nineteenth century? After 1851, the police and courts were responsible for making moral censorship legitimate and believable, but they had to do so in terms that resonated with public attitudes. In Berlin, the police drew on popular fears of urban danger as they worked to interpret the law regarding indecent publications. Legal language often involves the use of metaphor, and the police were able to draw parallels between the threat posed by immoral writings and other kinds of urban dangers. Because the law provided little interpretive

---

The Well Ordered Police State: Social and Institutional Change through Law in the Germanies and Russia, New Haven, CT: Yale University Press, 1983; and Alf Lüdke, *Police and State in Prussia, 1815–1850*, trans. P. Burgess, Cambridge: Cambridge University Press, 1989. Historians who have studied the theory and practice of *'Polizey'* argue that there was a link, particularly in Protestant areas, between the goals of religious authorities and those of the police.

[13] Raeff, *Well Ordered Police State*, p. 82.

[14] P. Englisch, *Geschichte der erotischer Literatur, von Dr Paul Englisch*, Stuttgart: J. Püttmann, 1927.

guidance, the police had to ask themselves a series of questions. Which books fell under the legal definition of indecency? Whom were they protecting? How could they legitimate censorship in a world in which authority was no longer absolute or God-given? Metaphor helped solve this problem. To say that the danger posed by books was 'like' other varieties of urban danger justified confiscations.

The police began their interpretive efforts on the urban streets. Reports from the police about their activities at mid-century described an urban landscape as unfamiliar as foreign territory. One of the essential changes noted in these reports was the city's exponential growth, from 242 000 inhabitants in 1830, to 962 000 in 1875. 'The extraordinarily rapid growth of the population and the expansion of the city's borders, particularly during the period from 1840 to 1860, was not matched by corresponding urban development.'[15] Under the direction of Carl Ludwig von Hinckeldey, Berlin's chief of police 1848–56, this arm of the government took an active role in documenting the city. They organized efforts to install a water supply, spray the streets, construct public baths and laundries, and establish a fire brigade. Urban fires, cholera outbreaks and statistics of infant mortality were carefully noted, as were questions of sanitation, cleanliness and physical safety.[16]

The most powerful metaphor used to describe the effects of immoral books was 'poison' (*Gift*). Already in the early part of the century metaphors of poison and physical contamination were used to describe the effects of books. The influential Catholic theologian Ignatz von Wessenberg warned readers that inferior novels were like 'a subtle poison, deadly to those who are not careful, that artlessly leaves its effects behind'.[17] During the nineteenth century, libraries in Germany created special collections of 'secret books', referred to as the *Giftschrank* or 'poison cabinet.'[18] The police were able to draw on this metaphor of books as poison, to form a link between sanitation and the elimination of morally dangerous substances. In the same way that the police set themselves the task of cleaning up the physical environment of the city –

---

[15] *Verwaltungs-Bericht des Königlichen Polizei-Präsidiums von Berlin für die Jahre 1871–1882*, Berlin: W. Moeser, 1882, p. 7.

[16] On the history of disease and cholera in nineteenth-century German cities, see R.J. Evans, *Death in Hamburg: Society and Politics in the Cholera Years*, Oxford: Oxford University Press, 1987; and P. Baldwin, *Contagion and the State in Europe, 1830–1930*, Cambridge: Cambridge University Press, 1999.

[17] Ignaz von Wessenberg, *Über den sittlichen Einfluß der Romane. Ein Versuch*, Constanz: 1826, p. 37.

[18] During the nineteenth century the *Giftschrank* of the Bavarian State Library contained hundreds of books on the themes of love, marriage, and eroticism. This collection included works in several languages. In 1924, most of the titles in this 'secret collection' were put back into circulation (see Bayerische Staatsbibliothek München, *Alte Remota Prohibita*).

focusing on poison, human waste, tainted water and fire – they took on the role of eliminating intellectual filth available in public spaces.

The metaphor of immoral books as harmful substances continued to inform regulation into the second half of the century. In 1879, a revision of Reich obscenity law drew on language protecting consumers from substances that harmed the integrity of the body. According to the logic of these revisions, selling indecent literature was akin to selling poison or harmful patent medicines to an unsuspecting consumer. A police circular explaining the changes to the law explained why this metaphor was appropriate. 'An analogy can be drawn between [substances that are harmful to the health] and the production and distribution of harmful intellectual sustenance. One can even say that the people's well-being is more damaged by the latter than by the former.'[19]

Comparing poisons to indecent books linked censorship to sanitizing the city streets. In a sworn statement to the Mayor of Bielefeld, the bookseller Velhagen denounced two of his colleagues in Hamburg, for selling 'immoral books' around the holidays. Velhagen was also concerned that male students from the *Gymnasia* (elite high schools), many from 'good' families, would buy these books. 'We have it from educated and credible sources that *these obscene books find their greatest audience among young men*. The fact that the Christmas season is misused for the purpose of importing this poison [*Gift*] into the family is particularly objectionable.'[20] Following the logic of Velhagen's complaint, he was concerned that the unclean public world would infect the private world of the family. An article from a religious periodical described advertisements in the press: 'Spicy! Interesting! Gallant! 150 printed sheets in 15 volumes of highly interesting and racy stories … . Is it not a scandal and a disgrace that this horrible filth – this pernicious poison of the soul [*Seelengift*], is offered freely while access to rat poison is regulated with such fear?'[21]

A second legal metaphor, that of contamination, also linked print to physical health. Fears of passing filth from one person to another was used to describe the dangers of the *Leihbibliothek*, or lending library. Unlike modern public libraries, use of these lending libraries was not free. They were often run by private booksellers, who offered popular titles for a few *Groschen* a day. For the price of one good volume, the thrifty reader could rent dozens of

---

[19] GStA, I. 77. 380. 7. Bd. 3, p. 224, *Entwurf eines Gesetzes, Betr. die Abaenderung des §184 des Strafgesetzbuchs.*

[20] Ibid., Bd. 1, p. 84. Letter to Interior Minister Eulenburg from the booksellers Velhagen and Klasing, Bielefeld, December, 1867.

[21] Ibid., 'auf der Wacht', *Die deutsche Wacht. Ein christlich-nationales Volksblatt für Nord- und Süddeutschland und aller deutschen Brüder draußen*, 4 April 1872. Article included in the files of the Interior Minister.

books. These popular sources of print were also seen as spaces of mental contamination. Publications available in lending libraries were often described as 'filthy,' or 'dirty.' The *Berliner Gerichts-Zeitung* described the link between physical and mental filth in these terms: 'The wife and daughter of a Privy Counsellor, who answers to the title "Excellency," are not embarrassed to read a book from the lending library directly after it has circulated among the domestic servants and through the stable. In its travels, the book has become dirty.'[22] A borrowed book, the article continued, could be identified by the smell of tobacco that lingered on its pages from the last reader. As they linked physical danger to mental harm, critics of immoral writings drew on the powerful analogy of ingesting something harmful from the outside. Through the lens of the police, public spaces and 'public life' were cast as suspect and dangerous.[23] After the occupation of public streets during the uprisings of 1848/49, popular suspicion of public spaces served the interests of the police.

While poison and filth were used consistently, other terms were added to the descriptive vocabulary of the police and courts. For instance, ideas of 'nature and 'the natural', as well as 'culture' and 'civility' were evoked to make a case against 'immoral' print. Both were used as more sophisticated legal definitions of obscenity were crafted. One definition condemned writings that 'offended the reader's sense of shame or morals' [*Schamgefühl und Sittengefühl*]. Disturbing this natural impulse of shame constituted a form of assault. Women were believed to be more vulnerable to these injuries, as their sense of shame was finer and more developed. Though the language of the law was gender-neutral, evoking offence of shame and morals implied a vulnerable reader, easily swept away or injured.

The idea of 'nature' also informed the evaluation of popular medical books, a genre that never failed to attract the attention of the police. These were inexpensive books and pamphlets that offered guidance on love, marriage and reproduction. Titles like Dr Römer's *No More Overpopulation*, and a mid-century favourite, *Amour and Hÿmen, or The Secrets of Love and Marriage*, offered advice on grooming, courtship and sexuality. Books of this kind had initially been difficult to prosecute, as defendants could often convince the courts that such works had medical value. By 1877, however, legal language had been introduced to make a case against such books. 'Immoral,' the police headquarters explained, 'is any satisfaction of the sexual instincts

---

[22] 'Die Beaufsichtigung der Leihbibliotheken'.

[23] It is interesting to compare nineteenth-century visions of public life with those of other periods. In classical Greece, for example, public spaces were associated with honour, privilege and citizenship. To confine oneself to private life was shameful. In the discussions of the police in post-revolutionary Germany, public spaces are associated with danger and shame, private with morality, vulnerable purity.

that takes place outside of marriage and the natural intermixing of men and women.' This definition of 'immoral' also included any deed or action 'which through *unnatural means prevents the natural consequences of intercourse*'.[24]

Confiscations

'Reading' began on the streets of Berlin, as the police looked for books with suspicious titles in store windows, colporteurs' boxes and publishers' warehouses. They combed the city looking for suggestive titles displayed in archways under trains and the windows of stationery stores. While the city's professional booksellers had little to fear from the police, their less respectable and itinerant counterparts endured regular searches and confiscations. Though it is tempting to focus on high-profile trials of famous authors and publishers, the great majority of obscenity cases in post-Revolutionary Berlin were levelled against figures who otherwise remained invisible: small-time peddlers and publishers, salesmen trying to make extra money selling illicit books, and colporteurs.[25] Ambulant booksellers often had no established residence or store, and they made their way from door to door, selling the books and pamphlets they carried with them. They inhabited the margins of society and cultivated anonymity and invisibility as a means of survival. Exploring the history of illicit print, we discover a world of pseudonyms, false imprints, publishers who moved constantly, and distribution through indirect and heterogeneous routes. This was a trade that necessitated the constant obfuscation and transformation of identity.

Simply by choosing to look in some places and ignore others, the police began the process of legal interpretation. Small, 'respectable' bookstores probably sold illicit literature discreetly 'under the counter', but such transactions rarely interested the police. The same was true of private collectors, who no longer feared police searches of their personal libraries.[26] Perhaps

---

[24] GStA, Bd. 2, p. 212. Report from police headquarters in Berlin to the Minister of Interior regarding the legal measures against advertising and displaying contraceptive devices (my emphasis).

[25] Some famous and well-documented obscenity cases include the trial of Gustave Flaubert for *Madame Bovary* in the 1850s, and the controversy surrounding Frank Wedekind's plays in the early twentieth century. For a thoughtful analysis of Flaubert's trial, see D. La Capra, *Madame Bovary on Trial*, Ithaca, NY: Cornell University Press, 1982. On the debates about obscenity in Bavaria that formed the context for Wedekind's trial, see R. Lenman, 'Art, Society, and the Law in Wilhelmine Germany: The Lex Heinze', *Oxford German Studies*, 8, 1973, pp. 86–113.

[26] During the eighteenth century, private book collectors were subject to searches and confiscations. Examples of books confiscated from private libraries are available in the Bayerische Staatsbibliothek, *A-Registratur B*.

this discreet trade was ignored because it did not intrude on 'public' spaces (the law condemned works 'distributed, displayed or attached *in spaces accessible to the public*').[27] But if the police ignored the 'respectable book trade', they kept a close watch on market places, city streets and the itinerant booksellers who inhabited both. By focusing on public spaces, the police attempted to prevent disruptions between the home and the street. The 'filth' of the urban environment could be contained, if not eliminated.

At mid-century, the police were preoccupied with books available in lending libraries. According to the historian Ronald Fullerton, there were 350–400 lending libraries in Germany in 1820, and the number had grown to 600 by 1842.[28] In 1859, the critic J.W. Appell lamented the dangers of the lending library: 'As everyone knows, in modern times these so-called lending libraries – which should be seen as *purveyors of poison rather than apothecaries of the soul* – have come under a certain degree of police control.'[29] Booksellers who had access to stock and a feel for popular taste could provide readers with new books every week.[30] Through the eyes of the police, lending libraries were 'public' in a way that private bookstores were not. This meant that the reading habits of those more likely to rent books – women, the working classes – were closely scrutinized, while those of elite men were not.

A case involving the proprietor of a lending library gives us some sense of the peculiarity of this institution. A report from Trier explained that *Casanova's Memoirs* had been discovered in the lending library of a bookseller named Sicius from Saarlouis. In addition to possessing multiple volumes of *Casanova*, Sicius was also caught lending *The Memoirs of Lola Montez*.[31] The second work was loosely based on the real-life adventures of Montez, the former mistress of the Bavarian king. Though he was caught circulating two illegal works, Sicius received exceptionally lenient treatment from local authorities. The district magistrate defended the character of the bookseller, 'the case of Sicius of Saarlouis appears to have been an occasion of igno-

---

[27] My emphasis.

[28] R. Fullerton, 'The Development of the German Book Markets, 1815–1888', PhD thesis. Madison, 1975, p. 115.

[29] J. W. Appell, *Die Ritter-, Rauber-, und Schauerromantik: zur Geschichte der deutschen Unterhaltungsliteratur*, Leipzig: Engelmann, 1859; reprinted 1967, p.6 (my emphasis).

[30] R. Engelsing, *Der Bürger als Leser. Lesergeschichte in Deutschland 1500–1800*, Stuttgart: Metzler, 1974. Engelsing argues that the period between 1500 and 1800 marked a transition in German reading habits from intensive to extensive reading habits. He also argues that readers moved from intensive reading of religious texts to a new taste for secular literature. If Engelsing's thesis is right, lending libraries were one place where readers could indulge their taste for extensive reading.

[31] Many popular memoirs and libels about the notorious Lola Montez circulated in the 1850s. Montez was the mistress of Ludwig, the king of Bavaria, who abdicated his throne in 1848, after his affair with her.

rance. He seems to be an *upright, orderly* man, who would not deliberately sell or lend books of this kind; nor is he the type likely to take a refractory stand against the orders of officials.' Sicius was judged to be an honourable and 'orderly' man, ignorant of the content of the books he lent.[32] In lieu of pressing charges, the district magistrate agreed to warn Sicius in person that the police would keep a closer eye on lending libraries in the future. The report also noted that the offending volumes had been safely deposited in the police station in Saarlouis, as it was usual to note the location of confiscated books.

Sicius's case alerts us to the way social status could play a role in decisions to prosecute a bookseller or publisher. Respectability and 'orderliness' (a high compliment in nineteenth-century Germany) could mitigate official perceptions of a crime. Status was particularly important in the initial encounter with the police, who made preliminary decisions about which books to confiscate and which booksellers to prosecute.

With no claims to respectability or orderliness, itinerant booksellers were favourite targets of the police. In 1855, the publisher, political activist and pornographer August Prinz warned contemporaries about the dangers of the ambulant trade. 'Among itinerant [book]sellers,' he wrote 'belonged peculiar people who were brazen and impudent. It they were thrown out of the house, they were not ashamed to reappear in another form.' As they were often financially desperate, 'when trade is slack, they are driven to steps of violence and temptation'.[33] Contemporaries distinguished between two varieties of itinerant booksellers. The first were street peddlers, or *fliegende Buchhändler*, who sold books and pamphlets on urban streets out of boxes they carried. Street peddlers had long been a fixture of urban life, and they had gathered for decades on busy streets and in market places to sell flowers, fruit, birds, cherries, and sometimes books. The popular 'street cries' genre of children's literature depicted city streets filled with the 'cries' of peddlers.[34]

Itinerant booksellers occupied a particular symbolic position as mobile occupants of the city streets. They inhabited the margins of society and had

---

[32] GStA, I. 77. 380. 7. Bd. 1, p. 59. Report from the District Magistrate in Trier to the Minister of Interior in Berlin, *die verbotene Schrift: Denkwürdigkeiten von Casanova betreffend*, 17 January 1857.

[33] A. Prinz, *Der Buchhandel vom Jahre 1815 bis zum Jahre 1843. Bausteine zu einer späteren Geschichte des Buchhandels*, Altona: Verlagsbureau 1855. There is an extensive historical literature on colportage. See, for example, R. Fullerton, 'Creating a Mass Book Market in Germany: The Story of the Colporteur Novel', *Journal of Social History*, 10, 1977, pp. 489–511.

[34] See, for example, the street cries genre: the 'Cries of Paris,' and the 'Cries of Berlin.' An excellent bibliography on the streets cries genre is available: K. Beall, *Kaufrufe und Strassenhändler: eine Bibliographie* [*Cries and itinerant trades: a bibliography*], Hamburg: Hauswedell, 1975.

few professional standards to uphold (or if they did, economic desperation made reputation a luxury they could not afford). Though they were required by law to submit a list of the books they carried to the police, they managed to slip illicit books into the boxes they carried with them.[35] Forbidden books sold, and itinerant booksellers were willing to take a chance. The danger attributed to peddlers seemed to confirm the fact that the city was filled with dangers, particularly for those who were new to the city.

The second variety of itinerant bookseller was the colporteur, who travelled from town to town, selling in communities where print was not widely available. These wandering booksellers walked long distances, carrying their wares in a box on their back. Usually these boxes contained almanacs, dream books and practical guides to letter writing or medicine; they might reveal French novels, sensational memoirs and tales of urban crime. Colporteurs often overlooked the orders of the police, selling the books that sold in spite of risks. Like urban peddlers, colporteurs inhabited the edges of society. In a culture that associated mobility with vagrancy and criminality, the colporteur was perceived as a dangerous, if also exciting, visitor.

By the time the police delivered confiscated books to the courts, they had made important decisions about the meaning of 'immoral writings'. They focused on figures who haunted the streets, and regulated the readers who bought or borrowed from them. The police were readers of a peculiar kind, as they emphasized context over formal analysis and paid little attention to the words on the page. Instead, their reading focused on the possibilities for unregulated reading provided by the city. They hoped that the freedom and anonymity of the city could be offset by determined regulation and accordingly they kept careful notes of all that beckoned vulnerable newcomers and seasoned book buyers on the city streets. Their preoccupation with disease, poison and physical dangers directed their vision to the social margins of city life. Animated by these concerns, the police made decisions about which books should be delivered to the courts.

The courts as readers

Although clues about the way the courts read must be teased out of terse reports of confiscations and trials, it is clear that they paid close attention to the words on the page. The task of the public prosecutor was to prove that a book in question was indecent or obscene by pointing to particular passages. Condemnations were not based on the spirit of the book, or even the context

---

[35] For an excellent discussion of the newcomer to the city in nineteenth-century America, see K. Halttunen, *Confidence Men and Painted Women: a Study of Middle Class Culture in America, 1830–1970*, New Haven, CT: Yale University Press, 1982.

in which it circulated, but rather on the words on the page. As a result, the court drafted decisions with a close eye to details.

A report of a trial in Neumünster demonstrates just how terse these court decisions could be. The report explained that in 1879 two colporteurs from Bremen were found in possession of the illicit novel *Louis XV and his Court, or the Marquise de Pompadour*. The colporteurs in question were working for a wholesale bookseller in Hamburg by the name of Kramer. The legal decision was focused, as it often was in such cases, on a brief passage from the book. The court reported that 'the immoral character of the second volume is beyond doubt. It is hereby established that that the two men accused sold and distributed immoral writings; they are therefore to be punished according to §184 of the Penal Code.'[36] In his defence, Kramer said that six years earlier he had submitted a copy of the condemned novel to the police in Berlin. On that occasion, police headquarters had reviewed the volumes and approved them for colportage. Because the story sounded plausible, the courts reduced their penalty. Nonetheless, the novels were declared illegal to print and circulate, and the booksellers were left to absorb the expense of lost stock.

Courts treated the voluptuous volumes they read with an analytic eye and a good deal of reserve. They matched florid language with formulaic decisions. Occasionally, however, trial reports lingered on the details of a decision, revealing clues about how courts read.[37] In late 1879, a report from Alta's police headquarters recounted the details of a trial of two booksellers, August and Carl Vaternahm. Both were accused of selling three 'obscene' pamphlets: *The Memoirs of the Marquise of Pompadour*; *The Memoirs of Catherine II, Queen of Russia*; and *The Memoirs of Jerome Bonaparte, a Love Story of the Wesphalian Court in Cappel*. The three pamphlets were all published in Berlin by a C. I. Leo, but somehow they had made their way into the coffers of booksellers in northern Germany.[38] Pamphlets of this kind were commonly found alongside the colporteur's standard offering of dream books and letter-writing manuals. The three confiscated pamphlets were initially tried by a local court in Altona, and then brought before an appellate court in Kiel. Among the hundreds of court reports generated by the campaign to suppress immoral books, this is one of the few that lingered on the court's process of

---

[36] GStA, 1. 77. 380. 7. Bd. 2, pp. 172–3, Copy of a report to Berlin from Neumünster on 6 May 1879. See also the trial report from Neumünster on 12 May, 1879, pp. 167–9 of the same file. §184 of the *Reichstrafgesetzbuch* Reich Penal Code, the passage concerning 'immoral and obscene writings,' followed the language of the 1851 Prussian Penal Code.

[37] Sometimes these cases were decided by a court of jurors, or *Schöffengericht*.

[38] GStA, 1. 77. 380. 7. Bd 3, p. 23. Copy of the proceedings against Rudolf Franz Vaternahm from Zechnow bei Landesberg and August Vaternahm, bookseller from Altona, September 9, 1879. Rudolf Vaternahm's occupation is illegible, but it is likely that he was a colporteur.

reading. First, the judge rejected the defence that the *Memoirs of the Marquise* were based on historical fact (scholarly merit was one viable defence):

> Following page 120, [the work] gives an exhaustive description of a scene in which the Marquise is shown to be nearly insane with lust. She is interrupted just as she is at the point of sexual abandon with the king. On the same day, she finds herself in the same situation with [another man], and is again disrupted. The scene ends with the observation that the poor little Marquise was interrupted twice in the same day with unfinished business – a bad break. ... No further argument is required to show that the goal of the work is not to elucidate historical truths, but rather to create the most indecent scenes. These [scenes] are more or less the product of the author's fantasy. Furthermore, both the form and the content are obviously calculated to rouse the sensuality of the reader.

The pamphlet was convicted based on its graphic references to sexual intercourse. Also, the work was largely fictional, and emerged from the imagination of the author. 'Science' and 'reality' could be defended, but fantasy could not. If we pay close attention to the language of the courts, we also learn about the shifting nature of legal authority. By 1879, the courts had worked out a more refined definition of 'indecent or obscene writing'. This definition appears at the end of the judge's commentary, where he states that the work was 'calculated to rouse the sensuality of the reader'. Cast in these terms, moral censorship was justified because it protected the vulnerable reader and expressed the values of the collective. The courts also began to focus on explicit representations of sexuality – in novels, books of advice for married couples, and pornography. By 1880, 'immoral writings' referred almost exclusively to *sexual immorality.*

The *Memoirs of Catherine II* were condemned on similar grounds. The judge wrote: 'On page 68, a caricature is described in an obscene manner, which refers to the sexual intemperance of the Empress Catherine II.' Like *Memoirs of the Marquise*, the work depicted a woman's search for sexual satisfaction with several partners. The argument that the book was historically accurate was again dismissed, as 'it is obvious that the work deals not with a faithful account of historical facts, but instead with an account assured to sexually excite the reader'. The third pamphlet received the same treatment, and was likewise condemned. In the text of his decision, the judge repeated his legal understanding of the legal term 'immoral and obscene'. The works *'rudely injure the feelings of shame and morality* by their tendency to arouse sensuality with representations of sexual pleasure.'[39] Human capacity for shame was seen as a 'natural' impulse, rather than a culturally conditioned response. Offending the 'feelings of shame' was thus an assault against both the mores of society and the integrity of the individual.

---

[39] Ibid., emphasis mine.

Concepts of obscenity had shifted considerably from the 1819 police rescript condemning books that 'offended religion, morality or *bürgerliche* Order.' At mid-century, the definition of 'immoral writings' had been broad and inclusive and encompassed materialist philosophy, Jewish and Catholic religious tracts and popular science. By the end of the 1870s, the courts of the German Reich defined obscenity almost exclusively in terms of sexuality and reproduction.

It follows that there were also shifts in the metaphors used to describe the effects of immoral writings. Dirt, filth and contagion were metaphors of disease and danger that drew connections between immoral writings and the city streets. Imagined in these terms, immorality, like disease, was something that could infect the innocent. Through contact with suspicious characters and their unsavoury wares, readers could be morally poisoned, and the private sphere might be contaminated. During the 1880s and 1890s, a new vocabulary began to animate the language of obscenity law.[40] Though metaphors of poison and dirt did not fall away entirely, the rise of psychiatry and genetic theories of disease offered new ways to describe the effects of immoral writings. In 1882, a new novel by the popular French novelist Emile Zola was reviewed by the German publicist Max Nordau. 'There exists a psychopathic disorder,' Nordau wrote, 'which psychiatry calls "moral insanity". The main symptom is the absence of any feelings of shame or morality. I cannot rid myself of the suspicion that Zola suffers from moral insanity.' Two days later, a letter from Wiesbaden urged the police in Berlin to confiscate and burn the novels of the 'morally insane Frenchman "Zola"'.[41] Psychiatry also led to efforts to link theories of criminality to 'immoral writings.' One report from the files of the interior minister explained that convicted criminals were interviewed about the books they read in the weeks before they committed a crime. After the 1880s, medical and psychiatric language continued to inform discussions of print culture and, later, other forms of media.

The campaign to suppress 'immoral and obscene writing' during the decades following the Revolution of 1848/49 was a unique attempt to explore a world of new realities and new rules. In a city that was larger, more diverse and filled with opportunities for illicit behaviour and heterodox beliefs, the police and courts could hope to have only partial control. The expanding trade of books and other writings, moving in and out of the city, available on city streets one day and gone the next, resisted order. The fact that authority was partial, subject to debate and permeable from below tells us something

---

[40] I am grateful to V.R. Berghahn for directing my attention to this shift in the sources.

[41] GStA, I. 77. 380. 7. Bd. 3, p. 73. M. Nordau, 'Pot-Bouille von Zola', *Morgenblatt der Frankfurter Zeitung*, 26 April 1882. The letter, from a Dr Schreiber in Wiesbaden, in the same file, p. 63.

about the nature of power in post-revolutionary Berlin. Because obscenity law was cast in terms of social good and the protection of the individual, stories, ideas and voices could be legitimately censored only if a convincing claim could be made that exclusion served the interest of the public. Between 1850 and 1880, confusions over interpretation and authority were slowly and unevenly worked out. By the 1890s, the campaign to suppress 'dirt and trash [*Schmutz und Schund*] in word and image' legitimately claimed the support of the public (or, at least, one version of 'the public').

Further reading

Peter Baldwin, *Contagion and the State in Europe, 1830–1930*, New York: Cambridge University Press, 1999.

Alec Craig, *The Banned Books of England and other Countries: A Study of the Conception of Literary Obscenity*, London: George Allen, 1962.

Carolyn Dean, 'Pornography, Literature, and the Redemption of Virility in France, 1880–1930', *Differences*, 5, 1993, 62–91.

Rolf Engelsing, *Der Bürger als Leser: Lesergeschichte in Deutschland 1500–1800*, Stuttgart: Metzler, 1974.

Isabel V. Hull, *Sexuality, State and Civil Society in Germany, 1700–1815*, Ithaca, NY: Cornell University Press, 1996.

Lynn Hunt (ed.), *The Invention of Pornography: Obscenity and the Origins of Modernity, 1500–1800*, New York: Zone, 1993.

Georg Jäger, 'Der Kampf gegen Schmutz und Schund. Die Reaktion der Gebildeten auf die Unterhaltungsindustrie', *Archiv für Geschichte des Buchwesens*, 31, 1988, 163–91.

Robin V. Lenman, 'Art, Society, and the Law in Wilhelmine Germany: The Lex Heinze', *Oxford German Studies*, 8, 1973, 86–113.

Alf Lüdke, *Police and State in Prussia, 1815–1850*, trans. Peter Burgess, Cambridge: Cambridge University Press, 1989.

Colin Manchester, 'A History of the Crime of Obscene Libel', *Journal of Legal History*, 12, 1991, pp. 26–57.

Marc Raeff, *The Well Ordered Police State: Social and Institutional Change through Law in the Germanies and Russia, 1600–1800*. New Haven, CT: Yale University Press, 1983.

Rudolf Schenda, *Volk Ohne Buch. Studien zur Sozialgeschichte der populären Lesestoffe, 1770–1910*. Frankfurt am Main: V. Klostermann, 1970.

Erich Schön, *Der Verlust der Sinnlichkeit, oder, Die Verwandlungen des Lesers: Mentalitätswandel um 1800*, Stuttgart: Klett-Cotta, 1987.

Gary Stark, 'Pornography, Society, and the Law in Imperial Germany', *Central European History*, 3, 1981, pp. 200–229.

Annie Stora-Lamarre, *L'enfer de la IIIe Republique: Censeurs et Pornographes (1880–1914)*, Paris: Imago, 1990.

Mary Lee Townsend, *Forbidden Laughter: Popular Humor and the Limits of Repression in Nineteenth-Century Prussia*, Ann Arbor, MI: University of Michigan Press, 1992.

Karl Klaus Walther, *Die deutschsprachige Verlagsproduktion von Pierre Marteau/Peter Hammer, Köln: Zur Geschichte eines fingierten Impressums*, *Zentralblatt für Bibliothekswesen*, vol. 93, Leipzig: VEB Bibliographisches Institut, 1983.

Albert Ward, *Book Production, Fiction and the German Reading Public, 1740–1800*, Oxford: Oxford University Press, 1974.

CHAPTER FIVE

Readers, browsers, strangers, spectators: narrative forms and metropolitan encounters in twentieth-century Berlin

Peter Fritzsche

When he was 23 years old, Jakob van Hoddis read his most famous poem, '*Weltende*' – 'End of the World' – in a Berlin cabaret. A few weeks later, he published it in the January 1911 issue of the literary magazine *Der Demokrat*. Nothing van Hoddis later wrote had the same impact as did these eight lines:[1]

> The bourgeois' hat flies off his pointed head,
> the air re-echoes with a screaming sound.
> Shinglers plunge from roofs and hit the ground,
> and seas are rising round the coasts (we read).
>
> The storm is here, crushed dams no longer hold
> the savage seas come inland with a hop.
> The great part of people have a cold.
> Off bridges everywhere the railroads drop.

Things no longer hang together in van Hoddis' rendering of the sensible world. Simultaneous juxtapositions and causal non sequiturs indicated a dishevelled universe, one that was folded and torn by surprise and shock. Just a few years after the great Messina earthquake of 1908, only months after Halley's Comet

---

[1] I have modified the translation of 'Weltende' from Michael Hamburger and Christopher Middleton (eds), *Modern German Poetry*, New York: Grove Press, 1964. The original reads as follows:

Dem Bürger fliegt vom spitzen Kopf der Hut,
In allen Ländern hallt es wie Geschrei.
Dachdecker stürzen ab und gehn entzwei,
Und an den Küsten-liest man-steigt die Flut.

Der Sturm ist da, die wilden Meeren hupfen.
An Land, um dicke Dämme zu verdrücken.
Die meisten Menschen haben einen Schnupfen.
Die Eisenbahnen fallen von den Brücken.

had brushed the planet in spring 1910, van Hoddis probed the supernatural behind the natural. Written a few years before the outbreak of the First World War, '*Weltende*' also anticipated the coming catastrophe, at least according to generations of literary critics for whom Jacob van Hoddis was a sensitive 'outsider' able to see turbulence beneath outwardly tranquil appearances.[2]

Indeed, van Hoddis' companions took his garbling words as revealed truths to be set against a deceiving order. Johannes Becher, later 'culture czar' of the German Democratic Republic, remembered 'Weltende':

> These eight lines seemed to transform us into entirely different people, to raise us out of a world of bourgeois convention … These eight lines seduced us again and again. We sang them, we hummed them, we murmured them, we whistled them … we shouted them at each other across the street as if they were battle cries.

Armed with these lines, Becher found the 'indifferent, horrible world' 'no longer quite so solid'.[3] Forty years after the fact, Becher mobilized van Hoddis against the bourgeois order to enlist him in the socialist politics of the 'other Germany'.

Yet this insurrectionary text also has a defining context. Berlin in 1911– 4 million inhabitants in a brand new industrial conglomeration – contained its own versions of disorder in which the fugitive appearances, unexpected encounters, and rapid fluctuations of the city challenged nineteenth-century certainties again and again. To account for this perceptual field, artists experimented with new representational techniques. The 'snap-shot' style of *feuilleton*, the anti-narratives of the modern novel, and the disruptions and displacements of Expressionist poetry have all been related to a distinctly metropolitan way of seeing at the turn of the century, which can be summed up as modernism.[4]

So perhaps it was not van Hoddis shouting at the city, but the city shouting back at van Hoddis. We know that the city was a powerful presence. The painter Ludwig Meidner used to take night-time walks with van Hoddis, who was actually born Hans Davidsohn, Jewish son of a Berlin physician. Together Meidner and Davidsohn walked until dawn along the edges of the city – Berlin Nord, Berlin Ost – where, amidst construction sites, newly erected tenements, and ramshackle carnivals and dancehalls, the crackling sense of things becoming metropolitan was most apparent.[5]

---

[2] See, for example, Helmut Hornbogen, *Jakob van Hoddis: Die Odyssee eines Verschollenen*, Munich: Hanser, 1986, p. 69.

[3] Cited in Hornbogen, *Jakob van Hoddis*, p. 72.

[4] Silvio Vietta, 'Grossstadtwahrnehmung und ihre literarische Darstellung. Expressionistischer Reihungsstil und Collage,' *Deutsche Vierteljahresschrift für Literaturwissenschaft und Geistesgeschichte*, 48, 1974, pp. 354–73; see also Heinz Rölleke, *Die Stadt bei Stadler, Heym, und Trakl*, Berlin: Schmidt, 1966.

[5] Quoted and translated by Eberhard Roters, 'The Painter's Nights', in Carol S. Eliel, *The Apocalyptic Landscapes of Ludwig Meidner*, Los Angeles: County Museum, 1989, pp. 75–7.

Van Hoddis, sensitive poet, or Davidsohn, metropolitan: these two figures can stand for two different, somewhat oversimplified, approaches to modernism. One draws attention to the experimentalism of an avant garde in rebellion, the other indicates the disorienting impact of the metropolis and thus the importance of a developed, industrialized context. But the poem '*Weltende*' provided an additional complicating factor, which insinuates itself between the insurrectionary experimentalist and the disorderly city. In van Hoddis' line: 'Seas are rising round the coasts (we read)', the parenthetical 'we read' signals just how much the press mediated and amplified the improvised and dangerously precarious nature of big-city surroundings. With his aside 'we read', van Hoddis suggested the extent to which metropolitans and readers lived in a second-hand universe composed of signs and images that were connected only incompletely to actual events and happenings. '(We read)': Modern cities had become inseparable from the commercial records, advertising broadsides, and newspaper stories that embellished them. 'We read' thus frames my own exploration of the modern experience, which, I argue, did not simply leave traces in popular texts but was itself fashioned by the reading, writing, and circulation of those texts.

It was difficult to use the city without reading through the city. Two interrelated processes were at work to bring the built city into correspondence with the word city. In the first place, with its streetcars and streetcar destinations, Berlin 1900 had become, in the words of Richard Sennett, a 'gathering of strangers,' a place where 'strangers [were] likely to meet'.[6] Workers no longer lived near factories and workshops, commuting to work became more and more normal. New industries and new migrants assisted in this disconnection between home and work, which not only meant that (still mostly male) workers and later (increasingly female) shoppers criss-crossed larger and larger parts of the city by streetcar but that families felt free to move from apartment to apartment around the city. The degree of mobility is astonishing. In the year 1913, for example, each Berliner took a total of 306 trips on streetcars, three times more often than had been the case in 1890.[7] In the last years before the First World War, no fewer than 750 000 and occasionally as many as 1.2 million commuters used the city's streetcars every day; thousands more rode motorized buses, underground subways and the suburban *Stadtbahn*, so that a daily average of nearly 2 million Berliners (out

---

See also Charles W. Haxthausen, 'Images of Berlin in the Art of the Secession and Expressionism', in *Art in Berlin 1815–1989*, Atlanta Museum: Washington University Press, 1989, pp. 68–73.

[6] Richard Sennett, *The Fall of Public Man*, Cambridge: Cambridge University Press, 1976, pp. 47, 39.

[7] Erich Giese and H. Paetsch, *Polizei und Verkehr*, Berlin, 1926, p. 20; Erich Giese, *Das zukünftige Schnellbahnnetz für Gross-Berlin*, Berlin, 1919, p. 32.

of a total of 4 million) were mechanically moved about the city.[8] Not surprisingly, the extensive transportation network became one of the distinguishing characteristics of the city. This mobility generated a new familiarity with the metropolitan aspects of the city and particularly its points of exchange and intercourse. Outlying commuters stitched central places such as Potsdamer Platz, Jannowitzbrücke, and Alexanderplatz into their individual itineraries. More and more Berliners came to use the city *as* a city.

The second process at work was the need to use secondary guides in order to use the city. It was almost impossible to make use of the metropolis (as opposed to the neighbourhood) without practical information on streetcar schedules, housewives' markets, and stock exchanges, without advertisements for Saturday-night theatre or Monday-morning jobs for hire, without reports on yesterday's sporting events or last night's family row down the street, and without warnings against corrupt marriage brokers or perfidious real-estate speculators. The big-city dailies that burst simultaneously on the scene at the end of the nineteenth century provided this sort of information, and mass-circulation papers such as *Berliner Morgenpost* or *Berliner Lokal-Anzeiger* quickly became everyday props in the city.

No metropolitan institution received quite as much attention as the *Grosse Berliner*, the city streetcar company. Newspapers were full of small items about new routes, extra cars, overcrowding, and collisions, as well as an unending stream of complaints and suggestions sent in by disgruntled commuters. As city people spent more and more time on public transportation, newspapers accordingly devoted more articles to questions of public behaviour – 'When should you pull the emergency brake?' or 'Should you get up or stay seated?'[9] Streetcars became part of the familiar interior of the city; articles reported on the life of streetcar conductors, told of the types to be found on the night bus, and examined the different ways in which passengers held their tickets.[10] In addition, a new genre of *feuilleton* articles detailed the flirtatious glances or awkward encounters among commuting strangers.[11]

---

[8] *Berliner Tageblatt*, no. 77, 12 Feb. 1907, reported that the biggest single day for 1906 was Sunday 17 June with 1 188 773 riders; the smallest, Friday 20 July, with 716 756. According to *Berliner Morgenpost*, no. 53, 3 March 1904, 1.6 million commuters used all types of public transportation each day in 1903, a figure which certainly reached 2 million by 1914.

[9] *Berliner Lokal-Anzeiger*, no. 557, 1 Oct. 1907; *Berliner Tageblatt*, no. 59, 2 Feb. 1906.

[10] See the series, 'Aus dem Leben der Strassenbahner,' *Berliner Morgenpost*, no. 249, 22 Oct. 1905; no. 255, 29 Oct. 1905; no. 260, 4 Nov. 1905; no. 270, 16 Nov. 1905; and 'Auf der Elektrischen, *Berliner Tageblatt*, no. 199, 21 April 1913.

[11] Heinz Knobloch (ed.), *Der Berliner zweifelt immer. Seine Stadt in Feuilletons von damals*, Berlin: Buchverlag der Morgen, 1977; Paul Schlesinger, *Das Sling-Buch*, Berlin, 1924, pp. 200–207; Johannes Trojan, *Berliner Bilder*, Berlin, 1903, p. 30; and 'Gespräche im Stadtbahncoupé,' *Berliner Tageblatt*, no. 285, 3 June 1907.

Moving about the city and reading about the city went hand in hand. The growing familiarity with streetcars indicated just how accustomed Berliners had become to moving about the city, and doing so not as neighbours but as commuters, strangers, and spectators. As city people circulated more widely and more frequently, the city in fact acquired an increasingly cosmopolitan quality. The busy commerce and restless recreations of the metropolis gradually overwhelmed the officious parade-ground ambience of the capital. Moreover, the delights of the metropolis attracted a large and socially diverse audience of proletarians and employees, men and women: it was no longer simply well-to-do *flâneurs* who were 'at home' in the city.[12] And as strangers and cosmopolitans, Berliners relied increasingly on the press for orientation. Local newspapers were not organized around work and it was only once the city became an emporium, a fairground, and a spectacle, in addition to a workplace, that Berlin's two biggest newspapers – Ullstein's *Morgenpost* and Scherl's *Lokal-Anzeiger* – attained their pervasive influence and came to be treasured alongside the '*Grosse Berliner*' streetcar company, the Wertheim department store, and Aschinger's beer palaces as quintessential Berlin institutions. With the extension of consumer culture at the end of the nineteenth century, Berliners came to see their surroundings through the perspective of the city newspaper and confronted the city as readers first.

While it is clear the city people became city readers, city readership also changed the city in important, though less obvious ways. Two local authors, Paul Gurk and Alfred Döblin, developed very different perspectives on city texts and they stand for two theoretical approaches to popular culture: one which regards reading and writing largely in terms of complicity, the other more generously in terms of subversion. This debate over the expressive potential of urban culture continues to be pertinent to this day, and Gurk and Döblin both recognized that cultural products worked in politically volatile ways. And both drew attention to the ways in which a culture of spectatorship had become as much a part of the city as the rhythm of factory work and the to and fro of raw materials and finished goods. The habit of enjoying the city as a spectator and seeing its contents as a spectacle had the effect of throwing a dazzling, superficial glaze over the city, and, as the mass media became more extensive and blurred the line between popular and high culture in the 1910s and 1920s, threatened to absorb history and memory in the sensation and surprise of the moment. Reflecting on 'the throngs that poured into the movie theatres night after night', Klaus Kreimeier contends that it was this 'Leviathan-like, voracious, everyday life of the city [that] gave Berliners

---

[12] Judith R. Walkowitz, *City of Dreadful Delight: Narratives of Sexual Danger in Late-Victorian London*, Chicago: Chicago University Press, 1992, pp. 16–18.

their equanimity and armed them against the impositions of history'.[13] It also provided the basis for a surprisingly open and tolerant and even democratic culture, particularly in the years before the First World War. It is worth examining the critiques of Gurk and Döblin.

At the end of Gurk's neglected Weimar-era novel *Berlin*, the itinerant bookseller Eckenpenn boards a streetcar which hurtles along the street like a screeching 'monster'. Eckenpenn sits down, pays his fare, and is at once blindsided by a newspaper that another commuter has suddenly unfurled in front of his face. This disregard accounts for Eckenpenn's demise. In a time when Berliners hurry along in streetcars and steal glances at newspapers there is simply no place left for books or booksellers. In a few masterstrokes, Gurk brings together the industrial schedules of the metropolis with debased regimes of reading and writing. As the bookseller travels about Berlin he encounters a city of readers, but, now mainly consuming newspapers in short intervals, this readership is driven by a relentless tempo that has obliterated contemplation and disenchanted experience.

Without adopting his heavy-handed tone, a number of modern critics more or less stand in Gurk's corner and regard newspapers, movies and other media as notable agents of homogenization and spiritual impoverishment. Cultural conservatives, Frankfurt School theorists, and Gramscian neo-Marxists apply the same broad strokes to their analyses: since the turn of the century, the culture industry has not only steadily abolished the intimate experience of reading books but gradually extinguished diversity as it has pulled various social groups into its vortex. In this view, men and women have been largely reduced to passive spectators who consume compelling images of a homogenized population in the pursuit of like-minded goals.[14]

In his analysis of discourse and counter-discourse in nineteenth-century France, for instance, Richard Terdiman identifies commercial newspapers as central sites in the production of the 'seamless serenity' of capitalism. Despite the juxtaposition of items on the front page, there was little about the modern newspaper, in Terdiman's judgement, that schooled readers to ac-

---

[13] Klaus Kreimeier, *The Ufa Story: A History of Germany's Greatest Film Company, 1918–1945*, New York: Hill and Wang, 1996, pp. 56–7. See also David Frisby, *Fragments of Modernity: Theories of Modernity in the Work of Simmel, Kracauer, and Benjamin*, Cambridge, MA: MIT Press, 1986, pp. 164, 170, 185; and Anton Kaes, 'Die ökonomische Dimension der Literatur: Zum Strukturwandel der Institution in der Inflationszeit, 1918–1923', in Gerald Feldman (ed.), *Konsequenzen der Inflation*, Berlin: Colloquium Verlag, 1989.

[14] Patrick Brantlinger, *Bread and Circuses: Theories of Mass Culture as Social Decay*, Ithaca, NY: Cornell University Press, 1983; James Naremore and Patrick Brantlinger, 'Introduction', in Naremore and Brantlinger (eds), *Modernity and Mass Culture*, Bloomington, IN: Indiana University Press, 1991; Richard Hoggart, *The Uses of Literacy*, London: Chatto and Windus, 1957; and Miriam Hansen, 'Early Silent Cinema: Whose Public Sphere?', *New German Critique*, 29, 1983, pp. 147–84.

tively perceive contradiction. 'In its routinised, quotidian recurrence, in its quintessential prosaicism, in its unrepentant commercialism,' the press flattened out and elided over difference and left power relations unquestioned. Newspapers 'seemed to go without saying,' representing the universe as a wonderfully complicated, colourful creation and doing so in a largely passive and utterly unchallenged way. Although Terdiman allows for counter-discursive interventions thanks to the occasional feuilletonist's sardonic irony or the caricaturist's bitter satire, these only highlight the hegemonic workings of the genre as a whole.[15]

There is much that is persuasive about Terdiman's analysis, and his observations about the way the newspaper calibrated readers to the operations of commodity culture are full of insight. Yet there is an overly serene, even static quality to his own portrait of the social text of the city. For the other Berliner, Alfred Döblin, by contrast, the social text itself has become unmanageable. The newspapers, handbills, advertisements, and stories he accumulates in the endless metropolis are anything but serene or seamless. In Döblin's big-city epic, *Berlin Alexanderplatz* (published in 1929), almost constant movement from all possible directions keeps the city in turmoil. From the very beginning of the story, when a page of newsprint grazes (but does not blindside) Franz Biberkopf on streetcar Number 41, texts interrupt and interject and jostle, and they continue to do so throughout the novel, disrupting again and again narrative coherence and mocking the idea of a stable, centred subject. What characterizes the city are fast-moving streams of information. The excessive number, simultaneous appearance, and rapid alternation of texts preclude any kind of metropolitan order. Under these turbulent conditions, Döblin's account of Franz Biberkopf in twentieth-century Berlin serves to discount the possibility of narration in the modern city.[16] Again and again, Döblin described the Berlin that inspired his writing with a diverse roll-call of characters whose versions and editions of the city were even more proliferate: 'two-thousand organisations,' he continued, 'ten-thousand newspapers, twenty-thousand reports, five truths.'[17] In our own time, Döblin has been echoed by Marshall Berman in whose *All That is Solid Melts into Air* the very great cities – Paris, St Petersburg, New York – are the turbulent places in which men and women must make themselves at home in conditions of

[15] Richard Terdiman, *Discourse/Counter-Discourse: The Theory and Practice of Symbolic Resistance in Nineteenth-Century France*, Ithaca, NY: Cornell University Press, 1985, p. 118, and generally pp. 118–38.

[16] I have found very helpful the summary analysis of Klaus R. Scherpe, 'The City as Narrator: The Modern Text in Alfred Döblin's *Berlin Alexanderplatz*', in Andreas Huyssen and David Bathrick (eds), *Modernity and the Text: Revisions of German Modernism*, New York: Columbia University Press, 1989.

[17] Döblin's response in 'Berlin und die Künstler,' *Vossische Zeitung*, no. 180, 16 April 1922.

perpetual change, a frightening but ultimately emancipatory challenge. For Gurk and Terdiman, Alexanderplatz – that odd, central Berlin square – might well stand for the order that is imposed violently on the city: slum clearance in 1906, Weimar-era design to keep traffic moving and city machinery humming, post-1949 East German plans to create a homogeneous socialist constituency in a one-dimensional living space, and now present-day insistence on 'world class' design for the newly unified *Weltstadt*. For Döblin and Berman, on the other hand, Alexanderplatz – that odd, central Berlin square – keeps slipping out of the frame imposed on it: it is a place that continually collects all sorts of debris and obstinately resists the designer. It remains kitschy, inappropriate, dangerous.

Alexanderplatz newspaper pages fluttered all around the place and they also littered Döblin's text. On page 269, for example: 'She went slowly back to the café, Prenzlauer corner, back again into the cafe. It was snowing ... On the Alex the newsboys were calling *Montag Morgen* and *Welt am Mittag*. She bought a paper from a strange boy, even looked at it.' Turn to page 274: 'He stepped into a little café, took a Kummel, thumbed the pages of the *Vorwärts* and the *Lokal-Anzeiger*.' And to page 279: 'Franz reads a copy of the *B.Z.* which is lying on the chair.'[18] Indeed, these ubiquitous texts provided Döblin with a miniaturized version of his entire project. Browsing over so many items, accumulating along the way such an array of stories, predictions, asides, and statistical data, and re-editing the city with each new edition, turn-of-the-century newspapers formally anticipated the structure and design of *Berlin Alexanderplatz*. Indeed, the manuscript copy of the novel reveals that Döblin wrote and pasted at the same time.

These texts – newspapers and newspaper stories – re-created a city that was ready-made for browsing. As turn-of-the-century newspapers discovered a metropolitan clientele and claimed to be institutions not simply *in* the city but *of* the city, reporters endeavoured to reproduce the meander of the *flâneur* who moved through the city without purpose or direction in order to slip into a shower of sensations. The metropolitan movements that Walter Benjamin and Franz Hessel celebrated in the 1920s were already long-established journalistic practices. By 1900, reporters and especially feuilletonists avidly collected the debris of the city – occasionals, incidentals, chance encounters – and wrote these up in an unsystematic way as 'snapshots' and 'sketches'.

---

[18] As Franz Biberkopf's movements around Alexanderplatz indicated, the habit of browsing among newspapers took place in cafés and restaurants as well. *BZ am Mittag*, no. 76, 30 March 1905, for example, advertised its availability in a total of 154 cafés in downtown Berlin. Café Josty on Potsdamer Platz even engaged a *Zeitungskellner* to select the latest newspapers for customers, and Café Bauer, on the famous corner of Unter den Linden and Friedrichstrasse, offered patrons a selection of more than 600 newspapers and magazines, each attached to a wooden pole in the Viennese manner.

The typical journey was simply to pass the day in a single place – the *Tiergarten* was a favourite location – and observe the timetable of contrasts unravel – boozers, businessmen, nannies, lovers, and teenage *Backfische* all had their routines and special spots. Social contrasts could be encountered even more dramatically by rambling through the entire city searching for variations on a theme. Eberhard Buchner, for example, made a study of popular theatre, and Hans Ostwald journeyed to a half-dozen different *Tanzlokalen* tucked into interior courtyards, clustered around the garish 'golden corner' at Oranienburger Tor, or scattered *'ganz weit draussen'* along the city's outer precincts.[19]

And while the practice of urban physiognomy imposed on the city a mechanical routine which made it possible to construct reliable schedules and accurate maps, the search for variation and colour provided the impetus for more digressive journeys that revealed again and again unpredictable aspects to the city. Snapshots could take up the most ordinary themes – Sunday afternoons, typists at their desks, commuters on the streetcar – in order to introduce 'everyday' people, particular individuals rather than social types. For example, a sketch of *Tempelhofer Feld*, the suburban park that doubled as imperial parade ground, presented readers with minor one-act dramas interspersed with mouthfuls of local dialect and political commentary: 'Willem hätte ja och mitjemusst. Und der Kleene veleicht och! Wejen Marokk'n!'[20] Again and again, excursions to music halls and cafés, encounters with kerbside vendors, or simply a walk across the street reported on the rough voices and individual manners of Berliners.[21] Long before Döblin, feuilletonists had begun working their way through the accumulation of litter that added up to the city and allowed readers to browse among charity-kitchen menus (main course: lung hash with potatoes), parade-ground songs ('Gestern noch auf stolzen Rossen, Heute durch die Brust geschossen'), working people's budgets, and even chalk traces of children's games ('Erich ... Kaiser; Hans ... König, Emil ... Junker').[22]

The descriptive attention to detail that made visible chalk marks on the sidewalk or audible gossip at Tempelhof was typical. *Feuilletons* trained

---

[19] Eberhard Buchner, *Varieté und Tingeltangel in Berlin*, Berlin, 1905; and Hans Ostwald, *Berliner Tanzlokale*, Berlin, 1905 – both widely excerpted in the metropolitan press.

[20] Lousie Schulze-Brücke, 'Ein Kinderparadies,' *Berliner Tageblatt*, no. 365, 20 July 1905.

[21] Walter Turszinsky, 'Im Theater der kleinen Leute,'*Berliner Tageblatt*, no. 84, 15 Feb. 1906; 'Strassenhändlerin,' *Berliner Morgenpost*, no. 175, 13 July 1909; Edmond Edel, 'Unsere Strassen,' *Berliner Tageblatt*, no. 279, 5 June 1906; and Victor Auburtin, 'Berliner Nachtleben', *Berliner Tageblatt*, no. 245, 15 May 1911.

[22] Erdmann Graeser, 'Auf dem 'Rummel,''*Berliner Morgenpost*, no. 125, 7 May 1911; Lousie Schulze-Brücke, 'Ein Kinderparadies,' *Berliner Tageblatt*, no. 365, 20 July 1905; 'Der Haushalt in teurer Zeit,' *Berliner Morgenpost*, no. 203, 30 Aug. 1905; and 'Am Krögel,' *BZ am Mittag*, no. 88, 14 April 1906.

readers to see and hear the jarring diversity of the city by striving for precision: by using just the right adjective, borrowing technical vocabulary to sharpen the portrait, favouring singular and proper nouns, introducing particular street-corners, giving names and addresses, and quoting Berlin dialect. Practised in this haphazard, unmindful way, physiognomy provided a method to collect the bits and pieces of the metropolis and to question any form-fitting cohesion that might be imposed on the city.[23] It would be a mistake to see physiognomy simply as a way of freezing city matters and rendering them harmless, a kind of 'botanising on the asphalt' as Walter Benjamin put it.[24] Physiognomy was a method that picked up difference, and the standard fare of entertaining physiognomical sketches made difference one of the constitutive attributes of the modern city. This effect was enhanced by layout philosophy and the daily re-edition of a dozen major papers. City stories not only rendered the city spectacular but inconclusive, in flux.

Emphasizing the movement, contrast, and transitoriness of urban inventory, the newspaper moved away from a textual or narrative organization of reality and constructed a visual or tactile encounter with it. Even without photographs, the early twentieth-century boulevard press generated image after image whose selection was made according to formal properties rather than thematic substance. Thanks to this basically cinematic appraisal, there was much about the city that was not reported on. To stand on Potsdamer Platz in the middle of Berlin and revel in the surprises and shocks of noon-time traffic, in the unlikely combinations of pedestrians and commuters, and in the ever-changing inventory of buildings and entertainments was to miss some very determinate and differentiating aspects of city life, such as conditions of employment, housing, and upbringing. As T. J. Clark and Christopher Prendergast have argued, the famous Impressionist 'blur' constituted a bold claim that modern life had become indeterminate but surely revealed as well a refusal to acknowledge class division and political conflict that would have clarified the very sensible and often sinister workings of the city.[25] Although feuilletonists journeyed to asylums and homeless shelters they did so to discover the traffic of unlikely characters. It was not the harsh social pictures of industrial settlement but the busy exchanges of the commercial metropolis on which big-city newspapers focused, and reportage accordingly led readers

[23] Michael W. Jennings, *Dialectical Images: Walter Benjamin's Theory of Literary Criticism*, Ithaca, NY: Cornell University Press, 1987, pp. 26–9; Peter Fritzsche, *Reading Berlin 1900*, Cambridge MA: Harvard University Press, 1996.

[24] Walter Benjamin, 'The Paris of the Second Empire in Baudelaire,' in *Charles Baudelaire: A Lyric Poet in the Era of High Capitalism*, trans. Harry Zohn, London: New Left Books, 1973, p. 36.

[25] T. J. Clark, *The Painting of Modern Life: Paris in the Art of Manet and His Followers*, Princeton, NJ: Princeton University Press, 1984; and Christopher Prendergast, *Paris and the Nineteenth Century*, Oxford: Blackwell, 1992, pp. 1–45.

to see the city's ephemeral aspect rather than recognize its 'other sides'. Kinds of difference were also inadmissible. By the end of the nineteenth century, newspapers had gone well beyond boulevards and cafes to talk about working-class districts, yet they continued to exclude the desperation of poverty, the routine of the factory floor, and other oppressive social settings where uniformity did not encourage browsing. Jews were also completely excluded from the table of variations, although this is somewhat paradoxical since so many editors and journalists were Jewish. As a result of peripheral points of vantage, front-page strategies of juxtaposition, the use of excessive detail, and the routine practice of exclusion, the newspaper choreographed city life as a grand, ceaseless parade in which difference and sameness coexisted on uneasy terms. The 'word city' rewrote the ontology of the metropolis and generally ignored its sociology.

By representing Berlin as a vast spectacle which provided pleasure and, at the same time, by rewriting difference and division in aesthetic and otherwise non-political terms, the major dailies invariably falsified urban reality. The preoccupation with exterior forms and surface textures – contrast, disconti-nuity, surprise – overruled the presentation of socially conscious themes and obliterated a cogent political analysis of the city. Nonetheless, to depict the city in a series of sharp, visually compelling images allowed readers to breathe life and complexity into a social formation that had been previously regarded as deadening. Berlin was not simply a wasteland of exploitation and impoverishment as so many Naturalist novelists and other urban critics indi-cated in the 1880s and 1890s.[26] Feuilletonists encouraged readers to repudiate single-minded renditions of the metropolis and to see it as a contradictory and surprising settlement in which anything could happen, and to approach it as an object of desire and imagination. The culture of spectatorship thus built a democratic, if somewhat sentimental foundation.

The spectator, like the *flâneur*, suggested the possibility of an exuberant accommodation with city life, its shocks, and its anonymity. Berlin's metro-politan dailies invited readers to assume the role of strangers and to move through the city as spectators, browsers, and, ultimately, as consumers. They did so not simply by looking but by looking at looking. Again and again, readers recognized themselves in newspaper reportage as urban spectators. A fascination with windows onto the city – *Litfasssäulen* (advertisement pil-lars), show windows, and the incidental glances among strangers – revealed the newspaper's awareness that looking at the metropolis had become a central part of life in the metropolis. Countless reportorial 'window shots' in which the 'frame' remained clearly visible did not so much provide views on

---

[26] See, for example, Andrew Lees, *Cities Perceived: Urban Society in European and Ameri-can Thought, 1820–1940*, New York: Columbia University Press, 1985.

the city – although they certainly did – than announce the secret pleasures of viewing.

In what became a staple of big-city reportage, stories about the *Litfasssäulen* – about 'blood-red' reward notices posted by the police or about private appeals for runaway children to return home – at once stimulated pleasure in the reader (by telling a story) and depicted the stimulation of pleasure for the reader (by showing the telling of a story). 'Whoever has time and inclination,' gushed the *Berliner Tageblatt*, 'should let themselves fall into the dream of these pillars.'[27] Other feuilletonists fell into the step of the urban *flâneur* by taking one of the handbills handed out on the street and taking advantage of the exotic services it promoted. Reports on the metropolitan's daily march past window displays, street vendors, and alluring strangers confirmed the newspapers' re-presentation to readers of their visual pleasures. Readers recognized themselves in the newspaper and they did so primarily as browsers along the boulevard. And while the presumed spectator was usually male, feuilletonistic items did occasionally take the *flâneuse* as their subject.[28] In a scene described by one reporter, a 'charming turbaned beauty' on Tauentzienstrasse was flirting with one young man, but, at the same time, cast glances at others coming down the street. She was no different than other strollers: 'they are all searching for the happiness that lies on the street!'[29] *Strassenbekanntschaften* (street-corner acquaintanceships) and *Strassenbahnbekannschaften* (streetcar acquaintanceships) were routine feuilletonistic items. Imagined encounters among strangers on streets charged the city with erotic possibility. 'Just looking' described the basic urban encounter that the paper recounted.[30]

There is little doubt that city people, both male and female, increasingly used the metropolis as browsers, spectators, and consumers. As the city's population continued to increase, more and more Berliners crowded downtown streets, visited department stores, travelled to entertainments and diversions and then read about themselves in and about the city in the next day's newspaper. Indeed, on any fair-weather Saturday or Sunday before the First World War, about one-third of all Berliners actually bought a streetcar ticket, left the *Kiez* (neighbourhood), and explored the metropolis. The public demand to 'look' was so insistent that municipal authorities were even forced to repeal regulations that had shuttered shop windows on Sundays. 'People are born with a desire to gaze,' explained the working-class *Morgenpost*, yet

---

[27] 'Litfasssäulen,' *Berliner Tageblatt*, no. 90, 19 Feb. 1910.

[28] See, for example, Anne Friedberg, *Window Shopping: Cinema and the Postmodern*, Berkeley, CA: University of California Press, 1993; and Walkowitz, *City of Dreadful Delight*.

[29] Gustav Eberlein, 'Der Tauentzienstil,' *BZ am Mittag*, no. 270, 16 Nov. 1911.

[30] Rachel Bowlby, *Just Looking: Consumer Culture in Dreiser, Gissing and Zola*, New York: Methuen, 1985.

'the people' only have Sundays 'to stroll and look about', the very day of the
week they were inhibited from doing so.[31] In this way, 'just looking' invited
an assertive, open, and unconventional approach to the Imperial capital.

As newspaper readers, Berliners discovered themselves to be constituents
of a common metropolitan public. Simply the daily reoccurring habit of
picking up a paper, repeated uncountable times in households, cafes, and
streetcars across the city, indicated the correspondence between readers and
metropolitans. At the same time, readers saw themselves reflected in attentive press accounts that identified and tracked movements of the crowd:
umbrellas on a rainy day, the streetcar commute to work, beers at Aschinger,
Sundays in the Grunewald. Stories such as these inserted individuals into
broader rhythms. In remarkable exercises of public stage management, the
city's big newspapers also physically reassembled their readership on the
street by choreographing huge city-wide events that attracted hundreds of
thousands of sightseers. In a mammoth promotional effort, Ullstein and Scherl
spent millions of marks staging rallies around technological novelties. In
1908, for example, Ullstein co-sponsored the great New York to Paris auto-
mobile race, happily won by the German entry. Scherl brought Orville Wright
and his 'Flyer' to Berlin the next year, and Ullstein organised Germany's first
big aviation rally in 1911. In these years, as streetcar ticket sales confirm,
upwards of one million Berliners crowded streets and stadiums to catch a
glimpse of Germany's bright technological future. The metropolitan press
thereby reversed the process of reportage, reproducing the sensationalism of
the front pages on the grand boulevards. Being in the city was becoming
much like reading about the city. When we consider how the 'word city'
organized the city, it was not so much by making the metropolis legible as by
creating for it an increasingly like-minded readership that encountered the
city as spectators, as an audience.

Both the ever-changing city that so manifestly transformed surroundings
and the ever-widening sphere of the mass newspaper were among the prodi-
gious 'machines of the visible'. Like the cinema that ultimately replaced
them, daily newspapers surveyed the world in sensual, tactile terms and
urged readers to see themselves as spectators and the world around them as
spectacle. City spectacles and the momentary detail and fame they bestowed
had the unmistakable effect of enfranchising city people who might otherwise been dismissed as an urban mass. Nonetheless, this 'frenzy of the
visible' always remained dubious. The digressive manner of the *feuilleton*
kept the status of legibility in doubt and the 'reality effects' of its aesthetic
detail produced as much blindness as sightfulness. A great deal of the terrain
of the city and its harsh economies was never successfully integrated into a

---

[31] 'Fensterpromenade', *Berliner Morgenpost*, no. 144, 29 May 1910.

spectatorial view. At the same time, the new collectivity of spectators was always tenuous. Berliners did not all at once drop allegiances to neighbourhood, or cast off identities as workers or artisans. And yet it is important to stress that the consumer 'public' that city texts pulled together was not just smoke and mirrors. Browsing and consuming became important, even overriding parts of the city economy.[32] Moreover, on the eve of the Great War, it was plausible for the mass-circulation press to celebrate the public of spectators as a new popular and patriotic subject beyond the confines of class and the hierarchies of the monarchy. To Ullstein and Mosse, the city of strangers, assembled in exemplary order under the banner of technical accomplishment, indicated the potential and grandeur of popular nationalism and seemed to entitle Berliners to greater political responsibility, as most big newspapers pointed out in their demands for a thorough revision of Prussia's antique three-class suffrage system. The press spoke in the name of a democratic city of browsers. The spectacle that was too much for Berlin's police president, Traugott von Jagow, for whom electric lighting on Behrenstrasse was too bright and street noise too loud, was the foundation of a new civic culture as far as the *Berliner Tageblatt* was concerned. If new street regulations were put into effect, editors jibed, police would have to confiscate the bells on Bolle's milk trucks, proscribe newspaper vendors from calling out the evening edition in anything but a whisper, and require garrisoned officers and soldiers to parade on tiptoe. What 'would happen to a city in which one could throw nothing out of the windows, neither dust nor noise?' the paper asked, a question that revealed a rather remarkable conception of the metropolis as a colourful, confusing, contradictory place that frustrated regulation from above.[33]

Imperial Berlin does have another story to tell, one that historians of Germany remain largely oblivious to. Dusty, noisy, it was a place where people moved about the metropolis as strangers, indulged in the pleasures of 'just looking', and approached one another with increasing measures of tolerance. They featured as crucial constituents of a public sphere in which strangers were likely to meet and actively exchanged opinions and goods. In this respect, browsing's visual thrills were an extension of commodity exchange and economic necessity. In style and substance, newspapers carried the message that cities were places where goods had to be efficiently stored, handled, and moved and they also fashioned a democratic space accessible to idlers, specta-

---

[32] Neil Harris, 'Urban Tourism and the Commercial City', in William R. Taylor (ed.), *Inventing Times Square: Commerce and Culture at the Crossroads of the World*, New York: Russell Sage Foundation, 1991, pp. 66–82.

[33] 'Das lautlose Berlin', *Berliner Tageblatt*, no. 588, 17 Nov. 1912. See also Arthur Eloesser, 'Die Blumen des Herrn von Jagow', 1913, in *Die Strasse meiner Jugend. Berliner Skizzen*, Berlin: das Arsenal, 1987 [1919], pp. 57–61.

tors, and strangers. Berlin's press did not simply represent the city in terms of spectatorship but vigorously favoured unrestricted access to city places. In the face of police infringements on the rights of pedestrians, newspapers championed the free flow of both things and people – of sale items and consumers.[34] Even as they remapped the metropolis as a field of visual pleasure, the print media reworked the political face of the German capital: diluting difference into merely formal variation, to be sure, but habituating metropolitans to thrive in a world of strangers and inconstancy and to participate in the restless activity of commerce, as well encouraging them to move about freely and haphazardly. Urban spectatorship, consumer capitalism, and democracy thus worked in surprisingly compatible ways. Berlin 1900 was a *Weltstadt* not only in that it attracted as many tourists every year as did Paris but because it defined itself in terms of the display of difference and the thrill of the spectacle.

Just how seriously this cosmopolitan tradition around 1900 ought to be taken can be revealed by a quick glance at the Weimar years, when the status of difference in popular culture shifted dramatically. After the hardship years of war, revolution, and economic distress, the crowds on Potsdamer Platz and Friedrichstrasse appeared to break up. To be sure, Berliners continued to replenish metropolitan culture during the 1920s. They still read the *Morgenpost* on Sundays, crowded the ever-popular carnival grounds at Lunapark and flocked to the movies; they wandered through the night-time city illuminated by thousands of lights in a gigantic municipal spectacle in February 1928 and hailed the return of the Zeppelin over Berlin the next year. Nonetheless, the metropolitan crowd assembled less easily than it had before the war. Partisan politics separated and isolated various parts of the public, making chance encounters more difficult and exclusive loyalties to social groups more important. The Sunday suit and everyman's bowler in which men browsed the pre-war city were exchanged, more and more, for exclusive party and paramilitary uniforms or for a distinctively proletarian wear like the balloon cap.[35] By the late 1920s, after political tensions between Communists and Social Democrats exploded in street battles, neighbourhood strongholds such as 'Red Wedding' nurtured protective subcultures. At the same time, the Great Depression hastened the psychological flight of the middle classes into such neighbourhoods as Wilmersdorf, Zehlendorf, Schmargendorf and Reinickendorf – which were re-imagined as idyllic villages between the folds of the dangerous metropolis.[36]

---

[34] William R. Taylor, 'The Evolution of Public Space in New York City: The Commercial Showcase of America', in Simon J. Bronner (ed.), *Consuming Visions: Accumulation and Display of Goods in America, 1880–1920*, New York: Norton, 1989, pp. 288–91.

[35] On the bowler, Fred Miller Robinson, *The Man in the Bowler Hat: His History and Iconography*, Chapel Hill, NC: University of North Carolina Press, 1993.

[36] Erhard Schütz, '"Kurfürstendamm" oder Berlin als geistiger Kriegsschauplatz: Das

In these circumstances, the various lines of difference and scattered points of exchange that had once excited the modernist imagination were increasingly regarded as troublesome. Dancehalls and boulevards, which before the war mixed a diverse metropolitan crowd, now threatened what was taken to be a healthy, but beleaguered *Volk*. Nowhere is this shift in the evaluation of difference more clear than in the popular writings of Hans Ostwald, a well-known Berlin feuilletonist. For Ostwald, Imperial Berlin had been an exciting journey of discovery and his *flânerie* challenged the pretensions of the Wilhelmine establishment with sympathetic portraits of prostitutes, vagabonds, and other metropolitan marginals. But after the First World War he mapped out a fearsome and disreputable cityscape in his influential *Sittengeschichte der Inflation* (*Tales of Inflation*). Many of the same characters introduced before the war reappear in the 1931 *Sittengeschichte:* criminals, gamblers, hustlers, prostitutes, musicians, occultists. But rather than exotic mutations on the shifting ground of the new industrial city, they are vilified as extraneous parasites. Rather than expanding the idea of '*Volk*' and bringing city people of all kinds closer together – the explicit goal of Ostwald's earlier journalism – this post-war narrative polices the borders surrounding the *Volk*, at once distinguishing and segregating the margins in an effort to make more sanitary the core.[37]

For more and more Berliners, the carnival of the city at the turn of the century had collapsed into a house of horrors. The modernist features of the city in 1924 recall those of 1904 – instability, mutability, uncertainty – but they are invoked to extinguish rather than celebrate difference. The colourful play on metropolitan identities and metropolitan niches has been subsumed by the grinding work of social homogenization which emphasized the virtuous sameness – the basic thrift and hard work – of the German people. This 'displacement of difference' takes the measure of the violence that ominous cultural projects of the post-war years exacted on what accordingly must be seen as the tolerance and urbanity of the pre-war metropolis.[38]

Textmuster "Berlin" in der Weimarer Republik', in Klaus Siebenhaar (ed.), *Das poetische Berlin: Metropolenkultur zwischen Gründerzeit und Nationalsozialismus*, Berlin/Wiesbaden: Deutscher Univsersitäts Verlag, 1992; 'Kleinstadt Berlin', *Reclams Universum*, **48** (50), 8 Sept. 1932, pp. 1840–41.

[37] Peter Fritzsche, 'Vagabond in the Fugitive City: Hans Ostwald, Industrial Berlin, and the *Grossstadt-Dokumente*', *Journal of Contemporary History*, 29, 1994, 385–402. See also Martin Geyer, *Verkehrte Welt: Revolution, Inflation, und Moderne, München 1914–1924*, Göttingen: Vandenhoeck and Ruprecht, 1998; and Bernd Widdig, *Culture and Inflation in Weimar Germany*, Berkeley, CA: University of California Press, 2000.

[38] Michael Geyer, 'The Stigma of Violence, Nationalism, and War in Twentieth-Century Germany', *German Studies Review*, Winter 1992, pp. 75–110.

Further reading

Rachel Bowlby, *Just Looking: Consumer Culture in Dreiser, Gissing and Zola*, New York: Methuen, 1985.

Anne Friedberg, *Window Shopping: Cinema and the Postmodern*, Berkeley, CA: University of California Press, 1993.

David Frisby, *Fragments of Modernity: Theories of Modernity in the Work of Simmel, Kracauer, and Benjamin*, Cambridge, MA: MIT Press, 1986.

Peter Fritzsche, *Reading Berlin 1900*, Cambridge, MA: Harvard University Press, 1996.

David Clay Large, *Berlin*, New York: Basic Books, 2000.

Vanessa Schwartz, *Spectacular Realities: Early Mass Culture in Fin-De-Siècle Paris*, Berkeley, CA: University of California Press, 1998.

William R. Taylor (ed.), *Inventing Times Square: Commerce and Culture at the Crossroads of the World*, New York: Russell Sage Foundation, 1991.

Judith R. Walkowitz, *City of Dreadful Delight: Narratives of Sexual Danger in Late-Victorian London*, Chicago: Chicago University Press, 1992.

CHAPTER SIX

Commercial spies and cultural invaders: the French press, *Pénétration Pacifique* and xenophobic nationalism in the shadow of war

Fay Brauer

'Nowhere is one more a foreigner', Julia Kristeva maintains, 'than in France'.[1] At no time was this so tellingly demonstrated than during the series of crises which punctuated the period Eugen Weber calls 'the *avant-guerre*', beginning with the 1911 conflict over Morocco between France and Germany.[2] From the moment the German gunboat *Panther* anchored at Agadir, a storm of vengeful nationalism, long festering since the humiliation of France by Prussia, and the German annexation of Alsace-Lorraine, was unleashed throughout the French press.[3] With the thirst for revenge directed at foreigners, this Morocco crisis marked a shift in public discourse from cordial welcome to a siege psychosis. This new wave of xenophobic nationalism was only intensified by the 'treasonous' *Accord*, the eruption of the first Balkan War and the state's policy of defensive militarist patriotism. From the time of the Morocco crisis paranoia was then deflected and projected onto the foreigner, in keeping with xenophobic mechanisms of persecutionary delusion – particularly onto Germans and Jews, who were invariably conflated into a single arch-enemy.[4]

---

[1] Julia Kristeva, *Strangers to Ourselves*, trans. Leon S. Roudiez, London: Harvester Wheatsheaf, 1991, p. 38.

[2] See Eugen Weber, *The Nationalist Revival in France, 1905–1914*, Berkeley, CA: University of California Press, 1968.

[3] Despite the Treaty of Algericas, signed on 7 April 1906, ensuring the independence of the Sultan of Morocco by Italy, Spain, Russia, Britain, Germany and France, and despite some commercial collaboration between France and Germany, rivalry had reached a peak by 1911. In March, Moroccan nationalism erupted in riots at Fez against the French. When General Monier was ordered to transfer 25 000 troops from Casablanca to Fez, without the consent of the other Algericas signatories, this violation of the Treaty provoked the German counter-occupation of the ports of Agadir and Mogador.

[4] I am drawing here on Sigmund Freud's views on paranoia and jealousy and their subsequent reworkings by Lacan and post-Freudians. According to Freud, in his essay 'Some Neurotic Mechanisms in Jealousy, Paranoia and Homosexuality' (*The Compete Psychological Works of*

In the press and in the speeches of politicians, a metalanguage of persecutionist paranoia developed in which such keywords as *l'étranger* and *le métèque* were employed to refer to a newcomer or resident foreigner.[5] Far from connoting benevolent visitors enriching the life-blood of France, these terms had the resonance of racist equivalents such as 'wop' or 'wog', connoting an alien contamination and life-threatening incursion from the outside. Cast in the role of menacing outsider and dangerous rival, *l'étranger* came to be projected across the entire spectrum of politics and the press, as an alien threatening to invade and corrupt France.[6] Once this stereotyping spread with the speed of rumour, it was no longer used only by right-wing politicians or Royalist, virulently anti-Semitic publications such as *L'Action Française*, but also by the anarchist journal *L'Assiette au Beurre*, and the moderate, centrist and Radical press led by *Le Matin*.[7] Yet rather than attack the aliens for their open and visible occupation of French terrain, these papers accused them of invading France invisibly and insidiously. The alien was represented not as overpowering France territorially and militarily, but as infiltrating it industrially and commercially in what the nationalist press, following Charles Maurras at *L'Action Française*, called *'pénétration pacifique'* (peaceful infiltration).[8] Once this penetration threatened to extend to French art, and the nation's very culture also began

---

Sigmund Freud, Volume XVIII, Hardmondsworth: Penguin, 1991, pp 228–9): 'Jealous and persecutory paranoiacs project outwards onto others what they do not wish to recognize in themselves. ... The relationship is based upon a love as well as hatred of the other in oneself and oneself in the other'. In her essay entitled 'Every Picture Tells A Story: Art and Theory Re-examined', (in Gary Sangster (ed.), *Sighting References*, Sydney: Artspace, 1987, pp. 16–17), the post-Freudian philosopher, Elizabeth Grosz maintains that because the Other is not treated as a positive complementary, but negative counterpart, the Other is always perceived as threatening to expose the deficits in the first Subject.

[5] Raymond Williams, *Keywords: A vocabulary of culture and society*, London: Flamingo, 1976. On page 15, Williams remarks that particular words become indicative of forms of thought, which bind together ways of seeing culture and society.

[6] With the new freedom of press legislation passed on 29 July 1881, there was no restriction to politicians writing, let alone owning newspapers. Once Deputies and Senators occupied positions as directors, editors, sub-editors, writers and financial backers, the press became, I argue, directly political. The correlation of the political order with the press is theorized in the first chapter of my 'L'Art révolutionnaire: The Artist as Alien. The Discourses of Cubism, Modern Painting and Academicism in the Radical Republic', PhD thesis, Courtauld Institute of Art, University of London, 1997.

[7] See Eugen Weber, *Action Française, Royalism and Reaction in Twentieth-Century France*, Stanford, CA: Stanford University Press, 1962. See also D. Cottington, *Cubism in the Shadow of War. The Avant-Garde and Politics in Paris 1905–1914*, Yale University Press, 1998 – from which part of the title of this article derives. Cottington argues that this collapse of the political spectrum began with the parliamentary downfall of the Bloc des Gauches in 1905.

[8] Charles Maurras, 'L'Alliance Républicaine Démocratique', *L'Action Française*, 8 July 1911, p. 1. The full French term used was *pénétration pacifique de l'étranger*.

to appear vulnerable to such infiltration, the issue of the alien presence in France erupted into a parliamentary controversy.

In 1882 there had been a proposal on the part of the Radical Republicans to extend foreigners' rights by reforming the citizenship law. It had been blocked, however, by the *jus sanguinis* lobby, who had stipulated that French nationality could only be granted to those who had French ancestral blood.[9] It was not until 1889 when legislation was passed extending *jus soli* to second-generation foreigners and amending working restrictions for immigrants, that the foreigner's rights were brought closer to those of the French citizen – although, as Kristeva points out, political rights were still denied them.[10] The granting of civil liberties signified that the foreigner was welcome in the Radical Republic, particularly from 1901 when Radical politicians, in alliance with Socialists, Anarchists and Feminists, achieved periods of dominance in the French parliament.[11] It signified that the Radical Republic identified itself with the spirit of internationalism promoted by the labour movement. Yet by the time of the 1911 Morocco crisis 1.16 million had come to live in France, making it second to the United States as a destination for immigrants. Yves Lequin argues that it then began to appear that the 1889 legislation had fostered a 'pacific invasion'.[12] For Charles Maurras, who subscribed to an absolute principle of *jus sanguinis*, it was proof that French citizenship should only be transmitted by descent.

A nation's unity was defined by Maurras as hereditary, deriving from an uninterrupted continuity of race. Since this was personified by a king, the monarchy was pivotal to his concept of *integral* national unity, while the alien and the Jew were the opposite. Because they had neither descended from a French bloodline, nor sprung from roots in French soil, but had originated from a different patriality, neither the alien nor the Jew could,

---

[9] See Roger Brubaker, *Citizenship and Nationhood in France and Germany*, Cambridge, MA: Harvard University Press, 1992, pp. 88–112. Brubaker recounts how reform of the citizenship law grew out of an original proposal in 1882 and tortuous debate, particularly from the *jus sanguinis* lobby, with Camille Sée haranguing the Senate: 'Nationality must depend on blood, on descent, [not on] the accidental fact of birth in our territory'.

[10] After eight years, Republicans were eventually able to convince the Chamber of Deputies and Senate that the extension of *jus soli* would eliminate the privilege of long-settled foreigners avoiding conscription and prevent the formation of nations within the nation. Legislation stipulating the new rights of foreigners was then passed on 26 June 1889. Kristeva, however, refers to political constraints, particularly over suffrage.

[11] See Madeleine Rebérioux, 'A Radical Republic?', in Jean-Marie Mayeur and Madeleine Rebérioux, *The Third Republic from its Origins to the Great War, 1871–1914*, trans. J. R. Foster, Cambridge: Cambridge University Press, 1989.

[12] See Yves Lequin, *Histoire des étrangers et de l'immigration en France*, Paris: Larousse, 1992. In *Histoire de la vie française, VII, L'Essor 1870–1914*, Editions de L'Illustration, 1972, 172–3, André Armengaud indicates that the foreign population grew by 56 per cent between 1872 and 1911, while the French population increase was only 10 per cent.

according to Maurras, relate or contribute to the French heritage.[13] For Maurras, both the alien and the Jew were precluded by their racial differences from sharing French patrial blood-bonding, even when naturalized: they were, then, not just outsiders, but potential traitors.[14] However, when the Morocco crisis was followed by what *L'Action Française* called the treasonous '*Désaccord*', and Germany's withdrawal from Morocco was negotiated in exchange for the French Congo, the focus of Maurras's attack was no longer the rootlessness of the alien and the Jew. Instead *L'Action Française* ran a series of articles in which scaremongering tactics were relentlessly deployed to convey the impression that France was in a state of siege. The alien and the Jew were conflated into a single traitor, conspiring with Germany to sabotage France not just militarily, but industrially, commercially and culturally.

From 17 September 1911 until the outbreak of the Great War, *L'Action Française* regularly published, as if it were indisputable empirical evidence, totally unsubstantiated reports of German–Jewish conspiracies under the ominous headline 'Jewish-German Espionage'.[15] The newspaper identified the French Jew as a direct conduit to Germany, the German and the Jew being portrayed, from the first article, as conspiring to bring about the invasion of French forts in the East and the conquest of Normandy. They were also represented as conspiring to sabotage France financially. By the time of the Balkan War, when *L'Action Française* was well into its second series, readers had been warned against French corporate take-overs by such German businesses as the Schinnelpfeng Institute; against German capitalists such as Auguste Thyssen; against the exploitation and sabotage of the French Diélette mines by the huge German cartel Krupp; and against the German 'infestation' of French car distributors.[16] On top of this, readers were warned that infiltration extended to major governmental positions. This was supposedly demonstrated by such isolated examples as Berthold Frischauer's purported manipulation of the Zola Monument Committee and Solomon Reinach's promotion to Deputy Director of the National Museums.[17] In order to inten-

---

[13] Charles Maurras, *L'Action Française*, 21 March 1909, p. 1.

[14] As the deputy Delahaye bluntly put it: 'Vous avez deux patries ... la Judée et la France!', *Journal Officiel de la Chambre des Députés*, 9 Nov. 1910, p. 955.

[15] This was a series entitled *L'Espionnage Juif-Allemand*, which ran from 17 September 1911, initially as a weekly series, but which changed towards the end of the following month when reports on Jewish–German espionage began to be published every two to three days for nearly a decade.

[16] 'L'Espionnage juif-allemand II', *L'Action Française*, 14 Aug. 1912; 25 Aug. 1912; 1 and 7 Sept. 1912; 16 Aug. 1912; 11 and 19 Sept. 1912; 15 and 18 Sept. 1912. These were all front-page reports.

[17] Léon Daudet, 'L'Espionnage Juif-Allemand', *L'Action Française*, 17 Sept. 1911, p. 1. An ardent anti-Dreyfusard, Daudet not surprisingly opposed any monument being erected to the notorious Dreyfusard, Zola.

sify this atmosphere of siege and conspiracy, readers were in turn urged, as a dire patriotic necessity, to furnish *L'Action Française* with fresh evidence of Jewish–German infiltration.[18] With crisis seeming to feed upon crisis, their espionage campaign gathered momentum. While there was an increasing number of informers (and indeed subscribers), similar campaigns began to be run by diverse sections of the national press. Although *L'Action Française* had once been dismissed by the centrist, Radical and Anarchist press as extremist right-wing rumour-mongers and anti-Semitic conspiracy theorists, these newspapers now began similar xenophobic – although not necessarily anti-Semitic – campaigns, spurred on by France's seeming dependence upon German manufactured commodities and technological expertise.

In the autumn of 1911, *L'Action Française* headlined the admission of German 'thieves' to the Paris stock exchange on its front page;[19] but then so did *Paris-Midi*, where the item was also accompanied by a cartoon entitled *La Caricature à l'étranger*, which became a regular feature.[20] They were joined, but not immediately, by another newspaper, the Anarchist journal *L'Assiette au Beurre*. It suggested – in both text and image – the possibility of many more German 'invasions' facilitated by the French Jew, masked by what this satirical journal revealed as sinister strategies of dissimulation.

German counterfeiting of French products was initially conveyed in *L'Assiette au Beurre* cartoons exposing how champagne in perfectly faked bottles looked French, but did not always taste French.[21] Other cartoons suggested that it was not just French gourmet products which suffered this fate. In a cover by Ricardo Floret where English toothpaste, American shoes and Egyptian cigarettes were set out alongside cases marked *champagne de Paris*, and beneath the caption, 'La Contrefaçon Allemande (MADE IN GERMANY)', Germany was portrayed as counterfeiting other nations' commodities which it then exported as forgeries (see Figure 6.1) This idea was reinforced by another cartoon, where the Kaiser was depicted proudly announcing that all 'Made in Paris' products were fabricated in Nuremberg. Only when country of origin needed to be divulged, did the Germans reluctantly do so – as signified by another cartoon depicting this disclosure by showing a Jew wielding a paint-brush over packaging, to create the words,

---

[18] Ibid. Such anxieties were not restricted to the series 'L'Espionnage Juif-Allemand'; *L'Action Française* also reported that the Ministry of War was supposedly endangered by the employment of foreign 'domestics', while such Jewish appointments as Fernand David's to the Ministry of Commerce allegedly demonstrated how German espionage was infiltrating the Government.

[19] Léon Daudet, 'Le Bilan du Trimestre', *L'Action Française*, 4 Oct. 1911, p. 1.

[20] The front-page headline of *Paris-Midi* on 15 Sept. 1911 read 'L'Introduction des voleurs allemands à la Bourse de Paris'.

[21] In this cartoon which appeared in *L'Assiette au Buerre* on 23 December 1911, one gentleman had remarked on sipping his *coupe de champagne*, that it was not French, while his companion had retorted that it nevertheless looked French.

6.1 Ricardo Floret, *La Contrefaçon Allemande (Made in Germany)* – German Forgery: 'Made in Germany', cover design for *L'Assiette au Beurre*, no. 559, 30 December 1911. © Bibliothèque Forney, Ville de Paris.

'MADE IN GERMANY'.[22] According to these cartoons, German manufacturers treated the issue of country of origin simply as a matter of simulating the appropriate signs, which deception they undertook in collusion with Jews. A spate of further *L'Assiette au Beurre* cartoons insinuated, however, that German fakes were not just limited to such commodities.

Four months before the Morocco crisis, *L'Assiette au Beurre* had parodied the way in which President Fallières's colonial business policy in Tunisia constituted what it called 'la pénétration pacifique', under the guise of a 'civilizing mission'.[23] Seven months later, it applied the same term to the 'infiltration' of France by German nationals. Hoards of Germans dressed as camera-hung tourists, businessmen, tradesmen, engineers, pick-axe workers, teachers, secretaries, chambermaids and hotel porters were portrayed pouring into France under the headline: 'La Pénétration Pacifique'. (Figure 6.2). Before the Franco-Prussian war, *L'Assiette au Beurre* claimed, German immigrants in France had generally been itinerant peddlers on the industrial fringes.[24] Now, it 'revealed', German women were taking positions as chambermaids, company secretaries and teachers, while German men were working on construction sites and the stock exchange, as well as in factories, restaurants and hotels in the French capital.[25] Subsequent cartoons portrayed German army captains in jobs as hotel porters, especially in venues where French officers congregated, while seemingly naive, camera-clicking German tourists were depicted focusing their lenses on naval ports and army barracks with captions indicating how they were doing the Kaiser a service by taking these photographs on behalf of German soldiers.[26] Other cartoons suggested that even German workers in France were 'counterfeit' by showing how German workers in Paris dressed specifically in order to be taken for French.[27] What seemed more disturbing to *L'Assiette*

---

[22] 'La Contrefaçon Allemande (Made in Germany)', *L'Assiette au Beurre*, no. 559, 30 Dec. 1911, p. [4].

[23] 'Fallières en Tunisie', *L'Assiette au Beurre*, no. 525, 22 April 1911. President Fallières's trip to Tunisia in April 1911, to pave the way for further French banking contracts, was topical. On page 907, Fallières is portrayed in front of a graveyard, saying to Le Bey (King of Tunisia until 1902), 'business is business'. On page 902, where he is depicted in a back-street brothel with a Tunisian woman, under the caption 'La pénétration pacifique', the term carried sexual innuendo – not insignificantly given the number of *maisons de tolérance* (brothels) in Tunisia for French officers and civilians.

[24] 'La Pénétration Pacifique', *L'Assiette au Beurre*, no. 554, 24 Nov. 1911, pp. [1–7].

[25] Ibid.

[26] Ibid. In a cartoon on page 14 depicting a German tourist/army sergeant's arrival at a French hotel, he is shocked to find that the porter was his Captain. Yet as the latter explains in the text, it was a strategic disguise in a hotel filled with French officers. On page 8, under the caption, 'Les Touristes Allemandes', two German tourists are shown taking photographs of French mountains, with fortifications.

[27] 'La Contrefaçon Allemande (Made in Germany)'. In the mock letter on the first two pages,

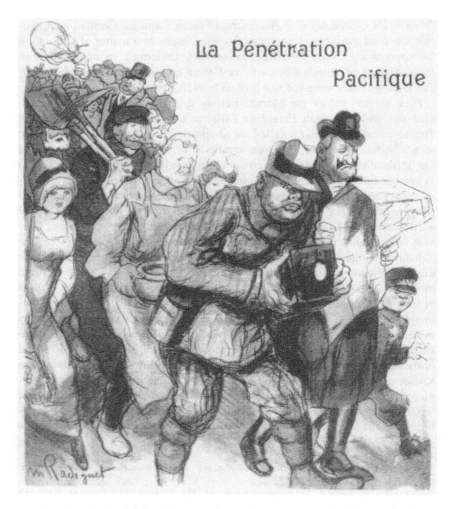

La Pénétration Pacifique

6.2   M. Radiguet, *La Pénétration Pacifique* – The Peaceful Infiltration, cover design for *L'Assiette au Buerre*, no. 554, 24 November 1911. © Bibliothèque Forney, Ville de Paris.

au Beurre, however, was the way the Germans' duplicity had increased their control. In other, similar, cartoons it was implied that they had infiltrated French professions to such a point that it had become simply

---

from a Germany chauffeur, Ludovic, to his comrade, he mentions gleefully how not only he, but the German tourists he escorted, were being mistaken for French.

impossible for French nationals to install a factory without the help of German engineers.[28]

Like the articles in *L'Action Française*, these cartoons seemed to seek to expose the Germans' subterfuge and to reveal the depth of their 'penetration'. Yet through their ironic use of exaggeration and distortion to caricature German coarseness and clumsiness, the cartoons also parodied the Germans' awkward attempts at subterfuge. Like the French humour of '*blague*' familiar from French theatrical reviews of the time, in which topical issues were travestied in skits, these cartoons were able to function as travesties or jokes.[29] As jokes, these cartoons were able to bring into the open things which would otherwise remain hidden. By exposing and ridiculing things which could not be discussed openly in polite terms, this kind of humour was able to use satirical breaches of decorum to make its point. Following Freud's theory on jokes, the cartoons in *L'Assiette au Beurre* were able to say in public, what was otherwise repressed, by encapsulating the paranoia about German infiltration in a publishable image, while at the same time expressing the urge for revenge through its caricatures of the enemy.[30] Other Anarchist satirical journals such as *Le Rire* also caricatured German 'infiltration'. However, the issue was most vigorously pursued in a series of cartoons and articles entitled 'Made in Germany', that appeared in *Le Matin* – a moderate centrist newspaper, notionally without political opinion, but which nevertheless championed the *Alliance démocratique*.[31]

In Henri Zislin's cartoon for *Le Matin*, entitled 'When Jacques Bonhomme does business with the Teuton', Jacques Bonhomme, the everyman of French business, is depicted in the top five frames being warmly welcomed by his Berlin equivalent, Siefzke (Figure 6.3).[32] The lower frames illustrate the differences in their business relations once the German visits Paris. After

---

[28] 'La Pénétration Pacifique', p. [6].

[29] An examination of these theatrical reviews can be found in Jeffrey Weiss, *The Popular Culture of Modern Art: Picasso, Duchamp and Avant-Gardism*, New Haven, CT: Yale University Press, 1994. On the role of *blague* specifically in these reviews, see, Brauer, *L'Art révolutionaire*, ch. 3.

[30] Sigmund Freud, *Jokes and their relation to the Unconscious*, first published 1905; trans. James Strachey, Harmondsworth: Penguin, 1991. Freud, quoting K. Fischer, *Über den Witz* (Heidelberg, 1889, p. 51), maintained that jokes 'bring forward something that is concealed or hidden' (p. 44).

[31] The lead taken by *Le Matin* was acknowledged by Pierre Demoulin in *L'Action Française*, 21 Sept. 1912: 'L'Espionnage Juif-Allemand, 'Les découvertes du "Matin", L'exemple de la Russie. – Les espions'. While praising *Le Matin* for its exposures, *L'Action Française* also criticized it for not revealing the more important issue of espionage.

[32] Henri Zislin, 'Quand Jacques Bonhomme veut faire du commerce avec la Teutonie', *Le Matin*, 2 Sept. 1912, p.1. Zislin, a well-known French-Alsatian caricaturist, vehemently opposed to the German occupation of his homeland, was jailed many times for his polemical cartoons.

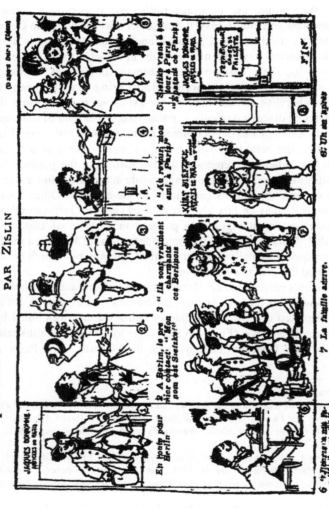

6.3   Henri Zislin, *Quand Jacques Bonhomme veut faire du commerce avec la Teutonie* – When Jack Everyman does business with the 'Kraut', designed for the front page of *Le Matin*, 2 September 1912. © Bibliothèque nationale de France, Paris.

Siefzke invites his family to join him there, they are then shown occupying Bonhomme's home. A year later Siefzke is finally portrayed after taking over Bonhomme's business, celebrating his success with a fat cigar in his hand. This takeover, representing a German conspiracy designed to invade France by peaceful means, was reinforced by a subsequent front-page cartoon in *Le Matin*. Under the caption, 'At the National German School', a German professor was depicted exhorting his students not to continue openly using politics as a weapon against France, but to deploy the more insidious, but more effective weapon of selling more German products to the French (Figure 6.4). While the Jacques Bonhomme cartoon signified how French businesses were being infiltrated by German businessmen, the German school cartoon signified how Germany's ambition to infiltrate France with its products formed part of its basic education – peaceful penetration having become such an official German strategy, that it was even taught in schools. These satires in *Le Matin* seemed to be corroborated by its fact-finding 'Made in Germany' reports.

The ingenious lamps invented by Rathenau, lighting almost every wall in Paris were, *Le Matin* reported, manufactured by AEG – not initials for a French firm, but the Allgemeine Elektrizitäts-Gesellschaft.[33] As the light and heating manufacturer Kœrting had a French chairman it was, *Le Matin* claimed, yet another German company masquerading as French, in order to flood the nation with its products. Moreover, since the radiators, fans and lights they manufactured were only ever delivered in parts from Hanover, German engineers were needed to assemble them.[34] *Le Matin* was soon followed by other national papers wishing to expose what *Paris-Midi* called the '*germanisation*' of France.[35]

According to *Le Radical*, the apparently all-French Compagnie Universelle de Télégraphie et de Téléphonie was actually underwritten by the Commerz-und Disconto-Bank, and was exploiting Julien Berthenod's invention with the equipment of the German Rudolph Goldschmidt.[36] *La Grande Revue* declared that most sewing machines sold in France were in fact German-made.[37] While the antennae on the Eiffel Tower, added *L'Autorité*, had originated from the German Kœrting Company, *La Libre Parole* alleged – in the spirit of the German counterfeit conspiracy promoted by *L'Assiette au Beurre* – that even

---

[33] 'Made in Germany', *Le Matin*, 20 Sept. 1912, 1. This company was most commonly known by its initials: AEG.

[34] '"Made in Germany", Comment M. Lebureau se chauffe et s'aère', *Le Matin*, 30 Sept. 1912, p.1.

[35] Eugène Destez, '«MADE IN GERMANY», Comment les Allemands «germanisent» la France', *Paris-Midi*, 31 Oct. 1912, 3.

[36] *Le Radical*, 29 Sept. 1912, p. 1, with specific reference to the Compagnie Universelle de Télégraphie et de Téléphonie.

[37] *La Grande Revue*, 15 Sept. 1912, p. 1.

A l'école nationale allemande

6.4 Anonymous cartoon, *A l'école nationale allemande* – At the National German School, designed for the front page of *Le Matin*, 8 October 1912. © Bibliothèque nationale de France, Paris.

the paper on French cigarettes purporting to be 'Made in Paris' came directly from the Rhine.[38] Reporting upon this escalation, *Le Matin* concluded that the whole press, regardless of political differences, was increasingly denouncing the economic danger posed by this insidious invasion: 'The protest against the insidious infiltration of anonymous German products,' it proudly declared, 'or those which masquerade under a French pseudonym, is mounting every day.'[39] Yet with what the press called 'the abduction of national treasures', *pénétration pacifique* became an even more serious issue. In an expression of paranoid anxiety about the sanctity of French art and culture, Germans and other aliens were allegedly prepared to go to any lengths to infiltrate France, as demonstrated by the mysterious disappearance of the *Mona Lisa*.

In the light of the country's potential industrial, technological and commercial eclipse by such rapidly modernizing nations as Germany, Italy and the United States, and the cession of some 265 000 kilometres of the Congo to Germany, art and culture appeared to be the one area in which France was still a world leader. Since what was at stake was the most precious jewel in the French crown, alien infestation here appeared far more serious. So when the most acclaimed of Western masterpieces, Leonardo da Vinci's *Mona Lisa*, suddenly disappeared from the Louvre in the middle of the Morocco crisis, there was – not surprisingly – a press controversy over the security of French art. There was a general suspicion, reinforced by rumours and jokes, that Germany was implicated in its disappearance. This was illustrated by the publication of a cartoon in *Paris-Journal* suggesting that France had traded the *Mona Lisa* with Germany for Morocco.[40] According to *L'Action Française*, the Morocco crisis, the loss of the Congo and the disappearance of the *Mona Lisa*, amounted to one coincidence too many.[41] Once these rumours and suspicions became fully-fledged reports, French art like French industry, trade and commerce, was also seen as vulnerable to *pénétration pacifique*.

In August 1911, the Louvre suddenly discovered that the *Mona Lisa* was missing.[42] On checking its collection against its inventory, the museum found that two Iberian sculptures were also missing. This, in turn, led to a

---

[38] *La Libre Parole*, 28 Sept. 1912, p. 1.

[39] 'L'opinion française commence à s'alarmer', *Le Matin*, 8 Oct. 1912, p. 1.

[40] *Paris-Journal*, 23 Aug. 1911, p.1.

[41] Daudet, 'Le Bilan du Trimestre'. The spate of these so-called suspicious coincidences included the sinking of the battleship *Iéna*, followed by the sinking of her sister ship, *La Liberté*, at the Port of Toulon on 25 September 1911.

[42] The disappearance of the *Mona Lisa* was announced by the French press on 21 August 1911. The painting was not found until 12 December 1913, in the Roman home of an Italian conservator, Vincent Perugia, who had been commissioned by the Louvre to undertake restoration on some of its sixteenth-century Italian collection. He had decided that it should be returned to its rightful home. The circumstances surrounding its discovery fuelled further xenophobia, *Gil Blas* suggesting that it had been taken in revenge for Napoleon's victories.

nationwide check of the state's art collections.[43] Although police complained of a baffling absence of clues to indicate what may have transpired, *L'Action Française* immediately announced that it was the result of a Jewish sabotage of the Louvre directed by Homolle, who owed his appointment as Director of National Museums to the influence of Solomon Reinach.[44] This report was subsequently embroidered by Charles Maurras' close friend and colleague at *L'Action Française*, Léon Daudet. He connected its disappearance not just with the supposed Jewish takeover of the Louvre, but with a long-standing Jewish cultural conspiracy that had begun with the pillage of treasures from churches, convents and bishoprics upon laicization.[45] This 'ritual murder of French masterpieces', Daudet suggested, was not just prompted by the profit motive, but was part of a Jewish plot to take over France.[46] The xenophobic dimension of these conspiracy theories was then pursued with a vengeance by the national press.

Once the disappearance of the *Mona Lisa* was identified as a theft and the hypothesis of a criminal conspiracy became established, there was never any suggestion by the national press that the picture might have been abducted by French nationals.[47] It was the work of an international network of thieves, not a French gang, according to *Le Matin* and other centrist dailies, which was acting on behalf of American collectors.[48] Not surprisingly, given the intensity of this paranoia, it was not a French citizen, legitimated by the principle of *jus sanguinis*, who stood as the accused, but an alien. More specifically in colloquial French, a *métèque* supposedly born in Poland of a Jewish family with German affiliations – Wilhelm de Kostrowitzky, otherwise known as the writer and Modern Art critic, Guillaume Apollinaire.[49]

It was because the police considered Apollinaire to be in league with one of the criminals from the international gang stealing museum art, *Le Matin*

---

[43] *L'Action Française* ran a series of articles early in 1912 entitled 'Les étrangers nous enlèvent nos œuvres d'art', highlighting the supposed abduction of French art by those it called 'envious aliens'.

[44] 'Au Musée du Louvre. La «Joconde» volée', *L'Action Française*, 23 Aug. 1911, p. 1.

[45] Léon Daudet, 'Le vol de la «Joconde», Le Louvre enjuivé', *L'Action Française*, 28 Aug. 1911 – Daudet called this the 'jewification' of the Louvre.

[46] Ibid. This was subsequently reinforced by Maurras; see Charles Maurras, 'Au Louvre', *L'Action Française*, 31 Aug. 1911, p. 1.

[47] In 'La Bande Noire', *L'Action Française*, 8 Sept. 1911, p. 1, Léon Daudet emphasized that this gang, which had been stealing art treasures for some years, was international.

[48] *Le Matin*, 12 Sept. 1911, p. 1.

[49] Apollinaire was arrested in the evening of 8 Sept. 1911. 'Les Vols du Louvre. Une Arrestation', *L'Action Française*, 9 Sept. 1911, p. 1, was the first of many references to Apollinaire being Jewish. This even included an accusation by his subversive friend, Arthur Craven, published in *Maintenant*, March 1914. This connection may have been prompted by Apollinaire's mother's long liaison with Jules Weil although, as Apollinaire explained in the letter cited below, anti-Semites could scarcely imagine a Pole not being a Jew.

explained, that they had suspected him.[50] This was comparable to the interpretation *Paris-Journal* had received from the Préfecture of Police, which had described Apollinaire as head of an international gang plundering French museums.[51] As Daudet put it, even if he had not actually stolen the *Mona Lisa*, he was highly capable of masterminding the theft.[52] That Apollinaire's alien status, along with his supposed Judaism, antipathy to French tradition and sexual deviance were the underlying motives for his arrest, was a factor of which he and his family were made all too aware. As Apollinaire recalled:

> I was the only person arrested in France for the theft of the Mona Lisa. The police did everything they could to justify their action; they grilled my concierge and my neighbours, asking whether I brought home little girls or little boys or whatever. If my life had been the slightest bit questionable they wouldn't have let me go, the honour of the corporation being at stake.[53]

Throughout Apollinaire's imprisonment, his brother Albert constantly had to correct allegations that they were not from a Jewish but a Roman Catholic family, had not received a foreign but French education, were not paedophiles but orthodox heterosexuals and were not hostile to, but supportive of French culture.[54] It was, as *Paris-Journal* explained, a supreme boon for the police to be able to arrest a suspect who was both a man of letters and an alien.[55] As attacks against Apollinaire continued unabated in the hope that discrediting him would simultaneously discredit the foreign intrusion into French art and literature which he represented, the alien artist – particularly the modern alien artist – was increasingly incorporated into invasion phobia.

Apollinaire's friend and colleague André Salmon drew attention to the simplistic nature of the concept of 'peaceful penetration'. It depended on an unsatisfactory analogy drawn between the 'invasion' of alien artists supposedly taking over French exhibition space and the usurpation of French manual

---

[50] 'Arreté', *Le Matin*, 9 Sept. 1911, p. 1.

[51] 'La Gaffe', *Paris-Journal*, 10 Sept. 1911, p. 1. As Apollinaire explained in an interview with *Le Matin*, (13 Sept. 1911), the police saw a connection between the theft of the *Mona Lisa* and the time his former secretary, Pieret, a prime suspect, had left his flat – despite Apollinaire's insistence that it was merely a coincidence.

[52] Léon Daudet, 'Diverses pistes et la bonne', *L'Action Française*, 13 Sept. 1911, 1.

[53] Guillaume Apollinaire, *Tendre comme le souvenir*, Paris 1952 (based on letters of 1915), p.7. In *Apollinaire, Poet among the Painters* (London: Rupert Hart-Davis, 1962, p. 220), Francis Steegmuller claims that Apollinaire was, in his lover Marie Laurencin's words, *worried sick* over being expelled from France as an undesirable foreigner. Knowledge of Apollinaire's pornographic writing and classification of eroticism in the Bibliothèque Nationale did not altogether alleviate his predicament.

[54] Ibid.

[55] 'La Gaffe', *Paris-Journal*, 10 Sept. 1911.

jobs by Italian 'navvies'.[56] Alien artists were also being accused of corrupting French art through their allegiance to such supposedly non-French Modern or Modernist art as Cubism, Fauvism and Futurism.[57] This issue was crystallized by the critical uproar unleashed by the Cubist's Room, the notorious number XI, opening at the 1912 Salon d'Automne with works of art by the Russian, Archipenko, the Czech, Kupka, the Austrian, Melzer, the Portuguese, Souza-Cardoza, the Pole, Louis Marcoussis, and the Italian, Modigliani. These were interspersed with works of art by the French artists Picabia, Metzinger and Le Fauconnier (all of which can be seen in the photograph reproduced from L'Illustration), as well as others by Duchamp, Gleizes, Léger, Marchand and Roger de la Fresnaye. (Figure 6.5).[58] This scandal was only exacerbated by the opening of the Cubist House at the Salon d'Automne a fortnight later, in which every aspect of bourgeois living – even the Salon or Louvre – seemed to have become cubified, as signified by Marcoussis' cartoon for La Vie Parisienne, called 'The Triumph of Cubism' (Figure 6.6).[59] While Salmon was not overly disturbed by such Royalist art critics as Louis Dimier adopting a predictably hostile stance in L'Action Française, he was perturbed when such criticism was rationally articulated by Thiébault-Sisson, the respected art critic of the centrist daily Le Temps, a paper reputedly above the sordid fray of politics.[60]

---

[56] La Palette, 'Les Artistes étrangers de Paris', Les Arts, Gil Blas, 1 June 1912, p. 4. Both Lequin (Histoire des étrangers) and Armengaud (Histoire de la vie française) point out that most immigrants came from Italy, Germany, Switzerland and Spain. By 1911 however, Italians represented 38 per cent of immigrants, displacing the Belgians and dominating the building industry.

[57] Ibid. 'Modernist' is the term currently used to denote experimental Modern Art, as epitomized by Cubism. The term Salmon used was 'l'art révolutionnaire', while Apollinaire used the French for 'Modern Painting', as indicated in Brauer, L'Art révolutionaire.

[58] The debates between Salmon and other critics, including his fellow writer at Gil Blas, Louis Vauxcelles, are discussed in Brauer, L'Art révolutionaire, Ch. 4.3. On the Cubists involved in this Salon, see Cottington, Cubism in the Shadow of War. The Avant-Garde and Politics in Paris 1905–1914, New Haven and London: Yale University Press, 1998, Chapter 6: 'Between Theory and Practice: The Meanings of Cubism'; see also Mark Antcliff, Inventing Bergson. Cultural Politics and the Parisian Avant-Garde, Princeton: Princeton University Press, 1993, esp. Chapter 4: 'The Body of the Nation: Cubism's Celtic Nationalism'.

[59] Louis Marcoussis, 'Le Triomphe du Cubisme', La Vie parisienne, no. 3642. 12 Dec. 1912. p. 366. For a detailed historical account of the Cubist House, see David Cottington. 'The Maison Cubiste and the Meaning of Modernism in pre-1914 France', in Eve Blau and Nancy J. Troy (eds), Architecture and Cubism, Cambridge. MA: Canadian Centre for Architecture/The MIT Press, 1997, pp. 17–40.

[60] By the time of the Radical Republic. Thiébault-Sisson had achieved the status of an establishment figure, having been granted honourable membership to various art societies and appointments to many governmental committees, including the prestigious Conseil Supérieur des Beaux-Arts. Regarded by his peers as neither conservative nor reactionary. but judicious. he was supportive of such ideologically 'radical' new ventures as the Salon d'Automne. from its inception in 1903. Presumably this is what made his criticism so much more perturbing.

6.5 The Cubist Room, No. XI, 10th Salon d'Automne, 1 October until 8 November 1912, at the Grand Palais des Champs-Élysées, Paris. Photograph reproduced in *L'Illustration*, no. 3633, 12 October 1912. © Bibliothèque Forney, Ville de Paris.

LE TRIOMPHE DU CUBISME

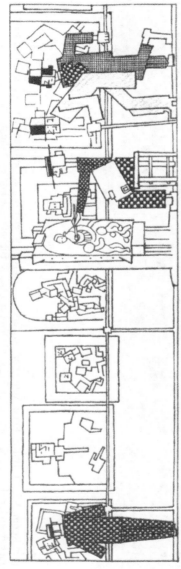

LE SALON CARRÉ... EN 1920

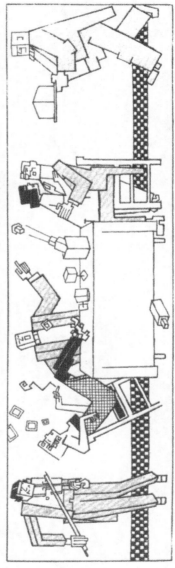

UNE PARTIE CARRÉE

6.6 Cartoon by Louis Marcoussis entitled *Le Triomphe de Cubisme* – The Triumph of Cubism – designed for *La Vie parisienne*, no. 3642, 12 December 1912, 366. © Bibliothèque Forney, Ville de Paris, ADAGP, Paris and DACS, London, 2001.

In what sounded like a cogent argument, Thiébault-Sisson claimed that Russian, Hungarian, Czech, Spanish and German artists were all invading Paris and forming isolated colonies in which they felt secure to indulge their instincts for nightmarish subjects in wild, untutored scrawls.[61] Once these so-called savages became civilized through learning the French language, he went on, they then felt sufficiently confident to enrol at a French art studio.[62] Yet the studios they chose were modern ones run by Matisse and the Cubists, which – in his view – merely provided a haven for alien artists and their indulgences.[63] These studios, Thiébault-Sisson argued, justified their experimentation as revolutionary; but revolutionaries, he went on, set out to overthrow the established order from a firm basis of knowledge of the great shifts in art, which these artists lacked.[64] Learning only specious principles, and with neither the ambition nor temperament to produce great art, the alien artists became servile copyists of a decadent dilettantism.[65] Hence Thiébault-Sisson portrayed these foreign artists as being as guilty of dissimulation as the German manufacturer, tourist and engineer. Armed with their imitations of Matisse and the Cubists, he suggested, they set out to penetrate French culture through its avant-garde salons – particularly the Salon d'Automne.

Of the artists who exhibited at the 1912 Salon d'Automne, Thiébault-Sisson calculated that 655 were French and nearly half as many again (315) were foreigners.[66] This overwhelming proportion of *métèques*, as he also called them, provided Thiébault-Sisson with a clear explanation as to why the prestigious Salon d'Automne, like the other avant-garde Salon, the 'Indépendants', had so heinously declined.[67] Since disproportionate numbers of aliens were not only taking over the exhibitions with an avalanche of abominations, but also dominating their organizational committees and juries, the result was what Thiébault-Sisson called 'The Crisis in French Painting'.[68] Coming as it did at the same time as the 'Made in Germany' campaign, this 'crisis' was seized upon by writers of the centrist press, and by politicians – and not necessarily neo-nationalists – as evidence of the massive infiltration of French art and culture.

---

[61] Thiébault-Sisson, 'Le Salon d'Automne: La Peinture', *Le Temps*, 1 Oct. 1912, p. 4.

[62] Ibid.

[63] Thiébault-Sisson, 'A propos des Indépendants, La crise de la peinture française, I', *Feuilleton du Temps, Le Temps*, 24 March 1912, p. 4. This was followed by, 'La crise de la peinture française, II', *Feuilleton du Temps, Le Temps*, 31 March 1912, p. 4.

[64] Ibid.

[65] Ibid.

[66] Thiébault-Sisson, 'Le Salon d'Automne: La Peinture', *Le Temps*, 1 Oct. 1912.

[67] Ibid.

[68] Ibid. Thiébault-Sisson, 'La crise de la peinture française, I' and 'La crise de la peinture française II', *Le Temps*, 24 and 31 March 1912.

In a front-page article in *Le Matin*, chauvinistically entitled 'For French Art', the distinguished writer Georges Lecomte railed against the alien artists' abhorrent deformations and the way they brought shame upon modern French art.[69] To privilege such ugly, filthy, vulgar art by alien artists in a national monument was, for Paul Omer at *L'Eclair*, so disgraceful that it committed a great wrong against the public and French art.[70] Whilst these denunciations were reinforced by *Les Annales*, the dominant word in its enquiry conducted into Cubism was 'invasion'.[71] For the academic artist, Léandre, it was a 'barbarous invasion'; for his colleague, Antonin Carlès, an 'uncontainable invasion of bad taste', while for Luc-Olivier Merson, the self-appointed leader of the resurrected academic 'pompiers', it was on a level with invasion by Australian savages.[72] Their attacks were politically compounded by the press, starting with the publication by *Le Matin* of an open letter to the Arts Minister from Pierre Lampué, the Socialist city councillor responsible for Paris art commissions.[73]

The alien artists at the Salon d'Automne were no better, Lampué exclaimed, than a gang of thugs, polluting French culture with extraordinarily ugly vulgarities.[74] It seemed that the state's most prestigious monument for contemporary art – the Grand Palais in Lampué's constituency – had been defiled by the most vulgar human deformations ever perpetrated in the history of French art. For Lampué, this was tantamount to the state's having abandoned its duty of protecting French patrimony and of preserving the nation's cultural glory. Hence Lampué argued that the state's loan of a public monument to such disreputable artists had not only compromised the Government, but also the nation. Having sounded this alarm, it was then picked

---

[69] Georges Lecomte, 'Pour l'art français, contre le défi au bon sens', *Le Matin*, 7 Oct., 1912, p. 1.

[70] Paul Omer, 'La Verité sur le Salon d'Automne où tout peut entrer', *L'Éclair*, 17 Oct., 1912, p 1.

[71] 'Enquête: Le Cubisme devant les artistes', *Les Annales*, 1 Dec. 1912, conducted by Henriquez-Phillipe.

[72] Ibid. The term *'pompier'* (literally 'fireman'), was applied to these classically academic artists on account of the fireman's antique helmet. Late in 1911, these artists formed a group, under the leadership of Luc Olivier-Merson, to organize exhibitions of their anachronistic wallowings in antique subjects. The first of these exhibitions opened in late January 1912.

[73] Pierre Lampué, 'Lettre ouverte à M. Bérard, Sous-secrétaire d'Etat aux Beaux-Arts', *Le Matin*, 5 Oct. 1912, p. 1. This letter is reprinted in full, as an appendix, in Brauer, *L'Art révolutionaire*. Acclaimed as the doyen of the Conseil Municipal de la Ville de Paris, Lampué had also been its president. As a Member of the state Administrative Commission for the Fine Arts and reporter of its Fourth Fine Arts Commission, Lampué had been responsible for the acquisition of art exhibited at the 'official' Salons: The Salon des Artistes Français and the Salon National des Beaux-Arts. Paradoxically, he exhibited his own photography at the Salon des Indépendants.

[74] Ibid.

up and pursued in state politics – not by a Royalist reactionary nor by a neo-nationalist, but by a Socialist politician: Jules-Louis Breton, the Deputy for Cher and nephew of the realist painter Jules Breton.[75]

While his choice of the title 'Against French Art' indicated a dialogue with Lecomte, Breton's deference towards Lampué also signalled support for his fellow Socialist.[76] He considered Lampué right to challenge the Government for permitting a national monument to be used for art in such bad taste. Like Lampué, he was concerned with the repercussions this would have upon the reputation of French art. Playing upon the French words for 'outsider' and 'alien', Breton then claimed that experience had proven that this term was merely a euphemism to justify admission of the most scandalous art, not just alien to the rules for French national art and alien to the marvellous French artistic tradition, but utterly alien to all sane and lucid artistic conceptions.[77] This very reiteration established 'alien' as the lynchpin of his argument. The problem, Breton maintained, was that the Salon d'Automne juries were dominated by aliens, whose taste was highly suspect. In this case, alien artists could legitimately be blamed for turning the Salon into what Breton called 'a lunatic asylum'.[78] As they could also be held responsible for ridiculing the French public and endangering the supremacy of the nation's culture with its very antithesis – as the title of his article put it – Breton recommended urgent state intervention.[79] However, rather than limit the issue to the domain of press controversy, Breton insisted it become a subject of concern to all the nation's politicians, to be raised as a matter of urgency in Parliament.

The opening salvoes of Breton's tirade in the Chamber of Deputies were largely a reiteration of his published text. His fellow Deputy, Auriol, had already alerted the Chamber to the danger to French art from the persistent efforts of neighbouring nations, particularly Germany, to eclipse its supremacy, and the way was paved for Breton's attack.[80] The greatness of France's artistic patrimony was, Breton told a captive Chamber, being damaged by the maddest eccentricities and hoaxes in the worst possible taste, which were passed off not just as new art forms, but as French art.[81] These hoaxes were even, Breton continued to cries of horror, being displayed in the nation's

---

[75] Surprise that a Socialist, rather than Royalist deputy, pursued this issue was registered by Léon Bailby, editor of *L'Intransigeant*, the 'independent' paper which employed Apollinaire as a critic: Léon Bailby, 'En passant ... Cubistes', *L'Intransigeant*, 15 Oct. 1912, p.1.

[76] J.-L. Breton, Député, 'Contre l'Art Français', *La Petite République*, 12 Oct. 1912, p.1.

[77] Ibid. Breton repeatedly used the word, *'étranger'*.

[78] Ibid. Breton accused *'les artistes étrangers'* of turning the Salon d'Automne into *'un asile d'aliénés'*.

[79] Ibid.

[80] For the Auriol debate, see *Journal officiel, Chambre des Députés*, 29 Nov. 1912, p. 2835.

[81] *Suite des Beaux-Arts, Chambre des Députés, Session extraordinaire de 1912, Journal Officiel*, 3 Dec. 1912, p. 2924.

public buildings, which had been made available by the government.[82] Having created sufficient suspense, Breton then proclaimed what was worse: that most of these hoaxers were not natives of France but foreigners, who had either unconsciously or deliberately set out to exhibit in these national public buildings in order to disgrace French art.[83]

Breton then departed from his article. Statistics, he claimed, citing estimates that bore a striking resemblance to those of Thiébault-Sisson, proved that it was the alien, not the French artist, who was to blame for the scandal at the Salon d'Automne and the degradation of French art.[84] There was no suggestion that the one might not necessarily have been the cause of the other. Although three aliens to every seven French artists would hardly constitute a takeover, let alone justify his paranoia about domination, these were the proportions Breton confidently cited, pointing out that of nearly 700 exhibitors at the last Salon d'Automne, more than 300 were aliens.[85] Although the 1912 Salon d'Automne catalogue reveals Frenchmen occupying the positions of President, Vice-Presidents and Secretary on the Painting Jury, with its Jury Committee equally balanced between French and non-French members, Breton wildly asserted that the Painting Jury directly responsible for the last Salon had been composed almost entirely of aliens. Although the only non-French Members of Office identifiable from the catalogue were J. Perrichon as President of Sculpture and H. Hamm as President of the Decorative Arts, nine of the Salon d'Automne's 16 Members of Office were also, Breton alleged, aliens. This explained why, Breton maintained, the alien artist had been able to take over the Salon d'Automne and generate such a scandal.[86] This explained why, he triumphantly concluded to thunderous applause, it was absolutely inadmissible for the alien's art, which was so clearly opposed to the lofty values of French culture, to be showcased in a French national building.[87] Although Breton's argument was cogently refuted by the Socialist deputy for Montmartre, Marcel Sembat, his response was

---

[82] Ibid.

[83] Ibid.

[84] Ibid.

[85] Ibid. In addition to the large contingents of Russian, German, Austrian, Swiss, Belgian, Spanish, Italian, Hungarian and Polish artists, the catalogue also lists Rumanian, Greek, Mexican, Uruguayan, Venezuelan, Brazilian, Swedish, Norwegian, Danish, American, Canadian and Australian artists. Such a vast diversity would seem to militate against any conspiracy amongst alien artists.

[86] Ibid.

[87] Ibid. As in his article, Breton recommended concession of national public buildings be conditional upon indispensable guarantees being secured by Salon Societies regarding their juries' constitutions. Should a Society not be able to fulfil such obligations, this would then permit the state to justify refusal of the Grand-Palais, he argued, and hence prevent any recurrence of this scandal.

rarely cited in the press.[88] Instead a range of newspapers, from *L'Action* to *L'Action Française* immediately reported a parliamentary consensus over Breton's position regarding the supposed domination of the Salon d'Automne juries, administration structures and exhibitions by the alien artist. This was soon followed by a drastic revision of the Salon d'Automne regulations, in keeping with amendments to the immigration laws.

Only one year after granting foreigners civil rights, legislation had been passed making it compulsory for them to register their location, profession and income with the local prefecture and police, in order to form a General Census of Aliens called *Carnet A*. From *Carnet A*, a second census of aliens suspected of endangering national security was compiled, called *Carnet B*. In September 1911, however, in the heat of the Morocco crisis and in the middle of 'treacherous' negotiations between France and Germany, a top-secret state document had been circulated that changed the terms of *Carnet B*.[89] With anti-militarism spreading, the criteria for inclusion in *Carnet B* were expanded to encompass the merest suspicion of espionage or anti-militarist sabotage conspiracies, including political ideologies antipathetic to patriotism.[90] In order to exercise surveillance over all military regions the list, which appears to have included about 2500 individuals, of whom a substantial minority were foreigners, was circulated not just to the police and prefectures, but also to the Minister of the Interior and all army commanders.[91] In November 1912 further instructions were issued requiring prefects to revise the list on an annual basis.[92] Suspects became eligible for immediate

---

[88] Ibid., pp. 2925–6. Sembat advocated a resolution in keeping with the Radical Republican policy of '*la liberté de l'art*'. This was the context for his oft-quoted statement to the Chamber, which may be broadly translated: 'In front of any painting, one has an incontestable right – not to look at it and to look at others; but one does not call the police!'

[89] Jean-Jacques Becker, *LE CARNET B, Les Pouvoirs Publics et l'Antimilitarisme avant la guerre de 1914*, Paris: Klincksieck, 1973, pp. 108–12.

[90] Ibid. In the secret circular of 18 September 1911, the registry was to include those suspected of espionage; those who purportedly aimed to sabotage mobilization, and those portraying unpatriotic political ideology. By this time, the three main anti-militarist positions were voiced through Jean Jaurès and Jules Guèsde and their respective Socialist Parties, and Gustave Hervé, editor of *La Guerre Sociale*. This journal, devoted to anti-militarism and anticolonialism, was launched just after Separation by Hervé and the militant anarchist representative of the International Antimilitarist Association, Miguel Almereyda. As particular Radical and feminist factions also supported antimilitarism, it was not confined to Socialism or Anarchism.

[91] Ibid., pp. 112–13. Becker mentions how these documents were to be produced in quadruplicate for the préfecture, the army, the police and the Ministère de l'Intérieur.

[92] Ibid., pp. 112–15. Issued on 1 November 1912, these instructions stipulated that reports focus upon individual attitudes and/or machinations likely to impede mobilization through sabotage or destruction of telegraph services, buildings of strategic importance, strategic railways, supply depots, and so on. The prefects of French departments continually revised the list of sabotage suspects to be immediately arrested upon mobilization, according to James Joll, *The Origins of the First World War*, London and New York: Longman, 1984, p. 179.

arrest in the case of mobilization. Changes to the Salon d'Automne regulations were consistent with the xenophobia, of which this legislation was also a part.

Immediately after the parliamentary debate, the under-secretary for the Arts, Léon Bérard brought pressure to bear upon the President of the Salon d'Automne, Frantz Jourdain, forcing him to amend the Society's statutes.[93] Through the introduction of three new statutes, only a restricted number of alien artists could be admitted to the Society for the Salon d'Automne; alien artists were prohibited from holding a majority on any Salon d'Automne committee and were also severely limited in the number of artworks they could exhibit.[94] As a compliant Jourdain confessed to Béraud, too much hospitality had led to the Salon d'Automne being invaded by the alien artist.[95] At the same time, Jourdain also pointed out that only 32 of the 1770 artists exhibiting at the 1912 Salon d'Automne were Cubists.[96] Under half of the exhibition consisted of work by alien artists, and despite the inclusion of such foreign Modernists as Archipenko, Kupka, Melzer, Souza-Cardoza, Marcoussis and Modigliani, the Cubists were, in fact, predominantly French. On top of this, as Sembat had pointed out in parliament, previous Salons had provided as much if not more cause for national scandal, without any repercussions. The puzzle for Jourdain, as for Sembat, was why political and press factions had joined forces in turning this particular Salon into a national scandal, making the foreign artists the scapegoats. In fact, at a time when France appeared most vulnerable to a loss of international status, foreign artists, like foreign engineers, had become central to the siege psychosis fostered by the press.

Despite its protectionist policy France had an adverse balance of trade with Germany by 1911. In spite of increased coal production in the Loire, the French iron and steel industry was still dependent upon massive supplies of German coal, much of which was mined in Lorraine. While the French government was reliant upon corporations like the Allgemeine Elektrizitätswerke

---

[93] As indicated by Frantz Jourdain's letter to the Under-Secretary for the Arts, dated 10 November 1912, reprinted in full, as an appendix in Brauer, *L'Art révolutionaire*, pressure was brought to bear before the controversy was debated in parliament. As the state's regranting of the Grand-Palais to the Salon d'Automne was conditional upon Bérard's stipulations becoming statutes, they were passed in the Salon meeting immediately following the parliamentary debates. The main instigator of Salle XI and the Cubist House, Jacques Villon, was forced to resign from the Painting Committee.

[94] These changes appear in Article 9 of the 1913 Salon d'Automne catalogue.

[95] Letter from Jourdain to Under-Secretary for the Arts, 10 Nov. 1912: 'Trop hospitalité, notre Société est actuellement envahi par les étrangers, de sorte qui au Salon National finirait par devenir un Salon d'étranger dans lequel on compterait quelques Français' (*sic* – Jourdain used a 'shorthand' form of written expression).

[96] Ibid.: 'Or, du 1770 numeros, nous étions affligés en tout de 32 Cubistes!' (*sic*).

(AEG) and Siemens for hydroelectric equipment in Lyons and the Rhône valley, it was also dependent upon German and other foreign labour.[97] The number of German engineers employed in the electrification of France was highest just before 1914, as were the numbers of German technicians engaged in the chemical industry at St Gobain.[98] Yet while their increasing numbers together with the incoming tide of German manufactured commodities nourished the press siege psychosis, German industrial and commercial experts, together with German raw materials and manufactured products were required to help modernize France and to prevent its technological eclipse. In fact, from 1906 the very functioning of the French economy was, as Armengaud shows, dependent upon immigration, and in particular on the recruitment of skilled workers from abroad.[99] In other words, France invited in German engineers, scientists and chemists because it lacked this technological expertise and was simply unable to produce comparable electrical and chemical products. Despite Renault, there was no French equivalent to Krupp. A similar paradox applied to French art and culture, although it was manifested in a different way.

The benefits to be gained from Morocco and other French colonies were, as Barraclough has shown, not merely financial, but necessary to the recuperation of a wounded and humiliated France.[100] Furthermore, they helped to alleviate the problem of France's relatively feeble birth rate and numerical inferiority compared with the philoprogenitive Germans. Art and culture were also central to the recuperation and restoration of French honour. While colonies represented a means of saving face, reclaiming honour and shrugging off any lingering taint of being a second-rate nation, so did the worldwide reputation of French art. With France seemingly in danger of being industrially, commercially and militarily eclipsed by its arch-enemy Germany, the accumulation of colonies was seized upon by the French press as well-deserved compensation for the wounds and humiliations inflicted upon France during the Franco-Prussian War. Similarly, the press seized upon the global superiority of French art.

The Balkans War, following so closely on the Morocco crisis, drew attention to the danger of France being territorially and militarily outmanoeuvred

---

[97] See Lequin, *Histoire des étrangers*; Armengaud, *Histoire de la vie française*.

[98] Lequin, ibid.

[99] Armengaud, ibid.

[100] Geoffrey Barraclough, *From Agadir to Armageddon, Anatomy of a Crisis*, London: Weidenfeld and Nicholson, 1982, p. 37: 'Trade was no longer the issue. What mattered now was property rights, mineral rights, mining rights, but above all else, financial control, for loans meant the right to control the wherewithal to repay the loans ... ' Delcassé, Delafosse and Barrès frequently extolled the virtues of the large labour force and enormous contingents of soldiers brought by France's African colonies. Through this, France could remain one of the first powers of Europe.

by Germany. The chorus of cultural chauvinism which resounded through the French art press was then a counterfoil to this threat: 'Art is one of our most uncontested supremacies,' Lecomte declared. 'No other country has shown such originality. Everyone everywhere is inspired by us and follows our direction.'[101] Through its art, France was supposedly not just able to cultivate its colonies and other nations but, more importantly, was able to preserve its place as a leader among first nations. France functioned not only as a centrifugal point from which art was exported, but also as a centripetal attraction, which brought foreign artists to its capital city. Consequently, the presence of such prestigious foreign Modernists as Picasso and Apollinaire was seminal to its image of itself as *the* cultural capital. Indeed, alien artists, like alien engineers, were not in France for the purposes of infiltration and insidious invasion – there being only ever flimsy circumstantial evidence for such a claim; in fact, they were there at the French behest.

Once France had lost one of its colonies to Germany and all-out war with its arch-enemy became imminent, the festering anxiety that it was losing control and global power, prestige and honour, reached a peak. Fear that France was declining – if not degenerating – into a second- or even third-rank nation in the global stakes, then became manifest through its press. In keeping with the Freudian theory of persecutionist paranoia, rather than this fear being openly acknowledged it was projected onto those perceived as threatening to expose the deficits in the French nation – the alien businessman and the alien artist. Consistent with this theory, the fear was deflected onto the alien, who was then positioned as a negative incursion threatening to control France through insidious invasion. Even though Modernism, particularly in the form of Cubism, was largely a French invention at this time, it was the alien artist who was accused of perpetrating it, to cause the downfall of French art and culture. Even though the German engineer was invited to France to generate its shift into electrical technology, this alien was also accused of insidious invasion. With the collapse of the political and press spectrum, and resistance increasingly isolated, the foreigner once welcomed by the Radical Republic became, within these discourses of xenophobic nationalism, the enemy. What the *Mona Lisa* theft and Salon d'Automne controversy, amidst this *pénétration pacifique* campaign, then ultimately reveal is that it was only within this siege psychosis, a psychosis that was so much a creation of the French press's making, that the commercial alien became a spy, and the alien artist became an invader.

---

[101] *Le Matin*, 7 Oct. 1912, p.1.

Further reading

Mark Antcliff, *Inventing Bergson. Cultural Politics and the Parisian Avant-Garde*, Princeton, NJ: Princeton University Press, 1993.

Geoffrey Barraclough, *From Agadir to Armageddon, Anatomy of a Crisis*, London: Weidenfeld and Nicholson, 1982.

David Cottington, *Cubism in the Shadow of War. The Avant-Garde and Politics in Paris 1905–1914*, New Haven and London: Yale University Press, 1998.

Jean-Marie Mayeur and Madeleine Rebérioux, *The Third Republic from its Origins to the Great War, 1871–1914*, trans. J.R. Foster, Cambridge: Cambridge University Press, 1989.

Francis Steegmuller, *Apollinaire, Poet among the Painters*, London: Rupert Hart-Davis, 1962.

Eugen Weber, *The Nationalist Revival in France, 1905–1914*, Berkeley, CA: University of California Press, 1968.

Eugen Weber, *Action Française, Royalism and Reaction in Twentieth-Century France*, Stanford, CA: Stanford University Press, 1962.

CHAPTER SEVEN

Neutrality under threat: freedom, use and 'abuse' of the press in Switzerland, 1914–19

Debbie Lewer

During the First World War, a 'Humorous Map of Europe in the Year 1914', published in Germany, depicted Switzerland as a tiny, isolated gingerbread chalet, sheltering motley residents in the midst of a marauding Europe personified by diverse oafs and barbarians straining at their own national boundaries. Lest the visual metaphor be lost on the viewer, an accompanying caption explained: 'Switzerland sits back in comfort and observes the world conflagration while providing a sanctuary for homeless Russian princes.'[1] Printed images representing Switzerland have often played on the small country's peculiar situation in Europe. Both in spite and because of its neutrality, there was enormous sensitivity during the war to these and many other kinds of printed text and image. The potential for printed material to upset the already delicate equilibrium of Swiss domestic and foreign relations after August 1914 came to be widely recognised. The map in question was just one example of the 'propaganda material' collected and monitored by the Swiss police during the war in an attempt to control partial, *'neutralitätswidrig'* (or 'anti-neutral') material. At that same time, one could also buy a postcard in Bern, the Swiss capital, showing an image of the country symbolized by its parliament building depicted as a rocky island surrounded by stormy seas. Evoking Switzerland's perhaps best-known painting, Arnold Böcklin's *Island of the Dead*, it too sought metaphorically to capture the political position of a small neutral country surrounded by international hostilities. Since 1901, visitors to the parliamentary chamber of the Bundeshaus have been greeted with the sight of Charles Giron's large mural depicting a timeless central Swiss Alpine landscape as the bearer of the Swiss state – *Cradle of the Confederation*. But Switzerland's position within Europe was much more complex than any of these clichéd images imply. The vision of Swiss stability, balance and unity even in the face of encircling crisis belies a reality that was critically fractious during the First World War. Switzerland's neutrality

---

[1] Map, 'Humoristische Karte von Europa im Jahre 1914', Dresden: Leutert and Schneidewind.

was more severely tested than usual from 1914. In cities especially, where the most intense publishing activity was concentrated, tensions were in many cases exacerbated by the production, dissemination and reception of particular printed items. This essay investigates how and why printed texts and images were regulated in Switzerland. It focuses on the problems that arose under the conditions of war and the uneasy alliance of neutrality, asylum and press freedom in Switzerland. It examines how material that transgressed official regulations could have serious implications for Switzerland's domestic and foreign relations during war. For reasons that will become clear, my discussion concentrates on cases of the French- and German-language Swiss press.[2]

Switzerland is so often described as a *Sonderfall* (special case) that this has become yet another of the clichés that surround it. Yet its peculiarities were indeed highlighted by both World Wars. In the context of a discussion of German nationalism, the historian J. P. Stern defined 'national identity' as 'a collective name for a group of similarities possessed by people who all call themselves by the same name; and who become recognizable to each other and to their neighbours by these similarities.'[3] Such a definition is not easily applied to the case of Switzerland and the Swiss. The Confederation has been accurately described as 'an egalitarian alliance between unequal partners'.[4] On the one hand, Switzerland is a unique entity in Europe, on the other, a highly particularized country of individual regions and linguistic communities, between which there has not always been significant contact. A defined sense of 'Swissness', such as it has existed, is often more closely linked with notions of liberty than with unity.[5] It has always been predicated on the rather artificial nature of the country's composition. Swiss nationality was (and still is) more a matter of citizenship within haphazard frontiers than one of race, blood, *Volk* or other romantic, 'organic' nineteenth-century notions of nation that informed post-Darwinist concepts of nation and national identity.[6] Hence, and especially during war in Europe, Swiss neutrality often served more as a statement of independence in the sphere of international power and politics than a means of uniting its own diverse peoples. Yet Switzerland is economically and culturally linked with its neighbours. Political isolation during the

---

[2] I am leaving aside the particular cases of the press in the Italian and Romansch-speaking regions.

[3] J. P. Stern, 'What is German?', in J. P. Stern, *The Heart of Europe: Essays on Literature and Ideology*, Oxford: Basil Blackwell, 1992, p. 297.

[4] J.-C. Favez, 'Between Myth and Memory: Swiss History and the Present Day', *Contemporary European History*, 3, November 1994, pp. 355–65; p. 360.

[5] J. Steinberg, *Why Switzerland?*, Cambridge: Cambridge University Press, 1996, pp. 212–13.

[6] For a discussion of the historical bases of the Swiss federal union and the contradictions inherent in questions of Swiss national identity, cf. Steinberg, *Why Switzerland?*, esp. Ch. 1.

war was impossible. Recognizing this, Otto Flake wrote of Switzerland in a Berlin newspaper in 1918: 'Neutrality is not a matter of keeping distance, rather of keeping equilibrium.'[7]

Paradoxically, while the powers in Europe respected, on the whole, the integrity of Switzerland's territory, the passions and national sympathies aroused by the First World War – particularly the opposition of the German Empire against France – exacerbated internal tensions within Switzerland. Prior to the war these tensions had been a broadly cultural division. Now they were heightened to a fractious state in which what was often called the *Graben* or trench between *Welsch und Deutsch* – the French-speaking West and German-speaking East – threatened to split the country. Shortly after the outbreak of war, the nervousness of the Swiss government was clear in its public call to the people to avoid overt sympathizing with one or other sides of the conflict. It urged the Swiss instead, to unite as a 'cultural community' regardless of race or language:

> We must make every effort to exercise maximum restraint in the judge-
> ment of external events and in the expression of sympathy for individual
> nations. ... However, even more important than consideration for the
> foreign nations is our own state's interest, as a matter of survival, in
> powerful restraint and unshakeable internal unity.[8]

As it happened, two of the gravest threats to 'internal unity' came from the highest Swiss offices themselves. First, two senior army officers were tried for passing secret information to the Germans and Austrians. Then, in 1917, it emerged that the Federal Councillor Arthur Hoffmann (he who had au-thorized the call for 'restraint' just quoted) had sought to negotiate a separate peace between Russia and Germany. Not only was this an embarrassing exposure of Swiss diplomatic bias, but it grossly contravened Swiss neu-trality, which forbids active foreign policy in any form. Hoffmann was forced to resign.[9] In an effort to counter-balance the incident, he was quickly replaced by a French-speaking councillor known for his general sympathy with the *Entente*. In the French-speaking western cantons of Switzerland there remained, however, widespread fear and resentment of the perceived unholy alliance between their German-speaking compatriots and Imperial Germany.

In the early months of the war, among the German-Swiss, support for Germany was widespread. In early 1915, a correspondent in Switzerland writing for the German newspaper, the *Vossische Zeitung* wrote:

---

[7] O. Flake, 'Schweizer Reise', *Norddeutscher Allgemeine Zeitung*, Berlin, 7 April 1918, no. 176: 'Neutralität ist nicht Fernhalten, sondern Gleichgewichthalten.'

[8] *Amtliche Sammlung der Bundesgesetze und Verordnungen der Schweizerischen Eidgenossen-schaft*, 30, for the year 1914, Bern, 1915, p.510.

[9] Cf. Steinberg, *Why Switzerland?*, pp. 54–5.

> Germans living here report that they are approached on the street by people they barely know, who shake them heartily by the hand in congratulation on the German victories ... The belief in the victory of the German armed forces is unshakeable here.[10]

To what extent this represents an accurate picture of Swiss sentiments or was rather more propagandistic is difficult to determine, but certainly in the early months of the war many Swiss Germans hoped for a German victory; it has been suggested so as to bask vicariously in the light of German glory. One German commentator estimated that around 75 per cent of the population of Eastern Switzerland were on the side of the Central Powers at the outbreak of war. For the Germans there was considerable propagandistic value to be gained from signs of foreign support for Germany, especially in Switzerland, where the country had a reputation for high principles and a noble moral tradition. However, as the war drew on, support for Germany waned. This change was in no small measure due to the German invasion of neutral Belgium, which caused widespread outrage and alarm in Switzerland, especially in the West, but also in the German-speaking East.

German-speaking Switzerland had close links with Imperial Germany. Many Germans lived and worked in Switzerland, and Swiss schools and universities employed a high proportion of German teachers and lecturers. In 1916, for example, according to one account, 14 per cent of school and university teachers were German, compared to 3 per cent French.[11] The Swiss army too, followed the Prussian model. Many other complex factors divided the Swiss along different lines. Class and religion defined some groupings, while the tension between the urban and rural Swiss became more marked under the impact of food shortages and price rises. However, by far the deepest rift was between the French- and German-Swiss. Linguistic divisions were significant factors. Not only was there the broad and long-standing problem that German-speakers often felt more affinity with German than Swiss culture, French-speakers with France and Italian-speakers with Italy, but in wartime, the fact that many German-speaking Swiss read German newspapers, while French-speaking Swiss read French newspapers, meant that these sections of the population regularly consumed highly partial and contradictory accounts of the war. Many believed that the only hope lay in the possibility of trilingual newspapers, but attempts in this direction were rarely successful.

---

[10] E. von Egidy-Thun, quoted in A. von Salis, *Die Neutralität der Schweiz*, Leipzig: Verlag von S. Hirzel, 1915, pp. 24–5: 'Hier ansässige Deutsche erzählen, daß sie auf der Straße von nur halb bekannten Leuten angesprochen werden, um unter kräftigem Händedruck Glückwünsche für die deutschen Siege entgegenzunehmen. ... Der Glaube an den Sieg der Deutschen Waffen ist hier unerschütterlich.'

[11] E. Steiner, *Wesen und Ursprung der 'Stimmen im Sturm'*, Zürich: Orell Füssli, 1916, p. 29. See also C. A.Loosli, *Ausländische Einflüsse in der Schweiz*, Zürich: Orell Füssli, 1917, p. 31.

Switzerland's neutrality and the accompanying principles of asylum and press freedom were already rigorously debated issues before the outbreak of war. The press in Switzerland has a symbolic significance. It is encapsulated in the shortest article of the Swiss constitution (article 55), just four words long, which in its entirety states: 'Press freedom is guaranteed'.[12] Switzerland was the first country in Europe to instate statutory freedom of the press. Defined broadly as 'the right to free expression of thought in printed text within the prescribed legal system',[13] the principle of press freedom is inextricable from the discourses of liberty in Switzerland. Paradoxically, during the First World War, it was this constellation of ideals and legislature that threatened their own tenability.

Pro-German sentiments in German-speaking Switzerland and pro-*Entente* sentiments in East Switzerland caused great concern for groups with varying political objectives within and outside Switzerland. Liberal patriots feared a disintegration of the spirit of Helvetian culture and the principle of neutrality under the formidable joint influences of French and German culture. The pro-revolution radical Left worked to counter partisan hostilities for other reasons. They saw in them a threat to the ideal of universal, international working-class solidarity. The Swiss socialist Fritz Brupbacher hoped to dismantle the kinds of patriotic sentiments that gave allegiance to the 'bourgeois' (Swiss) Fatherland or to Imperial Germany. He was dismayed by the enthusiastic reception the Swiss people had given the German Kaiser during his state visit in 1912, yet he also insisted that the Socialist should want just as little to 'defend the Swiss Fatherland'.[14] Brotherhood was to be found not with Switzerland's officials, but with 'Socialists of all countries. ... Each one who recommends to us that we defend the bourgeois Fatherland is a "national traitor" to our Fatherland, Socialism.'[15] The citizen middle-classes for their part recognized the potentially destabilizing effects of both international

---

[12] H. Tschäni, *Das neue Profil der Schweiz. Konstanz und Wandel einer alten Demokratie*, Zürich: Werd Verlag, 1990, p. 172. Article 55 was appended with two other conditions in 1848 and 1874 which guarded against the abuse of the press in general, and in particular against the confederation and its officials, though these were only established in the penal code in 1937.

[13] O. Wettstein, *Über das Verhältnis zwischen Staat und Presse, mit besonderer Berücksichtigung der Schweiz*, Zürich: Albert Müller's Verlag, 1904, p. 3: 'das Recht der freien Gedankenäusserung in Druckschriften innerhalb der gegebenen Rechtsordnung.'

[14] Brupbacher articulated these views in his address to the International Socialist Conference in Basel. The speech was published in the *Freie Jugend* under the title 'Wofür wir sterben würden' (What We Would Die For). Quoted in W. Münzenberg, *Die dritte Front. Aufzeichnungen aus 15 Jahren proletarischer Jugendbewegung*, (1930, republished Frankfurt am Main: LitPol, 1978), pp. 110–12.

[15] Ibid., p. 111: 'Der Sozialist läßt sein Leben nicht für bürgerliche Interessen und Ideale. Er stirbt nur für seine Ideale, nur für sein Vaterland, für die soziale revolution und die Internationale. Ein jeder, der uns empfiehlt, das bürgerliche Vaterland zu verteidigen, ist ein "Landesverräter" an unserem Vaterland, dem Sozialismus.'

socialism and German or French nationalism. There were well-founded fears that Switzerland would be spilt along social as well as regional axes, the West and East divided by partisan loyalties, and the working class alienated from the 'Swiss Fatherland' in favour of the 'International Fatherland'. National and political allegiances were therefore emotive and grave issues central to the tensions around Switzerland's unity and neutrality prior to and during the war.

The Swiss press in both regions was frequently accused from within the country of stirring up interregional antagonism. But perhaps more revealing of the importance of the Swiss press during war is that its newspapers and publishers were also very closely monitored abroad. This was carried out not only to detect signs of bias, inaccuracy or xenophobia relating to its reporting of foreign affairs, but crucially, to identify opportunities for influencing the tone and contents of the press in Switzerland. In this way, the British Foreign Office kept tabs on the Swiss press. The task, undertaken by the News Department, was difficult, since in 1916, for example, there were around 300 papers in Switzerland, in a number of languages. However, its files show too, that the department was concerned directly to *influence* what was published in the Swiss press. Switzerland's ostensible 'neutrality' was precisely the attraction for state offices seeking to proliferate partial accounts during war. The Foreign Office News Department in London was in close contact with British journalists based in Switzerland. Some appear to have acted as agents – monitoring the Swiss press, feeding its papers with articles and interviews and reporting back on successes and failures. Many items were initiated in Britain and sent, via the journalists, to be published in Switzerland.[16] Internal Foreign Office memos openly refer to such activities as 'propaganda'. The British sent investigators to Switzerland specifically to gather information about public opinion there, about the press and even about booksellers in various Swiss cities.[17] Contacts in Switzerland also sent reports to the News Department, which included snippets of information gleaned there about foreign affairs. If these were important, the News Department passed them on through the Foreign Office.[18] This kind of surveillance was carried out unofficially, but nevertheless, quite meticulously.

Germany too, supplied Swiss papers with 'news' material. Many newspapers in German Switzerland were fed by the numerous press agencies founded

---

[16] FO 395/35. All Foreign Office files (FO) are held in the Public Record Office at Kew, London.

[17] Cf., for example, report by Capt. Ralph Butler, 'Propaganda in Switzerland', dated 2 July 1916 (FO 395/33/131658).

[18] Cf., for example, letter from Julian Grande (in Bern) to Hubert Montgomery at the Foreign Office, dated 11 August 1916, relaying details of a private conversation with a Swiss adviser to the Swiss Society of Economic Surveillance relating to German supplies of coal and iron to Switzerland (FO 395/35).

and run by Germans in Switzerland with the purpose of providing the Swiss press with 'German facts'. Several items that appeared in the important *Neue Zürcher Zeitung* originated in press bureaux in Berlin.[19] And in England, one news agency claimed that:

> Ten million pounds (two hundred million marks) were paid by the German Government for press propaganda in foreign countries during the first two years of the war ... Approximately two hundred thousand pounds have been paid to newspapers in the German-speaking parts of Switzerland, principally in Berne, Basel and Zurich.[20]

Zurich, Switzerland's largest city, was perceived as extremely fertile ground for German propaganda. Known by many Swiss as '*Kleinberlin*' (Little Berlin) because of the pervasive Germanic influences in the city, Zurich was also the base of one of the most overtly pro-German papers during the war, the *Neue Züricher Nachrichten*. The Swiss themselves detected that German anti-*Entente* propaganda was widespread, infecting not only the press in Switzerland (publishers, editors and readers alike) but even extending to live entertainment in the *variétés* and cabarets of Bern, Zurich and Basel. For example, the Federal Justice Department received information that performers at the Cabaret Bonbonnière in Zurich (which catered for a fairly sophisticated clientele) were sent there from Germany on the condition that they perform certain material, 'in the service of propaganda', in exchange for their passage out of Germany to Switzerland.[21]

The best-known statement made during the war on the issue of neutrality and unity was an attempt to rouse the spirit of Helvetian unity and neutrality and, thus, to salve internal animosities. This was Carl Spitteler's speech, *Unser Schweizer Standpunkt* (our Swiss viewpoint). Spitteler delivered it in Zurich in December 1914. It was widely published in newspapers and in pamphlet form and it quickly became emblematic of the movement that sought to promote unity in the country – indeed, it is still widely known in Switzerland today.[22] The speech in Zurich was primarily directed at the German-Swiss, but Spitteler urged all Swiss to unite and to maintain a dignified distance from the coarse patriotism of the warring powers' sloganeering. Acknowledging that foreign propaganda posed a threat to Swiss unity, he emphasized the importance of impartiality and urged the press in particular,

---

[19] An example was the Wolff bureau. Its activities were also monitored by the Foreign Office (FO 395/35).

[20] The Wireless Press Ltd, London, 'How Germany Tells the Tale', 11 Oct. 1916 (FO 395/35).

[21] 'Propagandamaterial gegen die Entente' Band 1, Bundesarchiv Bern, E27/13893.

[22] Spitteler delivered his speech to the Zurich group of the *Neue Helvetsiche Gesellschaft* on 14 December 1914. It was subsequently published in the *Neue Zürcher Zeitung* on 16 and 17 December 1914 and has since been reprinted several times. Cf. W. Müri, *Carl Spitteler's Rede von 1914 rhetorisch betrachtet*, Bern: Verlag Herbert Lang, 1972.

to refrain from vicarious triumphalism, insult and *Schadenfreude*.[23] However, even this apparently conciliatory act was controversial. Intended to counterbalance German patriotism, and encourage a similar spirit of sympathy and understanding among the French-Swiss, Spitteler's gesture was interpreted by some merely as bald propaganda in the service of the *Entente*. The controversy was fuelled by the fact that the speech was made under the aegis of a meeting of the *Neue Helvetische Gesellschaft* (New Helvetian Society-NHG) in Zurich. This organization had been founded with the intent of promoting the historical principles of Swiss unity and neutrality. However, among German sympathizers and in parts of the conservative press, its activities were widely perceived as an ideologically-motivated *anti*-German campaign. The German envoy's office in Bern even claimed to have uncovered proof that the *NHG* was funded by the *Entente* as a cover to protect Allied interests.[24] In turn, another organization, the *Deutschschweizerische Sprachverein* (German-Swiss Language Union), founded in 1905, was widely suspected as a cover for German cultural propaganda.[25] The case highlights the paradox that, under the conditions of war in Europe 'neutrality' was always subjective.

By July 1915, almost a year into the war, there had been so many perceived infringements of neutrality in print that the Swiss Federal Council issued a decree specifically to hold in check the defamation of foreign powers. It stated that 'anyone who denigrates a foreign people, their authorities or their government in spoken or written word, in image or in representation, or who encourages hatred or mistrust' could face a sentence of up to six months, a fine of up to 5000 Swiss francs, or both.[26] The decree became the standard by which the Swiss press control commission operated. However, it was not easily enforced. In 1916, illicit postcards viciously caricaturing the Germans – so-called *cartes postales boches* – were still available, 'under the counter' in small tobacconists and other shops in French-speaking Switzerland. In German-speaking Switzerland, the irreverent fortnightly satirical paper

---

[23] Cf. C. Spitteler, 'Unser Schweizer Standpunkt', in ibid. p.593.

[24] Cf. D. Riesenberger, 'Deutsche Emigration und Schweizer Neutralität im ersten Weltkrieg', *Schweizerische Zeitschrift für Geschichte*, **38** (2), 1988, pp. 127–50.

[25] This claim was explicitly voiced in Steiner, *Wesen und Ursprung*, pp. 47–59. A Swiss report on German propaganda in the German-Swiss press speculated that the foundation of the *Deutschschweizerische Sprachverein* was probably intended to counter the influence of the *NHG*. Cf. 'Die Beeinflussung der Deutsch-Schweizerischen Presse durch die deutsche Propaganda' (typescript, undated), Bundesarchiv Bern, E27/13893.

[26] 'Verordnung betreffend die Beschimpfung fremder Völker, Staatsoberhäupter oder Regierungen', 2 July 1915, *Amtliche Sammlung Jahrgang 1915* (collected papers), vol. 31, Bern, 1916, pp. 249–50: 'Wer öffentlich, in Wort oder Schrift, in Bild oder Darstellung ein fremdes Volk, dessen Staatsoberhaupt, oder dessen Regierung in der öffentlichen Meinung herabwürdigt oder dem Hasse oder der Missachtung presigibt ... wird mit Gefängnis bis zu sechs Monaten oder mit Busse bis zu 5,000 Franken bestraft. Beide Strafe können verbunden werden.'

Nebelspalter articulated resentment towards foreign refugees. In doing so, it brought one of the most cherished symbols of Swiss humanitarianism into question, for 1916 was the year in which most casualties of war came into Switzerland; from then until the end of the war, 68 000 invalid prisoners of war were accommodated at some time in the country. The *Nebelspalter's* comment was made when it published the cover of a 1916 issue. It showed an endless stream of walking wounded, approaching from distant hills a garlanded gateway adorned with the Swiss cross, symbolizing the country's 'open' border. The caption reads: 'The Only Swiss Import – which now as then will be passed over to us with no compensation.'[27] And the same magazine was clearly dangerously close to contravention of the government's decree when it published four caricatures of national 'types'. The captions read: 'This is the German, who is happy he is in Zurich. / This is the Austrian, who is happy he is in Zurich. / This is the Russian, who is happy he is in Zurich. / This is the Swiss, who is happy he is tolerated in Zurich.'[28]

There was an important loophole in the government's decree. It goes some way to explaining why internal tensions could so often articulate vicariously national hostilities. The Swiss press control commission had jurisdiction over statements and images that were defamatory towards foreigners, but not those that played on *internal* tensions. Consequently, an editor or publisher in German-speaking Switzerland, for example, could be fined or imprisoned for insulting the French, but not for insulting the French Swiss. Indeed, it is clear that national antipathies were often deflected from the 'real' enemy, and projected onto the Swiss-French or Swiss-German from either side.

From 1914, censorship restrictions in several countries at war inhibited all but the blandest publications and editors were often forced to disguise political engagement under innocuous-sounding titles or the guise of 'art magazines'.[29] Many chose instead to go into exile to continue publishing from abroad. Neutral Switzerland was the most popular destination. Foreign envoy offices, especially the German delegation in Bern, kept under surveillance groups and individuals suspected of producing subversive literature or propaganda. Small magazines (such as Ludwig Rubiner's *Zeit-Echo*) and papers (such as the *Freie Zeitung* in Bern) produced by foreign exiles in Switzerland regularly aroused the suspicion of the police and foreign envoys.[30] These authorities tended to lump avant-garde writers and artists, such

---

[27] 'Der Einzige Schweizer Import-Artikel', *Nebelspalter*, Zürich, 6 July 1916.

[28] I am grateful to Raimund Meyer for bringing these two items to my attention.

[29] Cf. E. Kolinsky, *Engagierter Expressionismus. Politik und Literatur zwischen Weltkrieg und Weimarer Republik. Eine Analyse Expressionistischer Zeitschriften*, Stuttgart: J.B. Metzlersche Verlagsbuchhandlung, 1970, p. 8 and *passim*.

[30] Other examples range from small-circulation local papers, such as *Der Revoluzzer*, edited by Fritz Brupbacher and published in Zurich in 1915 and 1916, to more esteemed exile periodicals such as René Schickele's *Weißen Blätter* in Bern, and Henri Guilbeaux's *Demain* in Geneva.

as the Dadaists in Zurich, for example, together with left-wing political activists under the generic terms 'anarchists' or 'Bolsheviks'.[31] Records suggest that while many of these publications were carefully monitored, the investigators responsible for the work at ground level, both Swiss and foreign, were often ignorant or confused as to precisely where they had originated, how they were funded, or even as to the real identities of many of their contributors. Furthermore, any measures to curtail publishing activities had to be made through the Swiss authorities. The relative ease with which material could be covertly or anonymously produced and distributed meant that cities such as Geneva, Bern or Zurich remained attractive bases for all manner of publishing ventures, and fertile ground for many small literary and political papers. In turn, these relatively liberal conditions made for a diverse and dynamic publishing culture and a network of contacts between exiled publishers and writers.

The extensive foreign press in Switzerland was superficially tolerated, but increasingly became the cause of resentment. Some regarded the arrival in Switzerland of foreign papers and the journalists who worked on them as an invasion of its own kind. In more conservative and patriotic circles, the presence of foreign press ventures became a political and divisive issue. Just six weeks into the war, one of Zurich's petit-bourgeois weeklies appealed to the Swiss public to 'show stronger support for the literature (newspapers, illustrated press, [and] books) of German and Roman Switzerland, instead of reading ... foreign humorous magazines and newspapers, which are gradually poisoning the national, republican sensibilities of our people.'[32]

A year later, the same paper was still voicing such concerns. Evoking again the romantic ideal of an untainted *Volk*, it feared the foreign press threatened the purity and integrity of the Swiss national spirit. This time, it dealt with the numerous foreign Sunday supplements (claimed at 400 000 weekly), which caused concern because they were spread among the Swiss and, 'fluttering as far as the remotest Alpine hut', were read above all, by the 'mothers of our people and educators of our gentle youth'.[33]

During the war, Swiss cities were full of foreign correspondents. Numerous foreign press agencies were established and the trade in information was vigorous. It was common practice for some papers to reprint unquestioningly reports published in other papers, leading some observers to comment that many

---

[31] Cf. E21 / 10558, Bundesarchiv Bern.

[32] The appeal was originally made in the *Schweizerische Kaufmännische Zentralblatt* but was reported in the *Zürcher Wochen-Chronik*, no. 39, 26 Sept. 1914, p. 457: 'Es wäre heute für das schweizerische Publikum (auch für manche Vereine) wohl die Zeit gekommen, auch die Literatur (Zeitungen, illustrierte Blätter, Bücher) der deutschen und romanischen Schweiz kräftiger zu unterstützen, statt die ausländischen Witzblätter und Zeitungen, die unser nationales, republikanisches Volksempfinden allmählich vergiften, zu lesen und zu abonnieren!'

[33] *Zürcher Wochen-Chronik*, 25 Sept. 1915, p. 339.

editors' jobs consisted of little more than the cutting and pasting of clippings to make a 'new' paper. It is interesting that this practice itself was effectively exploited by the Dadaists in Zurich who, in 1919, made several wholly fabricated reports to the press who obligingly printed the stories as news and thereby ensured that other papers would take them up too. At a humorous level, the *Nebelspalter* took a cynical view of the war-correspondent's job in neutral Switzerland, caricaturing the foreign journalist who composes his 'front-line' reports from the safety of a Swiss tavern.[34] However, the trade in information in Switzerland was not always conducted along such apparently slapdash lines. Conditions in Switzerland made the country a major centre for black-marketeering and for international espionage. Valeriu Marcu, a young Rumanian in Zurich during the war, wrote: 'Every street-corner had ears, hands scribbled furtively in notebooks, every sound from abroad was picked up and passed on. Neutral [Switzerland] was the only window onto the enemy territory. No square millimetre of public life was unoccupied'.[35]

The press sometimes played an important part in these operations. Papers were full of small advertisements offering or requesting all kinds of products and services. The city councils regularly received complaints that illicit sexual and contraceptive services were being offered through the small ads pages of the press. Rather graver were the barely veiled offers of large sums of money for military secrets. A Swiss writer, C. A. Loosli, wrote a study of the press in Switzerland in 1917 in a pamphlet entitled *Ausländische Einflüsse in der Schweiz* (Foreign Influences in Switzerland), which aroused considerable debate. Here, he exposed such practices. He reported that a Prussian publisher by the name of Hans Rhaue, for example, had set up a press bureau in the lakeside village of Meilen, near Zurich. The bureau published a series of what were ostensibly specialist antiques journals. In one of these, *Die Internationale Antiquitäten-Rundschau* (*International Antiques Review*) several advertisements appeared, one of which read:

> *We pay up to 100,000 francs!* for valuable war collections and war documents of all kinds. We request immediate delivery of such items by express post. We pay cash, by telegraph if necessary. Only the most current documents are wanted, with authentication and exact details. Maps and walled defences of occupied zones are particularly sought.[36]

Loosli, a vocal commentator on politics and the press in Switzerland, also criticized native provincial and small papers. He attacked in particular third-

---

[34] 'Die spezial Kriegskorrespondenten', *Nebelspalter*, 16 January 1915.

[35] Valeriu Marcu quoted in D. Noguez, *Lenin Dada*, Zürich: Limmat Verlag, 1990, p. 41: 'Jede Strassenecke hatte Ohren, Hände schrieben verstohlen in Notizbücher, jeder Laut aus der Fremde wurde aufgenommen und weitergegeben. Das neutrale Land war das einzige Fenster ins feindliche Gebiet. Kein Quadratmillimeter der Öffentlichkeit blieb unbesetzt.'

[36] Reproduced in Loosli, *Ausländische Einflüsse*, p. 11.

rate local papers, which he suggested were run by dilettantes and often served little more purpose than to flatter the egos of frustrated schoolteachers anxious to see their tirades in print. Crucially, he identified too, a more ominous danger; that the financially precarious nature of small-circulation papers made them vulnerable to the influence of political parties and foreign groups who could exert control over the papers' contents.

News and the press were big business in Switzerland during the war. But it was not only the content of press material that gave rise to concerns. It is clear that the news business operated very much at street level, directly in the public, urban sphere. Police files record the public's objections to the tactics of newspaper vendors on the city streets, for example. There were complaints that the streets were becoming blocked by the vendors, who especially clustered along the world-famous Bahnhofstrasse connecting the main station to the banking heart of Zurich. According to a police report, many citizens found the overwhelming number of these vendors offensive, largely because of the 'inflammatory tricks of the trade used by newspaper sellers to attract customers with exaggerated, sensationalist, partially untrue and injurious proclamations'.[37] In response, in December 1914 the local police forbade such tactics as 'irreconcilable with the principle of neutrality'.[38]

In April 1915, the Federal Justice Department conducted a national investigation of contraventions of neutrality in Switzerland. It sought, in particular, information about the behaviour of foreigners in Switzerland and 'the distribution of printed matters, pictures, obscene or otherwise, that are either insulting to foreign states and their leaders, or liable to endanger the good relations among the Swiss population.'[39] That the initiative was formulated and worded in this way makes clear that there was official recognition that partisan or xenophobic material released into the public realm in Switzerland could have serious implications, not only for Switzerland's foreign relations, but also for its own internal security. Police records that were submitted in response to the investigation list a catalogue of further incidents perceived as public contraventions of neutrality. These range from a 1000 strong anti-Serbian demonstration led by Austrians in Zurich on the eve of war to a violent brawl in a city-centre tram which broke out when a drunken German out celebrating his birthday with friends attacked a French-speaking fellow passenger because 'he believed to have identified in him a citizen of a state hostile to his own nation'.[40]

In the mass media, the police were faced with the enormous problem of regulating film, image and text that represented events beyond or within the

---

[37] Abschrift, An die Polizeidirektion des Kantons, 3 May 1915, P239.12, Staatsarchiv des Kantons Zürich.

[38] Ibid.

[39] Ibid.

[40] Abschrift, Polizeirapport, 26 April 1915, P239.12, Staatsarchiv des Kantons Zürich.

borders. Most problematic for Switzerland in the longer term were the partisan polemics and small, independent political papers issued by groups and individuals in the form of small, cheaply produced pamphlets, flysheets and free papers. These often commented bluntly on the Swiss constitution, the loyalties of various sectors of its population and the implications of the war for Swiss unity. Many of these texts were distributed by subscription, or as unsolicited mail, or were placed in cafés and other public places to be read. The regulation of such printed matter was almost impossible. As the war progressed, class-based tensions mounted in Switzerland and military as well as police troops were deployed against Swiss demonstrators and strikers. Revolutionary groups relied upon printed items for quick distribution in order to organize their activities. Ephemeral printed items such as pamphlets and flysheets were especially difficult to control. Some survive today in police files, having been confiscated during the war. One example is a single flysheet calling on the workers of Switzerland to refuse conscription. It was confiscated on the streets of Zurich, but was of indefinable origin and anonymously produced.[41]

Material that contravened the principles of neutrality was just as difficult to regulate. Lacking the comprehensive censorship mechanisms that were in place in other countries, the Swiss authorities were often slow to respond to breaches of neutrality. Nonetheless, in response to public pressure and the showing of apparently uncensored film-footage in Zurich cinemas of French troops forced to dig trenches for the Germans before being executed, the police introduced patrols of the city's cinemas. After just two months of war, they noted that numerous illustrated magazines and postcards showing particularly gory scenes from the Front or caricaturing other nationalities, were displayed in shop windows and sold in large numbers in the city. Many of these were published in Berlin and imported into Switzerland. Certain issues of the Munich-based *Simplicissimus*, for example, were also categorised as '*neutralitätswidrig*' (anti-neutral). In response, the police made it an offence not only to offer such items for sale, but even to display them publicly.[42] Throughout the war, complaints continued to be made, and often at the highest levels, of offensive printed items in circulation in Switzerland. In April 1915 a memo was circulated from the Swiss Federal Council to the cantonal governments. It stressed first the duty of all civil servants to fight all attempts to confuse or poison the 'healthy spirit' of the Swiss people. Insisting that most of the offensive material came from abroad, it was nonetheless noted, with regret, that not all cantonal governments and police forces had been showing the necessary conviction to combat its distribution:

---

[41] Flysheet (undated), 'Arbeiter!', P239.12, Staatsarchiv des Kantons Zürich.

[42] Abschrift, An die Polizeidirektion des Kantons, 3 May 1915, Staatsarchiv des Kantons Zürich, P239.12.

Despite bans and confiscations, the flood of pamphlets, flysheets, illustrations, postcards etc., of part agitational, part pornographic nature grows. This ugly literature continues to be peddled [and] displayed in kiosks and bookshops. ... It can no longer be tolerated.[43]

It is clear that in Britain too, the Foreign Office was very aware of the effects that such material could have, though its interest was differently motivated. The News Department became concerned about the sensitivity of the 'dosage' of shock that could be effective in propaganda through the press. As Ralph Butler reported to the Foreign Office:

the Swiss believe on the whole in British news and British utterances, and this belief is based on the fact that we are supposed not to carry on any propaganda at all. To stomachs jaded with a surfeit of 'tendentious' news, from German and French sources the honest if stupid frankness (so it is argued) of England is not unpalatable. This consideration explains the attention which is undoubtedly paid to our communications to the Press through the Consulate General at Zürich. ... It is clear that, if this is so, we must not damage our credit by drawing too heavily on it. ... The atrocity market is particularly tight. To get the required thrill, the horror has to be piled up beyond the credibility limit.[44]

Indeed, such reporting sometimes overstepped the line and backfired. For example, overzealous reporting of the severity of French casualties transported from Germany through Switzerland to France inadvertently implied that the Swiss had not been able to look after them adequately, and this caused considerable local offence.[45]

The German envoys in Switzerland during the war kept a close watch on publishing activities in Switzerland too, though they concentrated their attention particularly on pacifist German intellectuals in exile in the country. The Imperial German envoy in Bern deployed a 'spy' who infiltrated German intellectual circles in the cafés and reported on their activities. House searches were carried out, mail was intercepted and contacts with Germans at home monitored. The envoy's office suspected the allied countries of supporting German revolutionaries and their propaganda in Switzerland. The Zurich-based Orell-Füssli publishing house was accused of disseminating pro-England propaganda.[46] The German diplomats kept files on many German intellectuals in exile in Switzerland and registered their suspicions. In these files, Leonhard

---

[43] Kreisschreiben, Der Schweizerische Bundesrat an sämtliche Kantonsregierungen, Staatsarchiv des Kantons Zürich, P239.12: 'Trotz Verboten und Beschlagnahmen dauert die Überschwemmung mit Broschüren, Flugblättern, Illustrationen, Postkarten usw., teils verhetzenden, teils pornographischen Inhalts, fort, unbehelligt wird diese hässliche Literatur kolportiert, in Kiosks und Buchhandlungen ausgestellet. ... Das darf nicht länger geduldet werden.'

[44] FO 395/33

[45] FO 395/33.

[46] Cf. Riesenberger, 'Deutsche Emigration', p. 131.

Frank, for example, who was based in Zurich for much of the war, is classified as 'a real coffee-house-anarchist, who sits all day in the Odeon Restaurant and preaches revolution in Germany'.[47] The Café Odeon in Zurich, by the riverbank had a reputation during the war as a 'European literature market'.[48] The coffee houses of Switzerland's larger cities were regarded with some suspicion by both the Swiss and foreign authorities; but the cafés frequented by émigrés were also regarded with disdain by many of those actively involved in revolutionary politics. Solzhenitsyn tells us: 'Lenin had hated cafés, those smoke-filled dens of logorrhoea, where nine-tenths of the compulsive revolutionary windbags were in permanent session' including 'blethering intellectuals, with their philosophical manifestos and artistic demonstrations, in revolt against they knew not what.'[49]

In 1916, one of the most serious and extensive controversies over a single printed item erupted. The case serves well to highlight the extremely delicate political relations within Switzerland during the war and the power of printed items to disturb their precarious equilibrium.

The *Stimmen im Sturm* (Voices in the Storm) was the slogan under which a series of pamphlets was published during the war by a group, ostensibly consisting solely of Swiss, on a range of contemporary issues. The forward to the pamphlets stated:

> Under the title *Stimmen im Sturm aus der deutschen Schweiz* a series of texts is published, in which Swiss Germans seek to express those concerns that move our people in the present difficult and grave international situation. Attempts have been made for months, from the other side, to distract our people from an apparently neutral position and to encourage a one-sided opposition to the German Empire, with which we have always enjoyed friendly relations, and to the German people to whom we are closely related. The daily press is incapable of working effectively against this pervasive propaganda. This failing is to be remedied by the *Stimmen im Sturm*.[50]

The titles in the series dealt with both national and international issues, chiefly, neutrality and Switzerland's relationship with Germany and France. They were often polemic in tone and intended to arouse strong feelings.

---

[47] Document dated 26 February 1918 of the Kaiserlich Deutschen Gesandtschaft in Bern, quoted in V. Grötzinger, *Der Erste Weltkrieg im Widerhall des 'Zeit-Echo' (1914–1917)*. Bern: Peter Lang, 1994, p. 255: 'ein richtiger Kaffeehaus-Anarchist, der den ganzen Tag im Restaurant Odeon sitzt und die Revolution in Deutschland predigt.'

[48] G. Huonker, *Literaturszene Zürich: Menschen, Geschichten und Bilder 1914 bis 1945*. Zürich: Unionsverlag, 1986, p. 27.

[49] A. Solzhenitsyn, *Lenin in Zürich. Chapters*, trans. H.T. Willetts. London: The Bodley Head, 1976, p. 95.

[50] H. Meier (pseud.), *Die deutschfeindliche Bewegung in der französischen Schweiz*. Zürich: Verlag der 'Stimmen im Sturm', 1915. p. 2.

However, the fourth pamphlet in particular led to a nationwide debate, investigation at cantonal and federal levels and to serious controversy. The pamphlet, entitled *Die deutschfeindliche Bewegung in der französischen Schweiz* (The Anti-German Movement in French Switzerland) appeared in Zurich in November 1915, but was subsequently read and discussed across the country over many months. The pamphlet was 36 pages in length, in which the author detailed evidence of 'fanatic' anti-German sentiments in Western Switzerland. He argued that not only did the French Swiss have close ties with France, but that, over the two decades prior to the war, French elements had been working to infect the Swiss with oppositional feelings to the German-speaking Swiss. To substantiate his claims that there was a pervasive anti-German movement in Western Switzerland, the author listed a catalogue of slights against all things Germanic in Western Switzerland from the colloquial use of terms such as '*boche*', 'sauerkraut-eaters' and 'German blockheads' used to refer to Swiss Germans, to instances of untrue reports in French Swiss newspapers of atrocities committed by the Germans in Belgium.[51] 'Meier' reported, for instance, that the Lausanne Gazette printed apparently untrue horror-stories of Belgian civilian refugees arriving in Swiss hospitals having had their eyes gouged out by German soldiers.[52] He also laid the blame for Allied tightening on Swiss exports on the West-Swiss press for its accusations of smuggling and economic links with Germany.[53] He singled out Geneva in particular as a stronghold of francophilia. Meier reported that its population included 32 000 French nationals, and many more whose ancestors came from France and noted that Geneva maintained strong trade links with its French neighbours.

Vehement objections to the pamphlet's overall sentiment and content were voiced almost immediately. Opposition was led by the press from both sides of the country. Finally, having received numerous public and private complaints, on 14 January 1916 the Press Control Commission brought the pamphlet to the attention of Bundesrat Hoffmann.

The pamphlet's author, 'H. Meier', was claimed by the *Stimmen im Sturm* to be a Protestant minister from Zurich, but in the course of the controversy it emerged that this was a pseudonym, that no H. Meier existed either as a Zurich minister or as a writer. Eventually it was discovered that the identity of the author was a Dr Edgar Schmid, a senior member of the *Deutschschweizerische Sprachverein*. Further details began to emerge that cast the *Stimmen im Sturm* under increasing suspicion. It was claimed that among those closely involved was the son of the pro-German army General Ulrich Wille. His own son, in turn, had as godfather none other than the German Kaiser himself. Further-

---

[51] Ibid., p. 8.
[52] Ibid., p. 6.
[53] Ibid.

more, it became known, through the press, that the offices of the *Stimmen im Sturm* publishing group, the address of which does not appear on their headed notepaper but which was revealed in the press, was in the same building as the German consulate in Zurich. When these details emerged, the military and police departments in Bern received several letters demanding that action be taken against Wille and his colleagues. One correspondent asked 'does Wille have nothing better to do than divide the Swiss people by means of this obscene publication and in so doing serve the interests of Germany, and all this because he is seduced by Prussian affectations and allures?'.[54]

In March 1916, Bundesrat Hoffmann wrote to the *Stimmen im Sturm* offices, reprimanding them for publishing this particular pamphlet 'under current circumstances', though not for producing the series as a whole.[55] In June, most likely influenced by the continued expressions of public indignation, and having evidently read the text for himself, he wrote again at greater length, objecting in particular to two passages.[56] In one, the author had claimed that the very neutrality of Switzerland was only ensured by the presence of German elements in Switzerland, without which Switzerland would already have been drawn onto the battlefields to fight for the French against the German 'barbarians'.[57] Second, and causing most offence, was the author's claim that if Switzerland had to use military force in a confrontation with the Allies, the loyalty of military personnel from Western Switzerland could not be fully counted upon. The 'evidence' cited to support this claim was that the mainstream press in Geneva and Lausanne consistently worked to stir up anti-German sentiment and to reveal military details of great use to French spies, and secondly, that in the French-speaking Jura, 'a large section of the educated classes desire to be separated from the canton of Bern and annexed to France itself'.[58]

In the meantime, the correspondence between the Federal Press Control Commission and the Federal Councillor himself indicates that the highest authorities had evidence that the pamphlets were funded and distributed by the German foreign offices. No direct punitive action was taken against the *Stimmen im Sturm*, but the episode undoubtedly soured relations within Switzerland and antagonism especially towards the city of Zurich, where there were accusations of 'arson at home'.[59]

[54] Typescript, author unidentified. Letter received by Swiss Military Department on 8 Feb. 1916. E27/13893/3, Bundesarchiv Bern.

[55] Abschrift, Der Chef des Schweizerischen Politischen Departements, dated 13 March 1916. E27/13893/3, Bundesarchiv Bern.

[56] Typescript, letter from Bundesrat Hoffmann to the *Stimmen im Sturm*, dated 6 June 1916. E27/13893/3, Bundesarchiv Bern.

[57] H. Meier (pseud.), *Die deutschfeindliche Bewegung*, p. 34.

[58] Ibid.

[59] 'Brandstifter am eigenen Haus', Aargauer Volksblatt, 22 Dec. 1915, p.1.

In international literary, political and art history, Switzerland during the First World War is too often characterized as an apathetic haven from which members of the European avant garde and political dissidents could operate in exile. In reality, those conditions that attracted so many celebrated figures from Joyce to Kraus, to Lenin and the Dadaists, such as the country's neutrality and asylum policies, also gave rise to some of the most serious contraventions of internal neutrality endangering its already tenuous unity. The cases outlined here are just a few of many, but they help to illuminate the ways in which linguistic and cultural diversity supported by, and reinforced through, a broad spectrum of print media with particular readerships cannot sustain distance, equilibrium, nor indeed neutrality. For when crisis conditions develop, it is in the realm of public discourse, especially in the press, that identities are formed and allegiances underlined, that cannot remain neutral.

Further reading

Walter Baumann, *Zürcher Schlagzeilen*, Zurich: Orell Füssli Verlag, 1981.

Edgar Bonjour, *Swiss Neutrality: Its History and Meaning*, trans. Mary Hottinger, London: George Allen and Unwin, 1946.

Peter Dürrenmatt, *Schweizer Geschichte* (2 vols), Vol. 2, Zurich: Schweizer Verlagshaus AG, 1976.

Willi Gautschi, *Helvetische Streiflichter. Aufsätze und Vorträge zur Zeitgeschichte*, Zurich: Verlag Neue Zürcher Zeitung, 1994.

Vera Grötzinger, *Der Erste Weltkrieg im Widerhall des 'Zeit-Echo' (1914–1917)*, Bern: Peter Lang, 1994.

Ulrich im Hof, *Geschichte der Schweiz*, Stuttgart: Verlag W. Kohlhammer, 1974.

Gustav Huonker, *Literaturszene Zürich: Menschen, Geschichten und Bilder 1914 bis 1945*, Zurich: Unionsverlag, 1986.

Hans Ulrich Jost et al., *Handbuch der Schweizer Geschichte* (2 vols), Vol. 2, Zurich: Verlag Berichthaus Zürich, 1977.

Walter Müri, *Carl Spitteler's Rede von 1914 rhetorisch betrachtet*, Bern: Verlag Herbert Lang and Cie AG, 1972.

Jonathan Steinberg, *Why Switzerland?* Cambridge: Cambridge University Press, 1996.

Oscar Wettstein, *Über das Verhältnis zwischen Staat und Presse, mit besonderer Berücksichtigung der Schweiz*, Zurich: Albert Müller's Verlag, 1904.

Sigmund Widmer, *Krieg und Krise, Zürich: Eine Kulturgeschichte*, Vol. 11, Zurich and Munich: Artemis Verlag, 1983.

CHAPTER EIGHT

The 'cultured city': the art press in Berlin and Paris in the early twentieth century

Malcolm Gee

In April 1900 Eduard von Bodenhausen wrote to his friend Harry Graf Kessler concerning their last-ditch plans to keep the periodical *Pan* afloat. They had considered merging with *Die Insel* and had won over Julius Meier-Graefe, who had been a key figure in the founding of *Pan* itself in 1895, to the idea. However, this project had fallen through. Bodenhausen believed that if Kessler were prepared to commit himself fully, they could obtain the necessary backing to continue publishing the journal on its present basis. Eduard Arnhold, the leading business figure and art patron, might be persuaded to put up major funds, he suggested, if Kessler and Wilhelm von Bode, the Prussian museum director and member of the *Pan* board, presented him with a clear plan. 'He has enormous Berlin local patriotism and is bound to support our side against Munich.' In the event Kessler remained reticent and *Pan* ceased publication, after five years during which it had set new standards for art and literary journalism in Germany.[1]

The case of *Pan* was in some respects unique. However, this incident brings out several aspects of the history of the art press with which this essay will be concerned. Personnel and backing were key. This type of publication was aimed at a restricted readership and its financial viability was precarious. On the other hand, a journal could articulate important interests: those of cultural leaders and regulators, art establishments and art innovators, intellectuals seeking to make an impact and a living, publishers who wished to add the high cultural values of the fine and applied arts to their range of output. The environments that nurtured these interests were urban. In France both art and publishing were highly concentrated in Paris. In Germany several cities had significant

---

[1] Hans Ulrich Simon (ed.), *E. von Bodenhausen, H. Graf Kessler. Ein Briefwechseln*, Deutscher Literaturarchiv, Marbacher Schriften 16: Marbach am Necker, 1978, pp. 54–5, letter of 6 April 1900. They had also had discussions with the Berlin publisher Samuel Fischer, also on the *Pan* board, about the possibility of taking on the journal. On the history of *Pan* see, Jutta Thamer, *Zwischen Historicismus und Jugendstil. Zur Ausstattung der Zeitschrift 'Pan' (1895–1900)*, Frankfurt am Main: Peter D. Lang, 1980.

publishing sectors and art production was spread throughout the Reich. Art journals needed to address activity across many centres; one of their functions, indeed, was to link individuals from different urban contexts together. At the same time, as Bodenhausen's comment indicates, they often related to specific local interests. The growth of the art press in Berlin in the early part of the twentieth century was part of the city's overall dynamism: it also reflected the ambition of various groups to promote the capital's cultural industries vis-à-vis those of other centres, notably Munich (and, in the case of publishing, Leipzig.) It is this nexus of interests, embodied in specific publishing initiatives, that forms the principal focus of this study, covering a period of dramatic change in Germany that also saw Berlin consolidate its dominance in the cultural life of the country. The character and role of the Berlin art press will be compared, in some key respects, with that of Paris, because Paris offered a model, throughout this period, of a successful art world system, one that German writers, publishers, and artists were constantly aware of.

The art press before 1914

Art periodicals were already a well-established sector in European publishing at the end of the nineteenth century. The period from the 1880s to the outbreak of the First World War was, however, one of expansion and change, generated on one hand by technological progress, particularly the development of photographic reproduction, and on the other by the spread of new ideas and practices in art and design, that elicited publishing initiatives of a wide range of types and ambition. (Both these factors also had an impact on the daily press and its treatment of art. This is not a theme that will be examined in detail here but, as we shall see, there were significant lines of interaction between the spheres of the specialist art press and newspapers.) Two broad categories of art periodical emerged at the end of the century that corresponded to different aspects of the art world as a whole and, to some extent, to differing national and urban contexts. A wave of publications in a number of centres, following the highly successful example of the London *Studio* (founded in 1893), promoted modern painting and sculpture in conjunction with the applied arts. A renewal of the decorative arts had formed part of *Pan*'s programme in 1895: after leaving the editorial group, Meier-Graefe went on to found *Dekorative Kunst*, published from Paris and Munich; in the same year (1897) Alexander Koch set up *Deutsche Kunst und Dekoration* as a complement to the Grand Duke of Hesse's efforts to promote Darmstadt as a centre of *Jugendstil* production.[2] The orientation of these journals was

---

[2] See H. Brill, 'The Fin-de-Siècle', in T. Fawcett and C. Philpot (eds), *The Art Press. Two Centuries of Art Magazines*, London: The Art Book Company, 1976, pp. 22–31.

primarily, if not exclusively, towards the visual arts, and while they represented the interests of contemporary practitioners engaged in the modern movement, they also related to the concerns of patrons and museum professionals. *Pan* itself, particularly in its early period, also had a strong literary character – in fact, striking a balance between different interests in this respect had been one of the causes of difficulties in editorial policy. Meier-Graefe's collaborator on the first, controversial issues, Otto Birbaum, went on to co-found a periodical, *Die Insel*, that focused on literary matters while also taking an interest in the visual arts.[3] *Die Insel* was an example of a second type of publication that became increasingly prominent at the turn of the century: edited by aspiring creative writers and aimed at a relatively small group of readers and sympathizers; committed primarily to contemporary, innovative production, and reflecting the community of interests between writers and artists that was a feature of cultural activity in many urban centres at the time, including Berlin and Paris.

Hans Brill has estimated that there may have been 1000 periodical publications in France in 1900 that engaged in one way or another with the visual arts.[4] The wide range, and enormous quantity, of writing about art in Paris played a major role in sustaining and moulding public awareness of the vitality of French art locally and internationally. Specialist journals ranged from the scholarly *Gazette des Beaux-Arts* to the popularizing *L'Art et les Artistes*; art reporting also featured widely in the daily press. The latter sometimes sensationalized, and politicized, art matters, as Fay Brauer's chapter here clearly demonstrates, but it was not totally unreceptive to modern art. Louis Vauxcelles, the combative supporter of Matisse's generation, was a professional journalist (he claimed in an autobiographical note to 'have worked for all the newspapers of France'). He ran the art column of the scurrilous society broadsheet *Gil Blas* and became the regular critic on *L'Excelsior*, an innovative illustrated daily founded by Pierre Laffite in 1910. The mainstream press provided a platform, and a useful source of income, for creative writers – Guillaume Apollinaire and André Salmon, poets who were closely in touch with the Parisian artistic avant garde, were, successively, employed as art critics on *L'Intransigeant* and *Paris-Journal*.[5]

The Parisian scene was also particularly rich in literary journals that engaged with the concerns of contemporary artists. During the 1890s *La Plume*

---

[3] *Die Insel*, Leipzig, 1899–1902. The publishing house continued (vey successfully) after the demise of the review. See *Die Insel. Eine Ausstellung zur Geschichte des Verlags*, Marbach: Schiller National Museum 1965.

[4] Ibid., p. 23

[5] For a general discussion of critical practice in Paris, see M. Gee, *Dealers, Critics and Collectors of Modern Painting. Aspects of the Parisian Art Market between 1910 and 1930*. New York: Garland Press, 1981, ch.4.

(1889), *Mercure de France* (1890), and *La Revue Blanche* (1889–1903) had articulated the interaction between literary and artistic circles in the city during the period when 'symbolism' was being propagated in both poetry and painting. Apollinaire and Salmon cut their literary teeth in this milieu, and developed their understanding and enthusiasm for contemporary art in it. Apollinaire's first text on Picasso was published in *La Plume* in 1905. His own review, *Le Festin d'Ésope* (1904), on which Salmon collaborated, and *Vers et Prose* (1905) where the latter was editorial secretary, focused primarily on literature, but as Cubism and associated avant-garde tendencies became prominent on the Parisian scene the association of contemporary literature and art was forcibly reasserted, notably in the second series of *Les Soirées de Paris* (1913–14), edited by Apollinaire and the baronne d'Oettingen, and in Ricciotto Canudo's *Montjoie!* (1913–14). It was in a long review of the *Salon des Indépendants* in *Montjoie!* that Salmon declared that their new poetic criticism of affirmation had killed off the old judgemental type, citing the role of the 'major and minor' press in giving it a platform.[6] While *Montjoie!*, with a broadsheet format, presented itself as a campaigning illustrated 'organ of French artistic imperialism', *Les Soirées de Paris* had a more conventional appearance as a small literary review, but its contents, reflecting the activities and connections of the Apollinaire-Picasso circle, dealt with the most experimental aspects of Parisian art and literature. The first issue of the new series (18) was illustrated by photographs of Picasso's collages and reliefs (provided by his dealer D. H. Kahnweiler); the last (26–7) featured Apollinaire's latest, hybrid, output, the '*idéogramme*'.[7]

The community of interests between the literary and artistic avant garde was a feature of the promotion of 'expressionism' in Berlin after 1910. During the first decade of the twentieth century, however, the main press locus for the defence of modern art in the city was the journal *Kunst und Künstler*, which was concerned almost exclusively with the visual arts. *Kunst und Künstler* was founded in 1902 by Bruno Cassirer, who had taken over the publishing activities of the joint business he had set up with his cousin Paul (who retained the art gallery) when they separated their interests in 1901.[8] Bruno Cassirer had been a founder member of the *Pan 'Genossenschaft'* and the journal was clearly inspired by *Pan*'s example (Cäsar Flaischlen, who had

---

[6] 'Le Salon', *Montjoie!*, 3 March 1914.

[7] See the studies of both reviews by Noëmi Blumenkranz-Onimus in L. Briony-Guerry (ed.), *L'Année 1913*, Paris: Klincksieck, 1971, vol. 2, pp. 1097–122.

[8] On the history of the review, see: Sigrun Paas, 'Kunst und Künstler 1902–1933. Eine Zeitschrift in der Ausseinandersetzung um den Impressionismus in Deutschland', doctoral thesis, University of Heidelberg, 1976; and Günther Feist (ed.), *Kunst und Künstler. Aus 32 Jahrgängen einer deutschen Kunstzeitschrift*, Berlin: Henschelverlag Kunst und Gesellschaft, 1971.

run *Pan* from 1896 to 1900 was joint editor in 1902–3, responsible for the look of the new review). However, Cassirer and his collaborators opted for a publication that competed directly with established art and design journals such as the Leipzig *Zeitschrift für Bildende Kunst*, with a similar type of coverage (and also price – 16, then 24 marks a year, compared to *Pan*'s extravagant 75), although one that was firmly oriented towards contemporary, 'progressive' production. *Kunst und Künstler* set out to be a source of high quality, critical opinion, and information, on modern art and its support structures, employing production values that emphasized its commitment to 'the beautiful'. A typical issue contained four to five illustrated articles presenting the work of contemporary artists (and sometimes architects), their nineteenth-century predecessors, a major exhibition or a topical genre of modern artistic production, such as prints, theatre design or furniture. The final pages (out of an average of about 45) were dedicated to a 'Kunstchronik' of listings and comment on exhibitions and auction sales in Berlin, other German cities and, less systematically, art centres abroad (see Figures 8.1 and 8.2). High quality colour illustrations appeared fairly regularly and original prints were used from time to time – as in, for example, a text by Max Liebermann of 1904 that presented two recently rediscovered woodcuts by Manet. One of the journal's explicit objectives was to provide insights into the ideas and working methods of artists, and texts by practitioners such as Liebermann were one of its distinguishing features.[9] However, most of the texts in *Kunst und Künstler* were either by progressives in the museum profession such as Max Friedlander and Alfred Lichtwark, or by professional critics such as Meier-Graefe and its editors, Emil Heilbut (to 1906) and Karl Scheffler (1906–33), who generally wrote at least one feature article per issue and provided much of the copy for the news section. Both Heilbut and Scheffler had some artistic training but had then moved into art journalism. Heilbut had established himself with a book on 'New Art' in 1887; Scheffler had acquired a reputation in the late 1890s as a writer on contemporary design, with the support of Meier-Graefe. Both had contributed to Maximilien Harden's journal *Die Zukunft*, which was the mouthpiece of the Berlin liberal intelligentsia – to which the Cassirer cousins belonged.[10]

Kunst und Künstler had a national ambition, and many of its contributors, particularly those in the museum world, were based elsewhere than Berlin. The journal was, nonetheless, firmly rooted in the specific context of the city. Its overall position, in favour of modernizing German art through the application of principles linked with naturalism and the recognition of recent foreign achievements in painting and sculpture, was pertinent to attitudes and

---

[9] 'Zwei Original-Holzschnitt von Manet', *Kunst und Künstler*, 3 (4), 1904/5, pp. 140–45. On the general policy of the review see the statement 'Zum Beginn', in 1 (1), 1902/3, p. 1.

[10] Paas, *Kunst und Künstler 1902–1933*, pp. 125–6 and 160–61.

MAX LIEBERMANN, KUNSTCHRONIK

BERLIN

Die Berliner Saison setzte sehr anregend mit der Ausstellung von sieben Boecklins bei *Schulte* ein. Es waren ausserdem ausgestellt Porträts von de la Gandara, Bilder von Axel Gallén, Otto Sinding, Arthur Langhammer; Emile Claus zeigte Landschaften und Hanns Fechner Pastelle. Vorher waren Bilder von F. von Uhde, Bürckel und L. Munthe ausgestellt. — Bei *Keller u. Reiner* hatte der Bildhauer Harro Magnussen eine Kollektivausstellung. Jetzt ist ein grosses Gemälde von Melchior Lechter „Die Weihe am mystischen Quell" mit anderen Arbeiten von Melchior Lechter zu sehen. Das Gemälde ist das Hauptstück aus dem von Jacob Pallenberg seiner Vaterstadt geschenkten Prunksaal im Kunstgewerbemuseum zu Köln. Wie hoch die Intentionen des Stefan George befreundeten Künstlers auch anzuerkennen sind, so hat er in dem Gemälde gewisse Unzulänglichkeiten, über die man nicht hinwegkommen wird. Der Künstler befriedigt eher dort, wo man ihn nicht ausführen sieht, in den Skizzen, in Entwürfen, als in dem ausgeführten Gemälde.

Bei *Paul Cassirer* ist eine kleine Anzahl von neuen Bildern Trübners, eine kleine Sammlung japanischer Farbenholzschnitte und eine Reihe von Bildern von Israels, Mauve, Jacob Maris und Breitner ausgestellt. — Im *Künstlerhause* sind Bilder von Mohrbutter, Alberts, le Sidaner, Carolus Duran (das Porträt von Gustave Doré), Daubigny, Munkaczy, Raffaelli, Gari Melchers und ein sehr umfangreiches Gemälde von Besnard ausgestellt, die „Insel der Glücklichen". An Böcklin denkt vor diesem Bilde wegen des Themas der Deutsche — an Watteaus göttlich schönes Bild „embarquement pour l'île de Cythère" der Franzose. Besnard bleibt unfassbar weit hinter den Erwartungen zurück. In einer Gondel fährt ein Mann, der ein Mittelding zwischen Christus und Richelieu ist, von zwei lockeren Frauengestalten begleitet, zur „Insel der Glücklichen" uns entgegen. Vorn scheint Sekt und Kaffee getrunken zu werden und eine Niederlassung von Schalen und Gläsern wie in einer Filiale von Art Nouveau etabliert zu sein. Ein Faun reicht seine Schale dar. Zwei Engel mit Loie Fullerflügeln hören einem Konzert zu, das von zwei Faunen mit Triangel und Castagnetten gegeben wird u. s. w. Das einzig Annehmbare auf diesem Bilde ist die Landschaft. Ihre Motive scheinen dem See von Annecy entnommen. In einem Nebensaal ist eine interessante Sammlung von Farbenholzschnitten ausgestellt. — Im Salon *Rabl* sind Bilder von Sperl, Leibl, Leistikow, Liebermann, Uhde, Hans Hermann, Lippisch und Schlichting und Tierstücke von dem Bildhauer August Gaul.

　　　　　＊

An Themen zur Diskussion über künstlerische Fragen der Zeit fehlt es im übrigen. Reinhold Begas' Auseinandersetzungen — über neue und alte Kunst, Schönheit und Hässlichkeit — sind zu

8.1 Kunstchronik. (Drawing by Max Liebermann.) *Kunst und Künstler*, **I**, 1, 1902, p. 31. © V&A Picture Library.

8.2 *Kunst und Künstler*, cover by Max Slevogt (**XXIX**, X, 1931). © V&A Picture
Library.

practice throughout the country, but had a particular resonance in the capital.
Kunst und Künstler had an open allegiance to the Berlin Secession and to its
leading artists, particularly its president Max Liebermann and Max Slevogt,
both of whom were personally linked to the publisher. They also sold their
work through his cousin's gallery. Bruno and Paul Cassirer did not get on;
Scheffler, as well as being Bruno's close associate, alienated Paul, the dealer,

by expressing reservations over the latter's assumption of the presidency of the Secession during the crisis of 1913. Nevertheless, in the overall pattern of the cultural life and politics of pre-war Berlin, the social, intellectual and business networks of the Cassirers intersected at key points. They were associated with the Secession, with the introduction of modern French art into Berlin collections, and the concomitant dismissal of the art favoured by the court and prevalent in the exhibitions of the Academy and Berlin Artists' Association. Their salons attracted a wide range of leading Berlin figures from the museum world, theatre, business, publishing and the artistic community.[11] In the early years of the journal, a sense of excitement, and success, pervaded this milieu: despite the 'backwardness' and crass nationalism of official culture, despite the 'ugliness' of Berlin (that Scheffler castigated in his book *Berlin: ein Stadtschicksal* of 1910), their values were in the ascendancy. As Scheffler recalled in 1928: '*Kunst und Künstler* was not successful with the general public, but it was in the circle it reached, because its programme was that of the times.'[12] When he wrote this, the journal was itself a representative of a conservative artistic establishment. The Cassirer–Scheffler 'position' was linked closely to 'naturalism' and, beyond that, to a belief in individual artistic character. Both factors made it difficult for them to see aesthetic quality in the work of the younger 'expressionist' generation that, as well as defying the principles of representation advocated by Liebermann and his colleagues, was promoted as a movement. From *c*.1910 onwards, *Kunst und Künstler* was operating a delicate balancing act between its role as a liberal forum for modern ideas and practices and its fundamental commitment to a set of aesthetic parameters that contemporary '*Tendenzkunst*' failed to comply with. The promotion of this art was undertaken by a very different kind of publication, above all Herwarth Walden's *Der Sturm*.

The common ground between literature and the visual arts was fundamental to the presentation and philosophy of *Der Sturm*, and to the concept of Expressionism that it played a key role in disseminating. In its first phase, in 1910–11, it was a literary and musical review, linked to the bohemian circles frequented by Walden and his then wife, Else Lasker-Schüler. Its focus shifted towards the visual arts as Walden's interests and promotional activity did, after the presentation of the Italian Futurist exhibition and the establishment of the *Der Sturm* gallery in 1912. Like *Montjoie!*, *Der Sturm* presented itself as a campaigning journal, using a broadsheet format and combining the

---

[11] Recalling the pattern of his working day, that included an afternoon meeting in the *Romanische Café* with Bruno Cassirer, Scheffler commented that even socialising in the evening involved work as he mixed with artists, collectors, dealers, journalists and officials who all had some connection with the journal: K. Scheffler, *Die fetten und die mageren Jahre*, Munich, 1946, pp. 186–7.

[12] 'Unser Programm. 25 Jahre Kunst und Künstler', *Kunst und Künstler*, **26** (1), 3, 1928, p. 3.

presentation of original literary and artistic work (prints, in *Der Sturm*'s case) with texts on contemporary art. *Der Sturm* was particularly distinctive on two counts: its direct links with a gallery (there were precedents for this and one other short-lived example on the Berlin scene at the time, the second *Pan*, founded by Paul Cassirer in 1910, but this was still relatively unusual), and its use of polemic and invective. Walden pursued a policy of self-definition through opposition, in which vilification of the rest of the press played a major part. Following the example of Karl Kraus, Walden and his collaborators attacked the superficiality of mainstream journalism, embodied above all in '*Feuilletonismus*'; when he moved into artistic promotion, negative reviews were collected and cited as proof of the philistinism and ignorance of professional critics (including Scheffler).[13] This was in many ways an effective strategy: it generated publicity and provided contributors and readers of the review with an appropriate sense of difference. However, the stridency and exclusiveness of Walden's position disturbed some of his artists. As early as 1913 Kandinsky expressed reservations, while acknowledging *Der Sturm*'s usefulness in the Berlin context.[14] Four years later in 1917, Paul Klee told Walden that the journal was fine for unknowns but no longer suited the needs of more established modern artists: 'Your *Sturm* is only the supplement to the periodical I would like … All the polemics in the literary section would be better off left out. I'm afraid I must also protest against the name, which is already out of date.'[15]

The First World War and its aftermath: Berlin

At the outbreak of war the art press in general reflected the surge of patriotic feeling in both communities. *Kunst und Künstler*, indeed, confirming its position as a cultural platform of the business elite, declared that German victory would result in its cultural, as well as economic and political, domination of Europe.[16] When the conflict dragged on this triumphalism gave way, in *Kunst und Künstler*'s case, to an attempt to 'normalize' report and discussion on the art world as art activity itself began to revive. In Paris after 1915 various new publishing ventures in the form of literary-artistic reviews

---

[13] See Volker Pirsich, '*Der Sturm*'. *Eine Monographie*, Herzberg: Bautz, 1985, pp. 605–16; and Maurice Godé, *Der Sturm de Herwarth Walden*, Nancy: Presses universitaires de Nancy, 1990, pp. 129–38.

[14] Letter of 31 May 1913 in: K. Lankheit (ed.), *Wassily Kandinsky/Franz Marc: Briefwechsel*, Munich: Piper, 1982.

[15] Letter of 30 June 1917. Sturm Archive, Staatsbibliothek Preussischer Kulturbesitz, Berlin. See discussion in Lutz Windhöfel, *Paul Westheim und das Kunstblatt. Eine Zeitschrift und ihr Herausgeber in der Weimarer Republik*, Cologne: Böhlau, 1995 pp. 101–4

[16] *Kunst und Künstler*, **13** (1), pp. 1–3.

were founded to promote the cause of modernism in the context of a growing optimism about the outcome of the war. In March 1917 Pierre Reverdy proposed, in *Nord–Sud*, that with victory now certain it was time to group around Apollinaire, the champion of innovation in poetry and painting, and the 'Latin' cultural tradition.[17] In Germany, in contrast, disillusion with the war contributed to a growth of appreciation of expressionism. Its inward-looking, antimaterialist character now seemed particularly appropriate, and its visionary quality could be linked with the growing aspiration for social and political change. Moreover, as inflation and a dearth of consumer goods fuelled the Berlin art market, the lack of foreign competition contributed to its commercial breakthrough. Klee's comments on *Der Sturm* were prompted, in fact, by the emergence on the scene of a new modern art journal, *Das Kunstblatt*, whose opening editorial statement by Paul Westheim made a lyrical claim for the necessity of the modern artist's rejection of external reality in favour of 'inner vision'.[18] Walden, whose publishing strategy had consisted in pouring scorn on the establishment and laying exclusive claim to the label 'expressionism', now found himself doubly discomfited, in that the art and literature represented by *Der Sturm* was entering the mainstream, but others were encroaching on his territory. One product of this situation was a long-running public feud with Westheim, initiated by Walden in December 1918 and pursued over the next three years, notably in a series of 'letters to Paul Westheim' by his collaborator Rudolf Blümner. *Der Sturm*'s principal accusation against Paul Westheim was that he was an opportunist latecomer to the support of modern art who had no real understanding of or sympathy for it. Westheim's response to these attacks was to question Walden's own judgement and probity, ironizing over his personal egotism and implying generally that the function of the periodical as the platform for the commercial interests of the gallery was improper – while also pointing out that the latter were suffering as different artists, and particularly the most distinguished ones, decided that Walden was impossible to work with.[19]

When *Das Kunstblatt* appeared Siegfried Jacobson commented, in an open letter to Karl Scheffler in *Die Schaubühne*, that 'It is perhaps not conceived as a rival to your art paper, but it may become one. It deals with the same field, appears with the same frequency, and has the same price'.[20] In striking contrast to *Der Sturm*, Westheim's journal was designed as a specialist review that would fulfil a similar function for the younger generation of modernists as *Kunst und Künstler* had for the leaders of the Berlin Secession.

---

[17] *Nord–Sud*,1, 15 March 1917, p. 2. Other modern reviews included *SIC* and *L'Elan*.

[18] 'Von den inneren Gesichten', *Das Kunstblatt*, 1917, 1, pp. 1–6.

[19] See 'Umschau', *Das Kunstblatt*, 1920, 10, pp. 312–18.

[20] Cited in Lutz Windhöfel, *Paul Westheim und das Kunstblatt. Eine Zeitschrift und ihr Herausgeber in der Weimarer Republik*, Cologne: Böhlau, 1995, pp. 50–51.

Walden had founded his own publishing house, declaring his contempt for the existing press; Westheim had secured the backing of a Weimar literary publisher, Gustav Kiepenheuer, who was keen to extend his range into the visual arts. A phase in publishing now opened up, mirroring that in the art market, in which 'advanced' modern art was enthusiastically promoted by a growing number of businesses old and new. *Das Kunstblatt* was one of the successes, and survivors, of this period, not least because its editorial base was firmly in the Berlin cultural milieu.

The Weimar period

On the occasion of the World Advertising Congress held in Berlin in 1929, the Ullstein Press published a lavish booklet informing delegates about the dynamism of modern Germany, the major role played by Berlin in sustaining it, and its own products. The section on 'Berlin as intellectual centre' concluded:

> The intellectual life of the city, organised in every detail, is reflected in the last analysis by the Berlin Press which, as an indicator of the development and the intellectual mobility of this cosmopolitan city, is centralising more and more and has so far attained its most comprehensive organisation in the Ullstein House.[21]

In 1925 Ullstein had taken over the urbane and innovative cultural review *Der Querschnitt*; in 1926 they published Carl Einstein's *Art of the 20th Century* as the latest volume in the Propyläen art history series. The business had survived the alarms of the Spartacist uprising and the Kapp putsch without too great difficulty; the hyperinflation of 1922–23, on the other hand, had caused severe problems. From the mid-decade on, however, prospects appeared good. Engagement with modern art fitted into a programme based on Berlin's position as a centre of change and innovation in the *Reich*, particularly in the cultural sphere.[22]

The art press in general was marked by the same phases: the political turmoil of 1919–21, the inflation, stabilization. The revolutionary period saw the emergence, and disappearance, of many ephemeral publications, including the lively Dada reviews, that mocked expressionist 'purity' and carried polemical writing to new heights; the economic chaos of 1922–23 caused other publications to close; the latter years of the decade saw general con-

---

[21] *Der Verlag Ullstein zum Welt Reklame Kongress Berlin 1929*, Berlin, 1929, pp. 49–56 (text in German, French and English).

[22] See Georg Bernhard, 'Die Geschichte des Hauses', in Max Osborn (ed.), *50 Jahre Ullstein 1877–1927*, Berlin: Ullstein, 1927, pp. 1–146; and, for a general study, Peter de Mendelsohn, 'Das Berliner Jahrzehnt', in *Zeitungsstadt Berlin*, Berlin: Ullstein, 1982 (1959), pp. 312–339.

solidation and several new initiatives, including *Die Kunstauktion*, founded by Walter Bondy in 1927 with the ambition of doing for Berlin what the *Gazette de l'Hôtel Drouot* did for Paris, and *Neue Kunst in Deutschland*, a product of the successful expansion of the Neumann/Nierendorf gallery in 1925. There were, however, important threads of continuity in the profile and activity of the Berlin art press throughout the republican period. A community of publishers, writers and artists, working through a handful of outlets, notably *Kunst und Künstler, Das Kunstblatt* and, after 1921, *Der Querschnitt* (and to some extent the quality daily press) generated a field of discourse in which artistic debate, and struggles for influence, could take place within a framework of understanding in which the balance of agencies and interests in the art world, and the aesthetic and subjective nature of art making itself, was taken for granted. Their effort was dedicated both to consideration of how art, and the infrastructure linked to it, should adapt to the new social, economic and political conditions of the republic, and, fundamentally, to the defence of an historically-informed and largely apolitical concept of art that these conditions arguably threatened. The art press contributed, therefore, to an ideological campaign to sustain bourgeois norms of cultural activity and understanding in the new 'democratic' Germany, in which Berlin's leading political, economic and cultural role was largely reinforced. This translated in practical terms into a broadly common pattern of reporting and presentation. The press were concerned with the nature and status of contemporary art movements, the character and originality of individual artists, the activities and achievements of exhibiting organizations, the acquisition and display policies of museums, the state of the art market, and the consideration of foreign, above all French, models of art practice. This pattern was very similar to the pre-war one: one of the functions of this activity was, indeed, to maintain links with the artistic life of that era. In 1919 Paul Westheim argued that current events had no fundamental significance for art, because it had experienced its revolution years before.[23] Scheffler expressed a similar opinion, that also marked the difference between them: 'The war changed nothing of art's essence; nor will the Revolution.'[24] *Das Kunstblatt*, for the next 14 years, set out to promote the modernist consequences of the artistic 'revolution' of the decade before the war; *Kunst und Künstler* warned against its excesses and defended the principles of the earlier 'naturalist' revolution. These positions marked out, in effect, the boundaries of debate in an intellectual community that rejected both materialist denial of the aesthetic sphere and the conservative nostalgia for a practice completely untouched by modernity (see Figure 8.3).

---

[23] 'Jenseits der Gräben weiter!', *Das Kunstblatt*,1919,1, p. 1.

[24] 'Die Kunst und die Revolution', *Kunst und Künstler*, **17**, 1918/19, pp. 165–7; Scheffler's rival editor, Georg Biermann of *Der Cicerone* (Leipzig) had taken a more optimistic, political, line: see 'Das Postulat der Kunst', *Der Cicerone*, **10**, 23/4, pp. 355–63.

DIE DAME

KUNSTSCHRIFTSTELLER in ihrem HEIM

Dr. Max Osborn.

Geheim-rat Max J. Fried-länder

Exzellenz Wilhelm v. Bode vor seiner Sammlung italienischer Majoliken.

Paul Westheim

Aufnahmen Roedecker

Karl Scheffler

Dr. Julius Elias.
Das Bildnis an der Wand: Porträt
seiner Gattin von Max Liebermann

8.3   'Kunstschriftsteller in ihrem Heim (Art critics in their homes)': including Paul Westheim and Karl Scheffler, *Die Dame*, 1925, 12. Ullstein.

For Karl Scheffler the art of the post-war era was characterized by a dangerous obsession with theory, neglect of sound aesthetic principles, and the
undermining of individual talent and feeling by endless 'movements': 'An art
periodical conscious of its mission could hardly do other than issue repeated
warnings – but in the clamour of the times this was perceived as a reactionary
appeal.' The journal, he declared in 1928, had the same principles as always:
'*Kunst und Künstler* ... has never *argued for* the 'will' in art, always only
knowledge and talent.'[25] The editorial line of the journal, established by himself with Bruno Cassirer's backing, did remain very consistent, marked by
loyalty to the values of 'naturalism' and its practitioners. Commenting in 1921
on Scheffler's attack on Ludwig Justi's introduction of 'Post-Impressionist' art
to the 'New Section' of the National Gallery, Paul Westheim argued 'Here ...
[he] is the spokesman of a specific group in the art world. Perhaps this is
merely the group of those who think it right to stick to the historically secure,
and who refuse everything more recent on the grounds of this questionable
security.'[26] Max Liebermann was at the core of this supposed group, and it was
the case that *Kunst und Künstler* offered virtually unqualified support for both
Liebermann's work and his policies at the Prussian Academy of Art, of which
he became president in 1920. However, like Liebermann himself, Cassirer and
Scheffler realized that it was impolitic (and indeed wrong) to reject 'Post-
Impressionism' and all its exponents out of hand. They secured the collaboration
of some slightly younger writers, notably Curt Glaser and Carl Georg Heise,[27]
who were more sympathetic than themselves to the art 'of the times', and while
the journal's reviews and periodic surveys of the art scene, usually written by
Scheffler, were frequently pessimistic, it singled out – often mirroring the
pattern of commercial promotion of their work – key figures in the modern
movement for sympathetic analysis. While highly sceptical of his post-war
success, Scheffler even acknowledged the talent of Max Pechstein in 1921. In
1920 he identified Kirchner as the most distinguished of the ex-Brücke group.[28]
In 1924, prompted by an exhibition of Kirchner's recent, Swiss, work at the
Paul Cassirer Gallery, Glaser argued that the artist had reached a new level of
maturity and synthesis.[29] Later in the same year Scheffler provided a very

---

[25] *Die fetten und die mageren Jahre*, p. 216; 'Unser Programm. 25 Jahre Kunst und Künstler',
Kunst und Künstler, **26** (1), 1928, p. 3.

[26] 'Broschürenkrieg', *Das Kunstblatt*, 1921, 10, pp. 313–18.

[27] *Die fetten und die mageren* Jahre, pp. 215–17. Glaser worked in the Prussian Print Collection and the Art Library; Heise was a rising star in the museum world, appointed to the Lübeck
museum in 1919. In 1916 he had negotiated with Kiepenheuer about founding an art journal,
and was indignant that Westheim had secured the publisher's backing instead. Between 1919
and 1921 he was co-editor of a luxury journal *Genius*, published by Kurt Wolff in Munich – see
Windhöfel, pp. 45–50.

[28] *Kunst und Künstler*, **18**, 1919/20, pp. 217–28.

[29] *Kunst und Künstler*, **22**, 1923/4, pp. 63–5.

positive assessment of Grosz's recent graphic output. He argued that precisely because the artist had shifted away from explicitly politicized work, he had allowed his personal artistic sensibility to assert itself. He reiterated this view in articles in 1926 and 1929, on the occasion of exhibitions at the Flechtheim Gallery and the Cassirer publishing house. Grosz's development, Scheffler claimed, showed his gradual acceptance of the true nature of art, which is to show and feel, not to rationalize and preach, and to transform the mundane into the universal. In 1929 he found that 'The struggle with the vilest raw material has been almost entirely resolved in favour of art.' Grosz's work could probably only come out of Berlin, but it had a European character, as a representation of modern urban experience.[30]

'The city's so-called art policy is quite simply a scandal', Scheffler claimed in an item considering the work of the Berlin art committee in 1926.[31] He suggested that their purchases should be put on exhibition to demonstrate what rubbish most of it was. Besides studies of individual artists and collections, exhibition reviews and auction reports, *Kunst und Künstler* commented regularly on art institutions, particularly those in the capital. These interventions reflected the liberal but elitist views of the Cassirer circle and were often highly critical. In particular, they used the platform provided by the review to challenge the policy and administration of the National Gallery under Ludwig Justi. This was an old quarrel, dating from the forced departure of Hugo von Tschudi from the directorship of the Gallery in 1909. The republican period aggravated the differences between Justi and the Cassirer–Liebermann 'camp', as Liebermann was president of the Academy and Justi embarked on a pro-modernist programme at the 'new Section' of the National Gallery in the Crown Prince's Palace. Scheffler launched an attack on Justi in *Kunst und Künstler* in March 1919, initiating a polemic that culminated two years later with the publication of rival pamphlets: *Museumskrieg* by Scheffler and *Habemus Papam* by Justi, in which the latter vigorously defended his record. Justi realized that he needed to counter *Kunst und Künstler*'s influence in the Berlin elites: when he clashed directly with Liebermann over the Gallery's advisory committee in 1924, he criticized the Academy in the *Deutsche Allgemeine Zeitung*, provoking Liebermann to call for his dismissal in a rival paper and a general debate in the Press.[32] Liebermann used *Kunst und Künstler* to reopen this topic in 1932, after the National Gallery had incurred a public protest – also published in the review – over its selection of a German art exhibition in Scandinavia.[33]

---

[30] *Kunst und Künstler*, **22**, 1923/4, pp. 182–6; **24**, 1925/6, pp. 354–9; **27**, 1928/9, pp. 269–73.

[31] *Kunst und Künstler*, **24**, 1926/7, pp. 158–60.

[32] See A. Hentzen, 'Die neue Abteilung der National-Galerie im ehemaligen Kronprinzen-Palais', *Jahrbuch Preussischer Kulturbesitz*, X, 1972, pp. 9–75, sections V and VII.

[33] 'Justi und seine Sachverständigen-Kommission', *Kunst und Künstler*, **31**, 1932, pp. 65–71;

The policies of the National Gallery were also frequently discussed in *Das Kunstblatt*. Westheim's journal generally welcomed the initiatives at the 'New Section' of the Gallery, while expressing reservations about certain aspects of them, including Justi's leadership.[34] Reporting on museum activity and reflecting on museum policies in respect of modern art figured largely in *Das Kunstblatt* in both its feature and review sections. The general structure of this periodical and its overall field of interests were not dissimilar to those of *Kunst und Künstler*. However, where the latter admitted modernists reluctantly into its purview and considered the enthusiasm of artists for the 'new' with disdain, *Das Kunstblatt* was, from the outset, a campaigning journal, oriented towards promoting the reception and production of innovative art. In 1925 Westheim published with some bitterness but also pride the letter he had received from the *Frankfurter Zeitung* effectively sacking him from his position as their Berlin art correspondent. They acknowledged that his unconditional support for new art had been influential and that such 'Productive Criticism' was appropriate for a journal like *Das Kunstblatt*, but found that it was unacceptable in a newspaper which sought to be a mirror of the entire range of artistic life.[35]

Das Kunstblatt aligned itself closely with Expressionism at first. As we have seen, this occupation of his critical territory enraged Herwarth Walden. However, the review quickly established its position as a platform for information and comment on the contemporary scene whose commitment was to the principle of creative originality in general rather than to a particular tendency. *Das Kunstblatt* did not support Dada but it published a first article on Grosz in 1917 and continued to feature his work and ideas throughout the 1920s. In accordance with its policy of investigating current trends, it devoted an issue to the theme of 'A New Naturalism?' in 1922 which reproduced the views of a wide range of artists, critics and curators – including G. F. Hartlaub, the organizer of the influential *Neue Sachlichkeit* exhibition of 1925. Commenting at the end of the decade on the lack of identifiable tendencies in contemporary German art, Westheim argued that this was not a weakness but in fact a strength: 'If we do not have a clearly defined movement it is because here everything is in movement ... Germany today has one of the most interesting art scenes in the world.'[36] Diversity had been a

'Ein Protest deutscher Künstler', ibid., p. 47. For a general discussion of Berlin art politics in the Weimar period, see M. Gee, 'The Berlin art world, 1918–1933', in M.Gee, T. Kirk and J. Steward (eds), *The City in Central Europe. Culture and Society from 1800 to the Present*, Aldershot: Ashgate, 1999, pp. 63–84.

[34] For example, *Das Kunstblatt*, 1919, 9, pp. 185–7; 1921, 10, pp. 316–18; and 1924, 8, p. 239 (preface to the survey 'Fünf Jahre Kronprinzen-Palais').

[35] 'Umschau: Musterbeispiel produktiver Kritik', *Das Kunstblatt*, 1925,1, pp. 25–6. They replaced Westheim with Meier-Graefe, by now an establishment figure.

[36] 'Neue Kunst in Deutschland', *Das Kunstblatt*, 1931, 4, pp. 100–110; for Westheim's general policy, see the editorial statement 'Zum 100. Heft', 1925, 4, pp. 97–100.

constant feature of the series of exhibitions organized by *Das Kunstblatt* itself between 1927 and 1930 with the support of figures in the Berlin art establishment with the intention of fostering new talent. In 1929 the review also ran a competition to promote new critical writing. These initiatives corresponded to two constant themes pursued by the review: the need to promote the next generation of German artists and the paucity of quality criticism of modern art.

As was the case with Scheffler at *Kunst und Künstler*, indeed more so, Westheim both set the editorial tone of the review and wrote a substantial proportion of the contents himself. However, he also drew on a wide network of contributors, that included Curt Glaser, G. F. Hartlaub and Paul F. Schmidt from the museum sector, and the writers Ernst Kállai, Willi Wolfradt, and Carl Einstein – mostly men still in their thirties at the end of the war who were instrumental in the promotion of modernist trends in the republic. Several of these regular contributors were based elsewhere than Berlin. Westheim set out to establish *Das Kunstblatt* as a national (and indeed international) platform for modern art that recognized the diversity of cultural activity in Germany. The journal reported regularly on exhibitions in Cologne, Düsseldorf, Hamburg, Frankfurt, Dresden and Munich, and carried features on artists based throughout the Reich. It was, nonetheless, a Berlin-oriented publication. Berlin art politics – arguments over museum policy, the exhibitions at the Academy, the Secession and other art associations – were a constant theme in the review, and its attention to the art market reflected the growing preponderance of Berlin in the art trade, and the personal connections that Westheim and collaborators such as Glaser and Einstein had with Berlin dealers.

Westheim in fact originally planned *Das Kunstblatt* with the art dealer, J. B. Neumann. However, Neumann's departure to the war in 1916 forestalled the realization of the project. The eventual publisher, Kiepenheuer, was based in Weimar (after 1919, Potsdam), but all editorial matters were dealt with by Westheim in Berlin. According to Ernst Rathenau, director of the *Euphorion Verlag*, 'Westheim was very unlucky with his publishers. When things were going badly financially, he sought to change and in this respect he was very capable. He always found a new publisher.'[37] In fact he was forced to switch three times: Kiepenheuer supported the review through the inflation period but decided in 1925 that they could no longer afford to publish it. After two years with the Athenaion Verlag in Potsdam, *Das Kunstblatt* spent an uncomfortable year in the hands of the J. M Spaeth Verlag before being taken up by Hermann Reckendorf, who also published the design review *Die Form*, linked to the Werkbund. Reckendorf was a progressive and expanding business –

---

[37] Cited in Windhöfel, *Paul Westheim und das Kunstblatt*, p. 57. Windhöfel provides a full account of the publishing history of *Das Kunstblatt*, ch.2, I.

Das Kunstblatt was able to organize exhibitions in the gallery of its new building, opened in May 1929, and undertake a programme of lectures and seminars around contemporary cultural issues. This promising new phase in the life of the journal was cut short by the slump and ensuing political crisis.

This shifting pattern of ownership contrasted with that of *Kunst und Künstler*, with its total integration into the Bruno Cassirer publishing business throughout its existence. Westheim did make some adjustments to the review in relation to its backers. Kiepenheuer originally took on *Das Kunstblatt* as part of a strategic move into art publishing. Between 1918 and 1922 they also published, under Westheim's editorship, a luxury print portfolio *Die Schaffenden*. This was ceded to the *Euphorion Verlag* at the end of 1922 and thereafter *Das Kunstblatt* carried, for a time, original literary work and literary and theatrical reviews, reflecting the publisher's other interests. The move to Reckendorf reinforced the journal's existing engagement with contemporary architecture and design. Overall, however, Westheim was able to maintain the independence and distinctiveness of *Das Kunstblatt*, a corollary of which was that for his different publishers it offered some prestige and even influence, but few profits.

The history of *Der Querschnitt* was very different. *Kunst und Künstler* and *Das Kunstblatt* apparently had a circulation of around 2000. At the height of its success in 1930/31 *Der Querschnitt* claimed sales of 25 000 copies a month.[38] In the first phase of its existence, however, between 1921 and 1924, this idiosyncratic review, founded in Düsseldorf by the art dealer Alfred Flechtheim, only printed 400–700 copies. In 1922 the editors announced that they were continuing production at their readers' request but reluctantly because, 'it costs us time and money. It will appear irregularly and only when there is something to say.'[39] In fact much of the tone and style of the review was established at this time: focusing on contemporary culture, avoiding ponderousness of all kinds, resolutely cosmopolitan and highly visual, combining graphic and photographic illustrations. 'This is the most undignified art journal that I have ever read, not only in Germany but anywhere', commented Hans Siemsen in the *Weltbühne*. 'But the few people in Germany for whom life is still as important as art and who prefer a good joke to a well balanced book should take a look at this "cross section".'[40] Albert Dreyfus, in 1923, prefaced an article on the recent work of Picasso with a quotation from the instructions he had received from the editor, Hans von Wedderkop; 'Art historical texts are frowned upon, particularly those of an analytical nature.'[41]

---

[38] Mendelsohn, *Zeitungsstadt Berlin*, Berlin: Ullstein, 1982 (1959), p. 259.

[39] Note by Alfred Flechtheim and Wilhelm Graf Kielmannsweg, *Der Querschnitt*, 1922, 1, p. 13. The third editor, Hans van Wedderkop, became responsible for the whole review in 1923.

[40] Cited in a review of its reception in the press, *Der Querschnitt*, 1922, 2, pp. 127–8.

[41] *Das Querschnittbuch 1923*, p. 56.

Whereas *Das Kunstblatt* campaigned in favour of modern art using a format that was largely based on established models of the genre, Flechtheim and his collaborators deliberately eschewed the high-mindedness and exclusivity of an 'art journal'. Articles were short and often anecdotal; the subject matter was almost exclusively contemporary and covered a range of topics besides art and literature, including ballet, cinema and ... boxing.

By 1924 *Der Querschnitt* had established itself as a distinctive voice on the German cultural scene. That summer van Wedderkop was able to refer to its 'Triumph'. He attributed its success to the breadth of its coverage and its striking visual style, and claimed that it was the only German periodical with a truly European stamp and an international readership.[42] Ullstein's decision to take it over that autumn was prompted by the realization, or calculation, that the sharp, modern outlook it projected could be developed to appeal to a wider market. Initially published in Düsseldorf, then in 1924 in Frankfurt, *Der Querschnitt* now became closely associated with Berlin, whose image as a centre of innovation and originality in the cultural sphere, as well as the economic one, was cultivated throughout the Ullstein group.

Der Querschnitt, the senior Ullstein editor Georg Bernhard commented in 1927, was aimed at people of refined taste, fully abreast of contemporary politics and culture, whose outlook led them to take particular pleasure in the unusual, curious and piquant aspects of modern life.[43] One man who met this description was the founder of the review Alfred Flechtheim. He had opened a branch of his gallery in Berlin in 1921 and moved there to live in 1923, making it the lynch pin of his commercial network. He remained a presence on *Der Querschnitt* after 1924: the activities of his galleries were regularly advertised and reported on, and he continued to make occasional contributions. In its incarnation as a monthly publication with a rapidly expanding readership the review shifted more towards entertainment and literature, but the textual and visual presentation of modern art remained a central feature of *Der Querschnitt* until the economic slump, and its choice of material and approach to it continued to be modelled on Flechtheim's; it was selective, oriented towards individuals not movements, and francophile. *Der Querschnitt* was distinguished by the range of its international coverage that included the USA, the Soviet Union, Spain and England as well as France. The art it illustrated, however, was almost exclusively either German or Parisian. Flechtheim, Wedderkop and their fellow contributors consistently derided what they saw as the provincialism and formal weaknesses of German art. In his preface (republished in the review) to an exhibition held in the refurbished gallery in May 1927, that showed the work of artists born around

---

[42] 'Der Siegeszug der Querschnitt', *Der Querschnitt*, 1924, 2/3, pp. 90–92.

[43] 'Die Geschichte des Hauses', *50 Jahre Ullstein*, p. 110.

1880, Flechtheim commented that, like Paul Cassirer, he had only imported foreign art 'whose quality needs to be seen in Germany' – by which he meant, notably, Picasso, Derain, Braque, Léger and Gris (with Cézanne and Renoir).[44] Surveying the Berlin season's exhibitions the previous year, Emil Szittya identified those of Daumier, the Impressionists, and the Douanier Rousseau as the most important, described Corinth's late work as tragic, and commented on a show of work by Pechstein and others at the Galerie Nierendorf that: 'These painters are today all trying to rediscover form but they cannot overcome the expressionism in themselves.'[45] Earlier in the year he had singled out Grosz as one of the very few German artists with confidence, a personal vision, and the ability to impose it: 'He constructs a Berlin, he americanises Berlin using French colours, and his formal power is such that through this Berlin remains Berlin.' Seeing the work one could even envisage that through it, one day, foreign observers would come to appreciate Berlin as they did Paris (see Figure 8.4).[46]

Berlin–Paris–Berlin

In an article on Picasso that appeared in *Das Kunstblatt* in May 1924, Alfred Kuhn reported that he and other Parisian artists had expressed an interest in contemporary developments in German art, together with some disdain for the older painters, whom they did know of, who persisted in trying to paint in a French manner. The text evidently caused a stir in Berlin. The July issue of *Das Kunstblatt* published an indignant letter from Walter Passarge blaming Parisian ignorance of original German modern art on a circle linked to 'a certain periodical', who chose to denigrate it in favour of French art and its second-rate German imitators. Flechtheim (the target of this attack) suggested, ironically, that to shame Purrmann, Levy, Grossmann et al. (the unnamed francophiles) into never showing their face in the Café du Dôme again, Kuhn should put on an exhibition in Paris of all those 'wild types' whom, he claimed, Picasso and his colleagues wanted to find out about.[47] Reporting on the Parisian scene was an important feature of the Berlin art press throughout the Weimar period. Scheffler, Westheim and Wedderkop, and their collaborators, held different positions on modern German art and its relationship with the French tradition, but they agreed that it was vital for German readers to be aware of developments in France. Several Paris-based writers, including Adolphe Basler, Florent Fels and Waldemar George, pro-

[44] 'Das Problem der Generation', *Der Querschnitt*, 1927,5, pp. 382–3.

[45] 'Ausstellungen des Winters', *Der Querschnitt*, 1926, 3, pp. 459–63.

[46] 'Nur einige Worte', *Der Querschnitt*, 1926, 3, p. 245.

[47] 'Bei Picasso', *Das Kunstblatt*, 1924, 5, pp. 128–33; 'Umschau', 1924, 7, pp. 233–4.

8.4 'Artists at Work (Matisse, Grosz)', *Der Querschnitt*, 1929. Ullstein.

vided copy for Berlin journals, and some German critics, particularly Westheim, Glaser and Einstein, visited Paris frequently.

As Kuhn's report indicated, there was not the same level of coverage in France of developments in Germany. The superiority of French – or at least Parisian – art was generally taken for granted by dealers, exhibiting organizations, and the press in the post-war years. The political and economic conditions that culminated in Germany with the inflationary crisis and the stark adjustment that followed it, reinforced Paris's situation as the centre of modern art production in the Western world. The Parisian art press both reflected and contributed to this dominance.

In May 1920 Louis Vauxcelles launched a new journal, *L'Amour de l'Art*, whose mission was the 'Defence and illustration of the independent French fine and applied arts, musical and literary lyricism'. Vauxcelles was a well-known opponent of Cubism, but this initiative, backed by the *Librairie de France*, was symptomatic of the acceptance of independent 'living' art by significant sections of the French establishment and public during the post-war era. *L'Amour de l'Art* was a well produced and illustrated specialist journal that combined solid interpretative essays and news with a focus on modern art and design, while building links to the past. In this sense, in fact, it was not dissimilar to *Kunst und Künstler*, to which Vauxcelles had occasionally contributed before the war. But *L'Amour de l'Art* did not adopt an overtly defensive line in relation to modern art in general. Vauxcelles recruited a young defender of modernism, Waldemar George, as assistant editor, and several well-known modernists contributed to the review. They included André Salmon, who was now established as an authoritative and influential interpreter of contemporary art. In another sign of the buoyancy of the art publishing scene, in 1925 the directors of *Les Nouvelles Littéraires*, linked to the *Librairie Larousse*, founded a new review that took up Salmon's term '*l'art vivant*' as its title. *L'Art Vivant* used a format and visual style similar to the popular illustrated press, and promoted the sensual figurative art associated with 'L'Ecole de Paris'.

Both *L'Amour de l'Art* and *L'Art Vivant* stood, to some extent, for a new '*juste milieu*' in French art. The period also saw an increase in the number and range of published outlets for resolutely advanced ideas. Numerous little reviews expressed the vitality of interaction between literary and artistic circles in Paris. *Littérature* and *La Révolution Surréaliste* (1924–29) were original and influential versions of the genre. The 1920s also saw the establishment of avant-garde reviews that specialized in the visual arts. *L'Esprit Nouveau*, founded by Ozenfant and Le Corbusier in 1920, associated 'Purist' art and design with a progressive rationalist ideology. In 1924 Léonce Rosenberg founded the *Bulletin de l'Effort Moderne* to propagate the work of artists attached to his gallery. At the end of the decade, the abstract art movement set up periodicals to disseminate its ideas: *Cercle et Carré* and

Abstraction Création. The most important initiative in this respect was the founding of *Cahiers d'Art* in 1926, by Christian Zervos, with the support (initially) of Editions Albert Morancé. This was a specialist art review with high production values and a clear orientation in favour of contemporary art that built on the achievements of Cubism, combining the 'French' tradition of formal values with creative daring and originality, as exemplified by the work of Picasso.

In 1929 Paul Westheim was concerned that *Das Kunstblatt* was falling behind in its coverage of the Parisian scene, as measured against the output of *Cahiers d'Art*.[48] Zervos's review rapidly established itself internationally as an authoritative source of information and critical assessment of the modern art scene. As such, it contributed to Paris' near hegemony in the field, although it was in fact cosmopolitan in its interests, playing, for example, an important role in introducing both Klee and Kandinsky to the French public at the end of the decade. Kandinsky was extremely conscious of the significance of this interest. He urged his Berlin dealer, Ferdinand Möller, to send a notice and photos of his 1932 exhibition to the review, and commented that it was vital that Will Grohmann's long article on contemporary German art appear there: 'It would be the first time that not just the French, but also the international public finally discovered what is being done in Germany.'[49]

In 1931 an issue of *Der Querschnitt* took 'Berlin and Paris' as its theme. The parisian artist Amédée Ozenfant wrote on 'Weekend Berlin': 'Thanks to the Northern Railway Company, Paris and Berlin have become neighbours.' Berlin, he noted, had learnt the lessons of 'L'Esprit Nouveau and Paris 1925'. It had become a showpiece of modern, international, aesthetics – and, consequently, of the contribution that artists could make to reconciliation between peoples. While Berlin did have 'American' aspects, it remained essentially 'European'. 'Paris is still the ideal capital city, but we need to move on. Berlin has something of Paris, something of New York.'[50] Since the turn of the century Berlin's cultural elites had sought to give the artistic life of the city the quality and prestige appropriate to its position as a modern *Weltstadt*. The art press had played an important role in this process. It had been severely impeded by the war and its aftermath but finally, at the end of the

[48] Letter to Emil Szittya, his Paris correspondent, cited in Windhöfel, *Paul Westheim und das Kunstblatt*, p. 266.

[49] Letters of 25 January and 5 March 1932, Ferdinand Möller papers, Berlinische Galerie, Berlin. In the event, this commissioned article did not appear in *Cahiers d'Art*. Zervos himself was at this point in severe financial difficulties owing to the economic crisis. See 'Vassily Kandinsky. Correspondances avec Zervos et Kojève', in Christian Derouet (ed.), *Les Cahiers du Musée National d'Art Moderne*, *Hors série/Archives*, Paris: Centre Georges Pompidou, 1992, letters 54–64; also, Georgia Illetschko, *Kandinsky und Paris: die Geschichte einer Beziehung*, Munich/New York: Prestel, 1997, ch. 2.

[50] 'Weekend Berlin', *Der Querschnitt*, 1931, 5, pp. 297–300.

1920s, Berlin could be represented as an art centre that, while it still lacked the wealth and variety of Paris, possessed a distinctive, impressive, engagement with modernity. But, of course, Ozenfant's vision was about to be proved wrong (or, at least, 70 years premature). Four months after his essay appeared, Paul Westheim was reflecting on the 'false economy, false politics' that had brought chaos to Germany again, and made art seem irrelevant.[51] Six months later his review was virtually extinct; *Der Querschnitt* dropped its price and changed orientation. By the end of 1933 Flechtheim and Westheim were in exile in Paris, and *Kunst und Künstler* had ceased publication.

Further reading

P. Albert, 'La Presse française de 1871 à 1940', in C. Bellanger, J. Godechot, P. Guiral and F. Terrou (eds), *Histoire générale de la presse française*, vol. 3, Paris: 1972.

T. Fawcett and C. Philpot (eds), *The Art Press. Two Centuries of Art Magazines*, London: The Art Book Company, 1976.

Günther Feist (ed.), *Kunst und Künstler. Aus 32 Jahrgängen einer deutschen Kunstzeitschrift*, Berlin: Henschelverlag Kunst und Gesellschaft, 1971.

Christian Ferber (ed.), *Der Querschnitt. 'Das Magazin der aktuellen Ewigkeitswerte' 1924–1933*, Berlin: Ullstein, 1981.

Malcolm Gee (ed.), *Art Criticism since 1900*, Manchester: Manchester University Press, 1993.

Heinrike Junge (ed.), *Avantgarde und Publikum. Zur Rezeption avantgardistischer Kunst in Deutschland 1905–1933*, Cologne: Böhlau, 1992.

Peter de Mendelsohn, *Zeitungsstadt Berlin*, Berlin: Ullstein, 1982 (1959).

Lutz Windhöfel, *Paul Westheim und das Kunstblatt. Eine Zeitschrift und ihr Herausgeber in der Weimarer Republik*, Cologne: Böhlau, 1995.

---

[51] 'Wirtschaft, Politik, Kunst', *Das Kunstblatt*, 1931, 9, p. 257.

CHAPTER NINE

Text and image in the construction of an urban readership: allied propaganda in France during the Second World War

Valerie Holman

From May 1940, large posters informed the citizens of newly-occupied northern France that under the German penal code, effective immediately, it would be a punishable offence to gather in the streets, publish and distribute tracts, or print any news that might be detrimental to the Reich. Acutely sensitive to the power of the press, the occupying forces clearly located the source of potential resistance in an urban environment. To a regime for whom propaganda was an essential element in the realization of a long-term project, it was evident that cities and towns held the key to success: urban spaces were where people congregated and exchanged information; where the imagined mass audience could materialize and see the effect of propaganda on fellow-citizens, and where the technology for printing and publishing was by tradition concentrated. Authors, publishers, printers, distributors and significant numbers of readers were assumed to be, if not necessarily the inhabitants of great cities, at least living in agglomerations large enough to constitute a community over which it was essential to establish control or with whom 'collaboration' was a prerequisite.

These assumptions, however, and later those of the British producing their own counter-propaganda, need to be tested against the actual social structure and demography of France, French levels of literacy and reading habits, and recent developments that had reformulated, but also reinforced, perceptions of difference between town and country.

Post-war analysis showed that 'in 1939 (peasants) were still by far the largest class'.[1] Despite the fact that their number dropped by half between the mid-nineteenth and mid-twentieth centuries, France still had more peasants than most other Western countries: 32.5 per cent as opposed to Great Britain's 5.7 per cent or even Germany's 29 per cent. Many lived in fairly large

---

[1] Theodore Zeldin, *France 1848–1945*, vol. 1, Oxford: Oxford University Press, 1973, p. 131. All figures are taken from chapter on 'Peasants', pp. 131–97.

communities, but, especially in the west and south-west, there were vast areas where 70 per cent of the rural inhabitants lived outside the main town or village of the *commune*. The fact that one-third of France's population was economically and financially worse off than the other two-thirds meant that the percentage of personal income they devoted to reading, for example, was proportionately smaller. A study undertaken in 1937 revealed that book borrowing was also difficult. Libraries in the provinces were few in number – 320 in 1930 – and poorly stocked: virtually nothing by twentieth-century authors had been bought since 1900.[2] The great period of social reform from 1936 to 1938 had seen the creation of a further 17, but much of France remained poorly provided for. In 1956 it was still the case that 'the peasants were ... forced to spend 10% less on food, 28% less on clothes and 50% less on culture and leisure than their urban counterparts'.[3] Books were a luxury item, and bookshops few and far between. It is important to bear these statistics in mind when reflecting on how the largely urban intelligentsia in Britain approached the problem of creating and distributing effective propaganda for the whole of France, especially after November 1942 when not only the industrial north, but also the predominantly rural south had become an enemy-occupied area.

Successful identification of, and communication with, a target audience depended not only on the acquisition of verifiable data. Less tangible factors came into play: the climate of opinion, and the unspoken assumptions that lay behind perceptions of otherness. Of potentially greater use than a knowledge of demography and access to recent research into reading would have been awareness of the *imagined* geographies of France, coupled with sensitivity to the latest developments in a series of long-running debates about France's self-perception as a nation. In his detailed study of French modernization at the turn of the century, Eugen Weber pointed out that the so-called 'Saint-Malo/Geneva line': 'was in effect the division between urban and rural France – better still, between the poor backward countryside and the areas of France, rural or not, that were to some degree permeated by the values of the modern world.'[4] Quoting in support of his assertion comments from the French press that had likened peasants to bourgeois in the north but to beggars in the south, he saw in the late nineteenth century a narrowing of the gap between elite and popular culture, but only in northern France, more

---

[2] See Denise Montel and Gorges Rageot, *Rapport sur l'Organisation de la Lecture Publique, du Commerce du Livre et de la Propagande Collective pour la Lecture et le Livre*, Paris: Comité Intersyndical du Livre Parisien, 1937; and André Guillou, *Le Book Business ou l'Edition Francaise contre la Lecture Populaire*, Paris: Tema-Editions, 1975, esp. p. 209.

[3] Zeldin *France 1848–1945*, p. 189.

[4] Eugen Weber, *Peasants into Frenchmen. The Modernisation of Rural France 1870–1914*, Stanford, CA: Stanford, University Press, 1976, p. 494.

marked by money and by modernity. However oversimplified, such ideas have remained remarkably tenacious, aided by precisely the type of urban newspaper to which Weber refers.

Celebrations in and of the city reached their apogee at the turn of the century, and 1900 has remained a pivotal date in subsequent analysis of the modern metropolis.[5] It was later, in the years between the two World Wars, that a number of official decisions and state-sponsored projects brought rural and provincial France into the limelight but in ways which often served to underscore the 'otherness' of the French peasant and reinforce the authority of the city. Literate – if at all – for barely two generations, peasants, like colonial subjects, became in the 1930s the object of sustained attempts to understand their mentality, collect their artefacts, categorize their rituals, and record their oral history – attempts officially sanctioned by the creation of the Musée des Arts et Traditions Populaires in 1937.[6]

There was a further issue which directly affected construction of the identities of both urban and rural Frenchmen: the perceived role of their capital city as the heart of France but also as an international centre, in direct contrast to the provinces which were often seen as peripheral and in some way deficient.[7] By 1937 there were indications that the pendulum was swinging away from greater centralization towards an emphasis on regional development. At the *Exposition Internationale des Arts et des Techniques*

---

[5] See for example Donald J. Olsen, *The City as a Work of Art. London, Paris, Vienna*, New Haven and London: Yale University Press, 1986; Peter Fritzsche, *Reading Berlin 1900*, Cambridge, MA and London: Harvard University Press, 1996; and more recently the Royal Academy of Arts exhibition in London, *1900. Art at the Crossroads*, 2000.

[6] Between the wars, 'the deserted villages of France' were much lamented, yet Emmanuel Le Roy Ladurie has subsequently sought to demonstrate that the longevity of French villages has always been more remarkable than their supposed demise. To write about disappearing rural life had a parallel in the fondness of ethnographers for describing all newly discovered tribes as 'vanishing'. As observed by James Clifford, 'ethnography's disappearing object is … in significant degree, a rhetorical construct legitimising a representational practice: "salvage" ethnography in its widest sense. The other is lost, in distintegrating time and space, but saved in the text … It is assumed that the other society is weak and "needs" to be represented by an outsider (and that what matters in its life is its past, not present or future).' In rural France too, the culture was still largely oral, and susceptible to 'saving' in text or through visual representation, which positioned the 'saviour' as both urban and literate. See James Clifford, 'On Ethnographic Allegory'. in, George E. Marcus and J. Clifford (eds), *Writing Culture. The Poetics and Politics of Ethnography*, Berkeley, CA and London: University of California Press, 1986, p. 112.

[7] Alain Corbin has explored in detail the changing relationship between spatial, social and psychological distance, pointing out, for example, that in the nineteenth century 'the new railway system was designed expressly to serve the needs of the capital. The invention of the telegraph meant more rapid dissemination of the news. This together with new modes of social control … reinforced centralization' (Alain Corbin, 'Paris-Province', in Pierre Nora (ed.), *Realms of Memory. Rethinking the French Past, Vol. 1. Conflicts and Divisions*, New York: Columbia University Press, 1996, p. 451).

appliqués à la Vie Moderne held in Paris, the Fair's General Commissioner announced: 'I have chosen a watchword, regionalism. Never [have] the provinces been invited to participate so directly in an international event.'[8] Identified both with modernity and internationalism, Paris was the city to which Frenchmen from the provinces had long migrated, and where many sought to reinvent themselves as cosmopolitan. Arguments for local autonomy, however, proliferated between the Wars, and in the early 1940s proved fertile ground for the Vichy regime's own regionalist policies and celebration of rural values grounded in an almost mystical attachment to the French soil. Pétain's emphasis on the timeless quality of the land has recently been interpreted as reflecting his refusal to face the modern world, showing how entrenched is the identification of metropolitan with modern, and its further association with positive change and progress.[9]

In England, not only had the Industrial Revolution and urban sprawl begun much earlier than in France, but the symbolism and personal qualities attached to town and country were markedly different: from the seventeenth century onwards, country people came to be seen as *morally* superior, for the city, despite its association with learning and civilization, was where money was spent and vice located. In France, the townsman chose to see the country as tranquil, but the peasant as grasping, whereas in wartime Britain 'the country' stood neither for virtue nor backwardness, but for safety, secrecy and isolation, even from surrounding rural life.[10]

On 12 October 1939, John Johnson, Printer to the University of Oxford, wrote to Stanley Unwin, one of the central figures in British publishing at that time, concluding his letter with the remark: 'And I am pleased to see that you do not write from some strange address in the country.'[11] This was probably a veiled reference to the Duke of Bedford's estate at Woburn which, throughout the War, remained the secret rural hideaway of a vast

---

[8] Edmond Labbé, quoted by Romy Golan in *Modernity and Nostalgia, Art and Politics in France between the Wars*, New Haven and London: Yale University Press, 1995, p. 120.

[9] See Pierre Deyon, *Paris et ses Provinces. Le Défi de la Décentralisation 1770–1992*, Paris: Armand Colin, 1992; and Philippe Burrin, 'Vichy' in Pierre Nora (ed), *Realms of Memory. Vol 1*.

[10] 'In Renaissance times the city had been synonymous with civility, the country with rusticity and boorishness. To bring men out of the forests and to contain them in a city was to civilize them ... The town was the home of learning, manners, taste and sophistication' (Keith Thomas, *Man and the Natural World: Changing Attitudes in England 1500–1800*, London: Allen Lane, 1983, p. 246). Raymond Williams has observed that in periods of rapid social change, however, city-dwellers have tended to mourn the passing of a rural way of life by writing in a pastoral or elegiac mode, and projecting an aura of timeless tranquillity onto the countryside and its inhabitants (Raymond Williams, *The Country and the City*, London: Chatto and Windus, 1973).

[11] Archives of Oxford University Press: John Johnson to Stanley Unwin, 12 October 1939, in John Johnson private letterbook vol. 42, p 292.

publishing enterprise that has never been fully documented.[12] Known initially as Department EH – after Electra House on the Embankment in London, the official postal address – the Department of Enemy Propaganda came into operation on the outbreak of war and, three months after the German occupation of Paris in June 1940, was responsible for the first aerial distribution of propaganda leaflets over France. At the end of that year, it also began producing the first regular airmail newspaper, *Le Courrier de l'Air*. Despite the British government having anticipated the need for a propaganda organization, its exact constitution, and the nature of its relationship with other essential organizations – notably the RAF – was subject to frequent change and considerable acrimony. What from August 1941 became known as the Political Warfare Executive, or PWE, was formed to undermine enemy morale, and brought together parts of the BBC, the Foreign Office, the Ministry of Information, and that section of the Ministry of Economic Warfare which had succeeded Department EH. A secret grouping operating under the cover of the Foreign Office Political Intelligence Department, it was ultimately responsible for producing and dropping over France alone 700 million leaflets.[13] At a time of strict paper rationing there were problems in obtaining raw materials; acquiring planes and finding pilots to undertake aerial dissemination; and locating printers with enough capacity to produce the huge quantities of material required in a very short time. Psychological warfare on this scale was not only a logistical tour de force, it also represented a major British investment in an activity whose efficacy remained hard to prove.

One of the most interesting aspects of the whole enterprise is the way in which those generating propaganda attempted to visualize and cater for their potential readers. At the end of December 1941, the Labour politician and Minister for Economic Warfare Hugh Dalton put down on paper some ideas suggested by a recent International Labour Organization conference in the United States, in which he sought to define both those to whom British propaganda should be directed, and the message it should be seen to convey:

> ... our best friends in Occupied Europe are not the bourgeoisie, much less big business, or generals. but the masses, and principally the indus-

---

[12] A good source of information on aerial propaganda is still Charles Cruickshank. *The Fourth Arm: Psychological Warfare 1938–1945*. Oxford: Oxford University Press. 1977. See also Valerie Holman, 'Air-borne Culture: Propaganda Leaflets dropped over occupied France in the Second World War', in James Raven (ed.). *Free Print and Non-Commercial Publishing Since 1700*. Aldershot: Ashgate. 2000.

[13] Official records are unclear as to whether the figures given are for publications dropped over Metropolitan France only, or whether they include French overseas territories. Public Record Office (PRO), FO 898/457.

trial workers ... We must show that we seriously mean to satisfy the hopes of working people everywhere for a new and better social order after the War.[14]

Not surprisingly, Robert Bruce Lockhart, the former diplomat who became Director General of the Political Warfare Executive (PWE), took exception to what he saw as Dalton's party political approach, and wrote a secret and personal memo to the Secretary of State for Foreign Affairs:

> I think our propaganda is already based on the hypothesis that in the occupied countries the broad masses have more of the stuff of resistance in them than has the bourgeoisie. The appeal, however, should not be based on Labour Party and Trades Union political thought and language. These are, I am convinced, out of date in most European countries.[15]

Recommending an appeal based on the idea of liberation rather than revolution, he particularly advocated an emphasis on democracy in sharp opposition to the Axis presentation of individuals serving the state machine.

Dalton's paper was circulated to Regional Directors for comment, and the resulting notes in relation to France spell out with much greater precision the intended readership.[16] In addition to industrial workers, 'our best allies' are defined as 'professional, technical and intellectual classes', that is to say those who may provide influence and leadership, and who are assumed to reside in the towns. 'The sentiments and actions of the agricultural population, preponderating in quantity, are less easy to ascertain, and propaganda access to them is less easy to obtain ... Over them, the influence of the subordinate clergy more particularly, and of the schoolmasters, is great.'[17]

In the 1880s, elementary education had been made compulsory and free, and every village in France with more than 20 children had had to have its own school. Teacher-training, regular inspections, and educational subsidies had ensured that standards were maintained, and the school certificate became for some a passport to escape from rural poverty. As Weber has pointed out, the main function of the modern school was to teach patriotism, to inculcate an awareness of one's country, not one's village, as an entity worth defending. The textbooks published to help newly-educated teachers in the late nineteenth century, especially those on history and geography, played a crucial role in the formation of a national and largely Republican, consciousness. For many rural

---

[14] Hugh Dalton, secret memo, 6 Dec. 1941 (PRO, FO 898/13).

[15] Robert Bruce Lockhart to the Secretary of State for Foreign Affairs, 8 Jan. 1942 (PRO, FO 898/13).

[16] Europe was divided into areas known as regions each with their own Director. The whole of Metropolitan France constituted one region.

[17] Notes on the memorandum by the Minister for Economic Warfare, by the Regional Director for France, 26 Jan. 1942 (PRO, FO 898/13).

French children, their schoolteacher would have been the main link to a wider world. Dalton's assessment proved absolutely correct: teachers, both men and women, are frequently mentioned as key figures in the Resistance, combining authority in the local rural community with a knowledge of urban culture, and hence uniquely well-qualified to form a bridge between the two.

From the earliest days of the PWE Planning Committee, a clear distinction had been drawn between what was perceived as the more influential and accessible segment of the French population – the town-dwellers, especially in the industrial cities of northern France – and the numerically, economically and socially significant population of the rural areas who were harder to fathom, and who could best be reached through more easily identifiable intermediaries such as priests and teachers. Only the fourth leaflet ever produced by PWE was directed to the workers of France. Dropped between October and December 1940, a single small sheet, it proclaimed 'this is the future reserved for you by your German masters'. Hitler wanted to make France into an agricultural country, as in the Middle Ages, it claimed. Essentially France still was largely agricultural, but this of course was not the message to encourage resistance from industrial workers.

Among the perceived needs and desires of potential resisters, second in importance only to expulsion of the Germans according to the Regional Director for France, was the issue of food. Its continuing dominance in Allied propaganda is illustrated by the ubiquity of the trick leaflet inside an envelope marked 'Voici l'Ordre Nouveau'. Captioned 'The German eats – the Frenchman looks on – this is the New Order', 1200 copies were dropped over Paris and Orleans in October 1941, and 5000 more, with the caption translated into colloquial Arabic, dropped over French North Africa (see Figure 9.1). Closed, it looked like a greeting card, and could be read as Hitler bringing food and drink to French women and children: opened, it revealed the true story, that the meal was for German soldiers.

Food was, however, not only the universal concern to which all French citizens could relate, but also a source of divisiveness. At the beginning of 1942 an illuminating note was drafted in an attempt to gauge the strength of European peasant resistance. It adopted a polarity which was to become familiar in many guises, in the use to which propaganda was put as well as the messages it was designed to contain: at its most crude, the town-dweller was interested in food for the mind, and the peasant in food for his belly.

> The 'booklearning' of the peasant is generally limited because he has the sense to realise that books won't make crops grow or produce fat bullocks ... In spite of what the townsman may call the peasant's 'lack of education', he is shrewd, often to the point of cunning. ... as a result of this shrewdness the peasant weighs very carefully anything he reads in the paper or hears on the wireless. From the propaganda point of view he is really a much harder nut to crack than the townsman.

9.1 'Voici l'Ordre Nouveau'. Trick leaflet in the form of a greeting card: (a) closed, (b) open. ©Royal Air Force Museum.

The report concludes:

> as a whole the peasants are far from being co-operative in helping to
> alleviate the food shortage in the towns. ... What makes the attitude of
> the peasants to the towns more significant and more indicative of the
> widening of the pre-war gulf between town and country is that the
> peasants themselves are in no danger of suffering from a food shortage.
> They are in fact holding on to surpluses for sale on the black market or
> for requisitioning.[18]

It was extremely important for the Allies to be aware of what danger and
deprivation their targeted readers, both urban and rural, were really experi-
encing, and of any sources of friction between them, as the conditions of
daily life were the most obvious factor which might affect the way their
propaganda was received. Given the perceived difficulty of reaching agricultural areas, and the pronounced regional differences in France, it was easier
to target specific urban groups such as factory workers or a single industrial
site where there was likely to be a commonality of feeling. Interspersed with
PWE productions are leaflets emanating from individual cities in the UK, and
designed as messages of solidarity with their fellow workers in an equivalent
position in France: a text from Durham coal miners to colleagues in Namur in
1940, or one from Coventry factory-workers, 200 000 copies of whose messages were dropped over Paris on 1 May 1941. Even more specific were
advance warnings of bombing to a potential target locality in France, and the
leaflets dropped in April 1942 showing RAF destruction of the Renault car
works and the Ford factory at Poissy, with the message: 'They were working
for Germany.'

Illustrated leaflets gradually changed between 1941 and 1943, as symbolic
representations of victory or France itself gave way to more specific depic-
tions of places and personalities, usually through the medium of photographs.
This was especially noticeable in the case of Allied leaders or the aftermath
of successful bombing raids such as that on the Ford and Renault factories.
Supported by such visual 'evidence', the textual message acquired an aura of
truth and precision. The change in approach can be traced through one of the
most ubiquitous and polysemous images in prints, postcards and propaganda
during the First World War, the Arc de Triomphe. Standing for the city of
Paris, for France, and later for the unknown dead whose symbolic tomb was
placed at its centre in 1920, it was reclaimed in the Second World War,
initially to evoke hope, victory and revolution against an oppressor, and often
crudely sketched as in a leaflet of 1941, *Victory on Four Fronts*. In 1942,
however, it featured in a sequence of aerial photographs taken by an RAF
flight lieutenant who, on 12 June, flew low over Paris and draped the arch in

---

[18] Note from Major Baker White, 1 Feb. 1942 (PRO, FO 898/332).

a French flag. Within three months, a further leaflet on the same theme had become worth 150 francs to those collectors who now preferred aerial propaganda to the more traditional stamps. Allied material had to make its mark in an urban context saturated with posters and pamphlets put out by the Vichy regime, whose fondness for just such familiar and evocative symbols as the Arc de Triomphe forced the British and Free French to adopt different iconography and alternative publishing strategies. Aimed largely at urban readers, it came to look less like propaganda than the type of magazine and journal regularly displayed by news vendors in peacetime.

What is doubly ironic is that the Germans had anticipated opposition being manifested on the ground in city streets (which initially it was), but it came increasingly from the air, not just from the arms parachuted into France, but from the leaflets disseminated by the RAF; and secondly, it came from the Maquis who, as their name implies, offered resistance from bases in the underpopulated rural areas, and used the rough terrain and scattered habitation to their advantage.[19] On 1 May 1943, a special leaflet was dropped by the RAF to keep Occupied France informed of what was being printed in secret in many different regions within its own borders. The product of a unique collaboration between de Gaulle and the British Political Warfare Executive, it was presented as a homage from the National Union of Journalists, illustrated with the front pages of nine prominent Resistance journals. These tended to be regionally based, and were not necessarily familiar to inhabitants of other parts of the country, so the leaflet not only gave information about activity in France itself, but it also conveyed the message that its producers were in touch with every one of the regions represented.

The same year saw a marked increase in the aerial distribution not just of political tracts, but of miniature magazines, printed on airmail paper in a reduced type size, mostly about 5 inches by 4 inches, and containing about 30 pages of contemporary literature or journalism. As specified by the *Instructions on Policy and Practice for Leaflets, Publications and Books* issued by the Foreign Office: 'This type of publication (periodicals) is designed to satisfy, at least to some extent the hunger of the educated Frenchman for unpolluted food for thought.'[20] Titles which were published on a regular basis included *La France Libre*, *La Revue du Presse Libre*, *La Revue du Monde Libre* and *Accord*. The role of the Political Warfare Executive had come to encompass far more than the provision of accurate and up-to-date news, advance warning of air-raids, or messages of moral support addressed to

---

[19] For a detailed analysis of the relationship between town and country in the history of the Resistance, see H.R. Kedward, *In Search of the Maquis. Rural Resistance in Southern France 1942–1944*, Oxford: Clarendon Press, 1993.

[20] *Instructions on Policy and Practice for Leaflets, Publications and Books*, n.d. [1943] (PRO, FO 898/435).

specific target groups. Through aerial dissemination of printed material, parts
of occupied France and North Africa gained access to the news, views, art
and literature that had been denied them since the beginning of the War.

In the Autumn of 1940, French publishers had been advised that 1000
books already published would be withdrawn from sale because they were
judged by the Germans or supportive French publishers to be poisoning
public opinion, and two further 'Otto lists' in 1942 and 1943 extended the
criteria for removal to include not just Jewish writers, but biographies of
Jews, and translations of works from English. Libraries were forbidden to
lend these books and, crucially, the publication of new titles was also subject
to a form of censorship in that not only had French publishers agreed to be
self-regulating – to anticipate what might offend the Germans – but from
April 1942 all new books had to be read and approved by members of the
Paper Control Committee, the body that allocated an ever-diminishing supply, reckoned at that date to be only one-tenth of what had been available
before the War. Bookshops such as W. H. Smith in Paris, which provided
access to an international literature in English, were in German hands.

To help fill this cultural vacuum, the editorial board of the PWE publication *La Revue du Monde Libre* declared: 'Our pages will be open not only to
French writers abroad, but to writers of all nationalities who may wish to
send you their messages.' In the Spring of 1943, the RAF dropped copies of
the fourth issue over a number of key cities in northern France: Lille 10 000;
Caen 44 000; Nantes 56 000, and Paris 33 500 (see Figure 9.2).[21] This miniature periodical opened with Eluard's poem now known as 'Liberté', first
published the previous year in Algiers, and also contained an extract from
what is probably the most famous wartime novel of all: *Le Silence de la Mer*
by an anonymous author calling himself Vercors. Into remote or rugged areas
of France such as the Vercors itself, however, were dropped arms for the
Resistance, and miniature books that looked like volumes of poetry but were
in fact sabotage manuals giving precise instructions on how to blow up a
train.

That autumn, the back cover of *Accord* showed a typical urban newspaper
kiosk, well-stocked with German and collaborationist periodicals over the
caption 'You want French newspapers Sir? Come back next year ... ' (see
Figure 9.3). Inside, solidarity between the rural populations of France and the
UK is suggested by an article on 'English Peasants' (actually Dorset small-
holders), illustrated with a photograph of an elderly couple, the labourer's
pose reminiscent of Millet's painting *Man with a Hoe* from the mid-nineteenth century (see Figure 9.4). Representations of city-dwellers favoured the

---

[21] Figures giving the quantity of leaflets dropped are held in the archives of the RAF
Museum. Hendon.

9.2 Front cover of *La Revue du Monde Libre*, no. 4. ©Royal Air Force Museum.

urbane, often young or middle-aged, sophisticated and relaxed *flâneur* featured as part of a crowd in an urban thoroughfare, in marked contrast to the image of an older, poorer, labouring individual or couple to signify the rural population of France in a particularly idealized form: 'La France Profonde', the French countryside as seen from the town, signifying lasting values as opposed to the rapid pace of change characterizing modern life. Peasants were often shown photographed frontally, in a static pose, much in the style of ethnographic portraits. Townsmen, on the other hand, were more usually represented from the side or even from behind, suggesting they and the viewer belonged to the same crowd of spectators, those for whom reading was a constitutive part of daily life.

At the end of 1943, 690 000 copies of *Les Cahiers de Libération* in miniature were dropped on major cities across Northern France: Amiens, Beauvais, Rouen, Paris and Orleans, all of which fall above the Saint-Malo/Geneva line. The publishers of the original limited edition stated that it had been compiled so that in addition to Resistance writing – in journals such as *Combat* or *Libération* – which was an act of war, there should be new writing formulating French ideas for a time of peace, which was why they offered 'a

" Vous voulez des journaux français, Monsieur ?
Vous repasserez l'année prochaine ..."

ACCORD, rédigé par des Français et des
Anglais, vous est apporté par vos amis de la
R.A.F.   Puisse-t-il vous aider à attendre le
jour où reparaîtront, dans tous les kiosques à
journaux de France, des publications libres.

La photographie sur la couverture est du commandant René et le Squadron
Leader Jock Charles, qui ont à leur actif le millième avion allemand abattu par
leur escadrille composée d'Anglais et de Français.

OCTOBRE. 1943   F145

9.3   Back cover of *Accord*, October 1943. ©Royal Air Force Museum.

9.4 Double-page spread from *Accord*, October 1943. ©Royal Air Force Museum.

forum to the intellectual élite'. Despite the much larger print-run of the airborne version, the leaflet was destined from the outset only for the urban population, and its distribution by air was limited to those cities that could be successfully targeted by the RAF.

The Allies were understandably concerned to know how their propaganda was being received, and the RAF monthly surveys of leaflet operations give fascinating, if unscientific, insights into the kind of information which guided those responsible for the production of propaganda, as their target readership spread from the industrialized north of France to the formerly unoccupied zone of the south and to North Africa.

Reports on rural reception of aerial propaganda are conflicting: on the one hand an 'educated Frenchman' wrote in 1941 that 'about 99% of tracts dropped by the RAF over France have not served any useful purpose. They are usually dropped in the fields and are used in most cases as kindling by the peasants.'[22] Alternatively they were used, or disguised, as wrapping paper for such unlikely food products as butter. However, in 1943, one informant 'stated that the peasants in rural districts are very keen about leaflets. He found one old man of 82 years studying the *Courrier de l'Air* with a diction-ary before spreading its contents to other less gifted friends.'[23] What this suggests, despite the enthusiasm recorded, is a tendency on the part of the informant to equate literacy with urban culture, and indeed another informant writing about a different area of France in 1944 said that 'in the country districts a certain amount of illiteracy prevails, and the peasants are reluctant to read more than a minimum'.[24]

In every case, 'the peasant' is at one remove, and there is no record of a direct first-hand response from those living beyond the margins of a town. It was concluded that they, and the populations of North Africa, would respond better to visual than to verbal propaganda which early in the War was some-times deliberately badly printed to suggest local production under difficult circumstances. Later, thinking on this issue changed: it was considered more effective to convey the subliminal message that the Allies had access to all the material they needed, and most aerial propaganda became better illus-trated, often with photographs, and extremely well printed.

Nonetheless, literacy, education, access to culture and leisure – all these continued to distinguish the urban citizen from his rural fellow-countryman. His interests were different, and he had more opportunity than the peasant to

---

[22] Extract from report by 'educated Frenchman' sent from Col. Sutton to Brigadier Brooks on 4 August 1941 (PRO, FO 898/444).

[23] Air Ministry, *Leaflet Operations for the Month of April 1943*, 6 May 1943. RAF Museum, Hendon. The peasant concerned, if born in about 1860, would have been too old to benefit from the educational reforms of the 1880s.

[24] *Evidence of Reception Report* for September 1944 (PRO, FO 898/463).

do exactly what had been forbidden by the Germans since the beginning of the war: further distribute by hand those leaflets he found in the street. This he did in a number of ways that were only possible in an urban environment: slipping them into a fellow-traveller's pocket on the metro; putting them under plates in a restaurant; passing one to every member of a community who gave blood at a donor centre.

Those who picked up tracts or booklets from the ground and ensured their further circulation could do so more easily in the anonymity of towns where close proximity to countless strangers facilitated the transfer of published material by unorthodox means. As early as June 1942, the Air Ministry reported: 'it can be safely estimated that one leaflet is read by a hundred readers.'[25] Indeed it was reported back to the British authorities that as time went on, the sheer quantity of aerial propaganda dropped over France bred a certain resignation in German officials, and citizens found in possession of leaflets became less likely to be penalized.

In order to reach and affect their intended readership, those who wrote, designed and published aerial propaganda for France in the Second World War had to create categories of imagined recipients based on pre-war perceptions, and what evidence of reception reached the UK, often long after the event. Furthermore, the British government needed to convince not only its own people that leaflet-dropping would help win the War, but also the RAF, reluctant to commit personnel to a project that was both dangerous and uncertain of success. The towns of northern France were a closer target, and given the concentrations of people, it was more likely that leaflets dropped there would be gathered and read. It is important to realize that the pattern of distribution across France had to conform to British needs as well as those of the target readership in Occupied France. Paradoxically, while British-published leaflets – notably miniature literary magazines – did indeed contribute to sustaining French culture in wartime, the very means of distribution that enabled so much news, debate and contemporary literature to reach so many individuals and circumvent the German prohibition on tracts, also reinforced Frenchmen's pre-war perceptions of their fellow citizens: it was primarily the towns of northern France who gained access to alternative publishing circuits, and intellectuals, still associated with urban culture, who, it was hoped, would generate new ideas for post-war France.

---

[25] Royal Air Force, *Leaflet Operations for the Month of June*, 1942 (Archives of Royal Air Force, Hendon).

Further reading

Michael Balfour, *Propaganda in War 1939–1945. Organisations, Policies and Publics in Britain and Germany*, London: RKP, 1979.

P.M.H. Bell, *France and Britain 1940–1994: The Long Separation*, London: Longman, 1997.

Jean-Louis Crémieux-Brilhac, *La France Libre. De l'Appel du 18 Juin à la Libération*, Paris: Gallimard, 1996.

Charles Cruickshank, *The Fourth Arm. Psychological Warfare 1938–1945*, Oxford: Oxford University Press, 1981 (1977).

Laurent Gervereau and Denis Peschanski (eds), *La Propagande sous Vichy 1940–1944*, Paris: BDIC, 1990.

Gerhard Hirschfeld and Patrick Marsh (eds), *Collaboration in France. Politics and Culture during the Nazi Occupation 1940–44*, New York and Munich: Berg, 1989.

Pierre Laborie, *L'Opinion Française sous Vichy*, Paris: Seuil, 1990.

Dominique Rossignol, *Histoire de la Propagande en France de 1940 à 1944. L'Utopie Pétain*, Paris: PUF, 1991.

David Schoenbrun, *Maquis, Soldiers of the Night. The Story of the French Resistance*, London: Robert Hale, 1990 (1980).

CHAPTER TEN

Structures of the typescript[1]

Catherine Viollet

Five thousand years have passed since the invention of the manuscript and 500 years since that of printing. The typewriter has been in existence for a little more than 100 years but the personal computer, which has become widespread only in the last few decades, has already more or less made it a redundant curiosity. Yet was it not the typewriter that first transformed the traditional conditions and practices of written production, literary or otherwise, that today only the general use of the personal computer appears to put into question? Has not the typewriter left its mark on twentieth-century literature, most of which has at one moment or another of its elaboration passed through its keys? Is the typescript comparable to the manuscript and if so to what extent? Is it possible to envisage a typology of writers' typescripts, comparable to that of manuscripts, and if so according to what criteria – the semiotics of the script? its genesis? Finally, as the first case of interaction between the machine and literary creation does the typewriter not have something to teach us about the writing processes that it generates? The starting point for this essay is the point of view of genetic criticism – the study of the origin of literary texts starting from the materials of their elaboration. However, if one wishes to define the role played by the typewriter in this field, it is necessary to take into consideration larger perspectives including historical, sociological, economic, cognitive, technical and – last but not least – epistemological.

A little-known tool

Heidegger's remark on this 'intermediate thing between tool and machine ... almost commonplace and which consequently passes unnoticed' seems to be still pertinent today.[2] In France there are only two collections of articles dedicated to a writing tool that has nonetheless marked the twentieth century very profoundly and one could say constituted the material base of its litera-

---

[1] Translated from the French by Malcolm Gee. A version of this essay, 'Ecriture mécanique, espaces de frappe', appeared in *Genesis* [Paris], 10, 1996.

[2] Martin Heidegger, 'Parmenides', *Collected Works*, vol. II p. 54; cited by F. Kittler, *Grammophon, Film, Typewriter*, Berlin: Brinkmann and Bose, 1986.

ture. The first brings together the papers from a conference organized by the
Institut de Livre (Institute for the Study of the Book) in 1980 and deals with
largely technical aspects;[3] the second appeared 15 years later and deals
essentially with the socio-economic consequences linked to the introduction
of the typewriter in the world of work – that is to say the arrival en masse of
women in the world of the office and the development of the so-called
service sector in cities.[4] In library indexes the key words 'typewriter' and
'typist' relate essentially to texts on learning how to type, together with a few
exhibition catalogues – minimal indications of the existence of an unexplored
continent.[5] It is very surprising that the typewriter has not found a place in
the history of writing or that of publishing; even more disconcertingly, the
history of the press seems to pass over it with disdain. It seems unlikely that
the history of the computer will treat it any better. Nonetheless the invention
of mechanical writing is very closely linked to other technical advances:
those tied to the book industry and the industrial manufacture of paper and
synthetic ink; or those in the techniques of reproduction like carbon paper,
the duplicator and the stencil. Yet the typewriter is equally contemporary to
the invention of means of communication that have not yet disappeared from
our civilization – radio, the telephone (also 1876) and the cinema – inven-
tions which have attracted more attention. In many ways is not the break that
mechanical writing introduced in relation to writing by hand equivalent to
that introduced by photography in relation to painting? The comparison
seems provocative but merits development.

A collective invention

Numerous inventors contributed to the development of mechanical writing
with a range of ingenious uses of materials and mechanisms. The oldest
patent registered in London, by the engineer Henry Mill in 1715, concerned
'a machine or artificial method ... for printing letters separately or in sequence just as in handwriting'. In 1833 Xavier Progrin's 'Kryptographic pen'
appeared in France; various initiatives followed in the 1850s in different
countries, amongst them the 'cenbalo scrivano', the 'balle écrivante' and the
'machine à barillet'.[6] It was precisely at this moment that the printer

---

[3] Roger Laufer (ed.), *La machine à écrire hier et demain*, Paris: Institut du Livre/Solin, 1982.

[4] 'Machines à écrire. Des claviers et des puces: la traversée du siècle', Monique Peyrière
(ed.), *Autrement*, 146, June 1994.

[5] For example, the catalogue *Un siècle de machines de bureau*, Brussels: Bibliothèque royale
Albert 1er, 1993.

[6] See W. A. Beeching, *Century of the Typewriter*, Bournemouth: British Typewriter Museum,
1990 [1974].

10.1 Typewriter *Dactyle c.* 1895. © Musée des Arts et Métiers – CNAM, Paris/ Photo.

Christopher Latham Sholes in the United States, assisted by Soulé and Glidden, developed a prototype which was of interest to industry. A manufacturer of arms and sewing machines, Remington, began to produce it in a series in 1873. These first machines had the same frame as sewing machines and had a pedal for carriage return. The main inconvenience was that the user could not see the text. Apparently Mark Twain was the first writer to adopt it, in 1874. In the following quarter of a century, patents for improvements multiplied. But it was only in 1898 with the Underwood that the decisive step was made: the typed line became entirely visible for the operator. Rapidly the typewriter spread in the United States and in Europe from 1882 onwards; used in France from 1885, it was only manufactured there from 1910. Already in 1900 there were more than 700 000 in use in the world; Remington would go on to produce 15 million units in the one year 1954. (See Figures 10.1 and 10.2.)

Usage

A standard typewriter is made up largely of three parts: a metal frame; a moveable part called the chariot carrying the cylinder around which is rolled the paper; and a printing mechanism controlled by keys, organized in a keyboard, that hit the paper through an inked ribbon. In order to obtain an

10.2   Lucien Lefebre, Poster advertising the typewriter *Yost*, 80.60 cm, 1892.
© Bibliothèque Forney, Ville de Paris.

imprint of the character, one strikes a key that activates a hammer having at
its end two characters, one of which strikes the paper through an inked ribbon
which rises up for each impression. While the hammer returns to its bed, a
step forward moves the chariot one space thanks to a cog and a spiral spring,
so avoiding double impression. A space bar allows one to move the chariot
on its own. This system is, of course, familiar to anyone who has used a
typewriter: however, very little research has been carried out to evaluate its
implications in terms of cognition, kinesthetics and psychomotor activity.

   The percussive striking of a keyboard generates – in contrast to the word
processor, where the strike and printing are disassociated – the immediate
inscription of the series of characters on the paper. Organized in discrete
units, these characters derive not from writing by hand but from typography,
and their design is specially adapted to this new tool.[7] They must satisfy
criteria of legibility (hence the choice of the '*mécane*' type with rectangular

---

[7] On this point, see René Ponot, 'Pica, Élite et les autres ou les caractères de la machine à
écrire', in Laufer, *La Machine à écrire*, pp.143–54.

bases) and – unlike typographical characters – they need to occupy exactly the same amount of space for each letter. Mechanical impression consequently reduces the infinite variety of handwriting and the lesser variety of typographical types to an extremely limited number of forms (pica, elite, and so on). Another consequence was the use of the QWERTY layout (adapted to AZERTY in French) based on the frequency of use of letters in English (an alphabetical layout leads to frequent tangling up of the hammers); although word processors use the same arrangement it does not correspond to any ergonomic criteria.

Among the different systems envisaged, the choice of the now familiar flat keyboard made a major contribution to the success of the typewriter – 'a piano for letters', 'a writing harpsichord', 'a sort of mechanical piano whose keyboard instead of producing sounds produces printed letters'.[8] Some old models imitated the layout of black and white keys of the piano, and in fact the very first typists were expected to be good piano players. Professional teaching (in France from 1892) developed a rigorous division of the keyboard in terms of each finger, and learning required the qualities of agility and speed but also of 'feeling' and 'touch' associated with musical virtuosity.

A vague terminology

How should we designate the bastard object that is produced by mechanical writing – now recently made redundant by 'information technology' and its word-processing programmes? The available terminology is pretty unclear on this point. Does the term 'draft' include documents produced by mechanical means? There is no a priori reason why not if one refers for example to the most recent glossary in this area: 'Draft: working manuscript of a text in the process of being constituted; usually covered with changes and crossings out.'[9] A 'typewritten' text can easily be used as the starting point for phases of rewriting and consequently be covered with crossings out. More paradoxical is the fact that the term 'manuscript' can also include typescripts: 'manuscript: any document written by hand: by extension one sometimes includes hand written or printed documents (the Proust manuscript archive at the Bibliothèque Nationale includes notebooks, books of drafts, books of final drafts, typescripts and corrected proofs).'[10] The truly ambiguous term 'manuscript' functions here as a generic noun, which could be applied despite its etymology to the products of word processing and printing since it seems

---

[8] *Journal des fonctionnaires*, 30 Oct. 1887; cited in *Un siècle de machines de bureau*, p. 21.

[9] Almuth Grésillon, *Éléments de critique génétique. Lire les manuscrits modernes*, Paris: PUF, 1994, pp. 241–6.

[10] Ibid.

to cover typographic output. If typewriting is not opposed to 'handwriting' how should one define its specificity? Certainly the hand plays a role, and usually indeed two hands. But from the point of view of psychomotor movements, it is not at all the case of the same kinds of gesture as those of writing proper, directly manual with a pen or pencil: the body engages completely differently. The product obtained by mechanical writing for its part has characteristics that are very different from a true manuscript. And, in fact, in French one encounters different terms to designate this object which indicate its unstable status in relation to writing practices as a whole: '*typoscrit*', influenced by German, linked to typography; '*dactylographie*', made up of the Greek *dactylos* (finger) and *graphein* (to write) – word for word 'to write with the fingers', linked to graphism (it designates in principle the 'technique of mechanical writing', the act and not the result – according to the *Petit Robert*: 'action of expressing oneself by touch'); dactylogramme' (text-object produced by 'dactylographie'); and the inelegant but widespread '*tapuscrit*'.[11]

In English, a composite term, 'typewriter' originally designated both tool and user, while the corresponding verb 'to type' emphasizes the technical specificity of the act, as in the French '*taper*'. The names invented for different models in the prehistory of typewriters also translate a noticeable imprecision: amongst them we find the 'kryptographic pen' (Xavier Progin, 1833), the 'chirographe' (Thurber, 1845), the 'printer keyboard' (Foucault, 1851), the 'writing ball' (Hansen, 1867), the 'Calligraph' (Yost, 1879), the 'Typo' (M. St Etienne, 1910), and the 'polygraph' (Burt, 1929). This is a terminological profusion that underlines above all the intermediate position of the typewriter – between manual writing and typography.

From 'keyboard for the deaf, dumb and blind' that the word '*dactylographe*' designated in its first usage (1836), it has become, according to the *Robert*: 'a person whose profession is to write or transcribe texts, using a typewriter (term used almost exclusively of women).' From object to women, the shortcut is striking: condemned to monotonous and repetitive tasks, women become in a sense the 'natural' users of the machine, to the point of merging into the object. The typewriter did open up the labour market to women, for reasons of profitability, but did so basically in a subaltern, auxiliary role. In fact, the pay of a (female) typist was, because of the creation of new conditions, half that of her male equivalent. Associated with the image of the female typist it is, consequently, the notion of 'transcribing tool' of anonymous copy that predominates in the perception of the typewriter. (That is to say, a tool used

---

[11] This term, which does not figure in dictionaries, is taken from a popularizing 1970s guide to the presentation of research work in typed form: M-L. Dufour, *Le Tapuscrit*, Paris: EPHE, 1971. (The use of '*taper*' for '*dactylographier*' ('to type') dates from 1923, according to *Robert*.)

for the 'insignificant' tasks of reproduction, and not the 'noble' ones of creation.) Roland Barthes seems to be one of the rare writers to have had a clear sense of this sociological aspect of the matter, both in terms of theoretical reflection and in relation to his own practice: 'The typewriter remains an instrument of class, linked to the exercise of power: this exercise supposes a secretary, the modern substitute for the slave of antiquity ... whose body is welded to the machine ... '[12]

These socio-economic considerations, far from being foreign to my purpose, probably partly explain, on an epistemological level, why, up until now, so little attention has been given to the typewriter as an instrument of writing itself. It is nonetheless the case that within a few decades, the rapid diffusion of the typewriter effectively transformed the practice of writing – dramatically in the administrative, industrial and commercial domains, but also in that of literature. The chief advantages of the typewriter are on the one hand its legibility (and, as a corollary, its effectiveness for reproduction – which links it to typesetting), and on the other, its speed and the advantage in time expended that it generates. Legibility is obtained at the price of the infinite possibilities of graphic expression and the individual characteristics of writing by hand. These allow one to identify the hand – how, indeed, without a witness, can one distinguish an 'autograph' typescript from another 'allograph', unless one employs a very particular expertise? And how has this implement, which as Barthes puts it 'expels a small piece of code' under the pressure of the finger, that breaks down language into discrete units (alphabet and punctuation), and disassociates elements that the hand, on the contrary, links together, influenced the relation of writer to the text being written? The gestures of writing themselves have an importance that goes beyond that of a simple instrumental practice: to what extent does technology induce its own strategies? We know Nietzsche's programmatic reflection on this, when he had a Malling Hansen sent to him in Italy from Denmark in 1882. It was meant to palliate his difficulties in seeing, although its output was, paradoxically, not immediately visible. He commented on the experience by saying 'Our writing tool is part of our thought processes'.

What writers say

As specific objects typescripts have been accorded little attention by '*généticiens*' or semioticians.[13] In the absence of any substantial works of synthesis on these matters, we have to turn to the direct witness of writers

---

[12] Cited in Jean-Louis de Rambures, *Comment travaillent les écrivains*, Paris: Flammarion, 1978, p. 15.

[13] '*Généticien*' here refers to someone who studies the origins, or genesis, of texts.

themselves. There are many writers who have discussed their relation to the typewriter.[14] They have emphasized different aspects of their practice of mechanical writing: clumsiness or virtuosity, awareness or not of the gestural, graphic and audible expression (comparisons between the typewriter and the piano – the 'letter piano', the 'literary piano' – are frequent); the inhibiting or stimulating role of the machine in the process of writing; the material and technical obstacles involved; the fetishistic and affective, using sensuality and even eroticism in the metaphors used to personify the object; referring to questions of rhythm, of the usefulness of typing mistakes. The aspect which I shall develop here is probably the most characteristic: it relates to the closeness – constantly emphasized by author-typists – of mechanical writing to typography.

For many writers the typewriter seems to be synonymous with a horror of crossings out. Even if it is a first attempt, the text must look like a 'finished product', 'clean', 'faultless', even if it means typing out again in full however many times is necessary. Use of the machine corresponds to 'a desire to see the book virtually ready, as it is being composed', says Serge Doubrovsky, to gain vis-à-vis the text 'a distance, where the hand does not seem to have intervened, where it leaves no trace'. Bernard Noel states: 'when I type I cross out in my head, you don't see it.' In contrast, texts by Ingeborg Bachmann contain an impressive number of typing errors, that seem to leave the author indifferent. Speed, an uncomfortable position, defective material, and probably a certain clumsiness, result in innumerable instances of overtyping or repetition of signs, perturbations and telescoping of word forms, to the point where they are sometimes illegible (for example, natprikch = *natürlich*, vertanadne = *verstanden*).

In fact, nothing prevents simple rewriting operations at the graphic level (deletions, normally through superimposed x's, and additions) carried out immediately or later; no doubt typescripts provide the same variety as autographed manuscripts (see, for example, the typescripts of F. Ponge). But it must be admitted that the mechanical tool is not per se suited to the more complex rewriting operations like shifting paragraphs, or to extended corrections. The machine therefore invites the writer to associate with typing, writing by hand put to one side, specific techniques of correction; self-correcting sticking ribbons, auto-sticking ribbons, sheet or liquid tippex ... The particular method linked to mechanical writing seems to be scissors or

---

[14] The following collections offer a survey of writers' experiences and reflections on the topic: Rambures, *Comment travaillent les écrivains*; André Rollin, *Ils écrivent. Où? Quand? Comment?*, Paris: Mazarine/France Culture, 1986; *Writers at Work: The Paris Review*, Harmondsworth: Penguin, 1st series, ed. M. Cowley, 1958, 2nd, 3rd, 4th series, 1977, 5th series, 1981, ed. George Shrimton; Ulrich Ott (ed.), *Literatur im Industriezeitalter*, 2, Marbach, Marbacher Katalog, 42/2, 1987.

paste (or pins, paper clips), – which corresponds precisely to the cut-and-paste function of word processors.

One reason why students of the genesis of the literary text have paid little attention to typescripts[15] is that usually the typewriter is associated with the final phases of the establishment of the text. However, it is not unusual – and not only among American authors like Hemingway, Miller or Burrows – for an author to make use of the machine from the moment of taking notes or drafts, or indeed to write entirely on the machine. Doubrovsky again underlines the fact that for him the typography plays an important role: spaces, blanks, the material layout of the language, all are part of written expression. For other writers phases of handwriting and typing – usually in that order – alternate, with different degrees of volume from one page (Nathalie Sarraute) to a quantity corresponding to one day's output, or a chapter or an entire text. Usually the typing phase is followed by a handwritten revision finalized by a further typed version. But this alternation of typing and writing may correspond to other criteria, which derive not from a rigorously programmed scripting process but rather from a dynamic that is intrinsic to writing. John Dos Passos, for example, recounted that while he had written some texts entirely by hand, his usual practice was to begin chapters writing by hand and finish them on the machine: 'it becomes such a mess that no-one except my wife can transcribe it.'[16]

Ingeborg Bachmann is one of those writers who very early wrote directly on the machine at least in prose: quite quickly she came to use handwriting only for complementary research, sketches or corrections. We know that Paul Valéry only employed handwriting when writing 'for himself' (in his *Cahiers*), whereas he typed directly works destined for publication; for him also the machine was linked to the 'faculty of exteriorization'. Inversely the mechanical phase can be used as a start-up device before going on writing by hand, or again, the passage from one to the other technique can occur, so to speak, unconsciously. If authors who prefer typing directly to writing in longhand are quite common, it is nonetheless true that the typewriter has very often a function of control, reformulation, finalization of the text – a decisive role, when one thinks, for example, of typescripts revised by Proust such as the typescript D2 of 1909, on which there is added by hand, replacing a crossed-out phrase, the inaugural phrase of the novel, together with the title 'Le Temps Perdu', or again the recently rediscovered typescript of *Albertine disparue* where Proust suppresses the equivalent of two handwritten note-

---

[15] An exception: J. Neef's analysis of 'les commencements chez Samuel Beckett', in *Genèses du roman contemporain. Incipit et entrée en écriture*, Paris: CNRS Éditions, coll. 'Textes et Manuscrits', 1993, pp.121–50. This text shows an awareness of the dialectic between handwritten and typed text in the process of creation.

[16] *Writers at Work*.

books. It is also true, as Marianne Bockelkamp has stressed, that this phase, whether 'autographic' or not, has been imposed on writers by their editors since the 1920s, essentially for reasons of legibility and economy through a significant reduction in typesetting costs.[17] In this case the typescript is generally the work of a typist, whose role in the matter is not always as slight, in fact, as one might imagine. Think, for example, of Maria Van Rysselberghe, Gide's 'Petite Dame', or again of the valuable correspondence between Joyce and his typist Harriet Weaver during the writing of *Finnegan's Wake*.[18] Here typing – properly speaking transcription of the manuscript – modifies the point of view of the writer on the text, that is to say the process of reading: it introduces a distance between the author and the text, the author 'sees what he has written'. Some writers, like Kafka, appreciate the fact that the impersonal standardized machine 'effaces' the author; at least in terms of the individual dimension that a handwritten text embodies through its very nature. They all emphasize that the machine metamorphoses the text in rendering it objective and concise, and therefore allows a more critical read-ing – outside the narcissistic reflection and intimacy of all handwriting. Christiane Rochefort: 'I type the text myself, of course. It's in my interests. The machine is a good judge, a very cruel one; ... it isn't very creative but it is a terrific tool for revision.'[19] There are also interesting cases of *mimesis* taking place in the graphic process itself. Stefan George and Friedrich Nietzsche, for example, imitated mechanical writing in some manuscripts, to avoid 'all trace of intimacy'. In Nietzsche's case this practice was apparently explicitly linked to disappearance of the notion of the author.[20]

The two extreme positions – direct typing in the initial stage of the writing process, or typing as the final stage of the establishment of the text – have as their common point the fact that they highlight the fundamental characteristic of mechanical writing, deriving from the mobility and standardization of the elements that make it up: its proximity to typography, to the finished product which is the printed book. F. Kittler rightly insists on the fact that the typewriter is the first tool which disassociates the body of the writer and the text support in the phase of production itself (whereas in typography, it can only be a phase of reproduction of a text that is already written). The interme-diate stage between the alpha and the omega of the literary work, the typescript seems fitted to confer on the text a 'provisionally definitive' status, to make production and reproduction of the text more or less coincide. Amongst

[17] Marianne Bockelkamp, 'Objets matériels' in, *Les Manuscrits des écrivains*, Paris: Hachette/ CNRS, 1993, pp. 88–101.

[18] See Claude Jacquet (ed.), *Genèse de Babel. Joyce et la création*, Paris: CNRS, 1985.

[19] C. Rochefort *C'est bizarre l'écriture*, Paris: Grasset,1970.

[20] See Martin Stingelin, 'Kugeläusserungen. Nietzsche's Spiel auf der Schreibmaschine', in H. U. Gumbrecht, *Materialität der Kommunikation*, Suhrkamp, 1988, pp. 326–41.

others, and each in his own way, Roland Barthes and Serge Doubrovsky, bring this out:[21]

> As far as I am concerned it is necessary to distinguish two stages in the process of creation. First of all there is the moment when desire asserts itself in a graphic impulse, generating a calligraphic object. Then there is the critical moment when this object offers itself to others in becoming in its turn, a typographic object (and it needs to be admitted, a commercial one. It starts already there). In other words, I first write the whole text with a pen. Then I redo it from beginning to end on the typewriter. (Barthes)

> A manuscript would be too different from the final book. I need to see my text. I need to distance myself from it, all the more since it has an autobiographical basis. Typing, and then the photocopying which follows the completion of each section, are processes that move it closer to the final product ... No doubt it is the mechanical side that fascinates me in this. The book in the process of becoming ... on the plane of fantasy. (Doubrovsky)

In fact the typewriter is in some instances substituted to typography; the most convincing example of this is probably Arno Schmidt who published his extraordinary typescripts directly in facsimile. The form of his prose itself – these 'skeins' of intermingled text – is inextricable from its typed presentation: columns organized in threes, windows, frames, plays on lines.[22] These textual strategies are tied to the knowingly calculated visual aspect of the artisanal layout, and propose multiple ludic reading paths 'whoever wants literature, must want the typewriter', he claims.[23]

The 'architecture' of the typescript

Let us consider, briefly, some specific examples of the organization of the typed space, of the possible 'architectures' of the typescript. Writing on the machine eliminates the expressive movements of writing by hand, the graphic traces of scripted impressions. Although it is subject to very restrictive constraints – the principal parameters of which are the horizontal direction of the writing (normally fixed but which can be loosened, particularly at the end of pages), the margins and the (changeable) line spacing – the organization of graphic space does leave an element of initiative to the writer, of play, even of transgression of these parameters, that is widely used by practitioners of concrete poetry. For Cendrars, for example, typescript did not mean absence

---

[21] Rollin, *Ils écrivent*.

[22] See Claude Riehl, 'Mise en page parlante', *Revue de littérature générale*, 96/2 digest.

[23] *Zettels Traum*, Zettel 16.

of a personal 'mark': 'You can see easily that I typed it/there are spaces that only I could make … '(*Au Coeur du monde)*. In fact most writers seem to associate mechanical writing with a desire to saturate the graphic space 'to put as much as possible into the smallest space' (Sollers) – to achieve a compact density where the page coincides as far as possible with a textual unity, and where the processes of page layout are reduced to a minimum, so allowing a free flow of writing. For Guyotat, for example, 'the page is entirely filled up, there is no margin, it really begins at the edge of the sheet'; the space is saturated to the point where one typed sheet corresponds to three printed pages.[24]

Using a vertical division of the sheet, common in the nineteenth century, is rare today. Uwe Johnson does employ this method, typing directly on to the right-hand side of the page, leaving the left free for corrections. In Bachmann's case, the typescripts allow us to identify a prosody that is specific to mechanical writing, to sense the distinctive rhythm of striking keys. The A4 sheet appears to be too small for her, its limits seem to get in the way of the fluidity of the writing act; the text as it is written usually spills out of the page, to the side or at the bottom – this generates, at the bottom of pages, words (maybe lines?) in the void, rarely taken up on the following sheet. A famous, and probably unique, case is the typing on continuous paper, the 'hundred foot roll', on which Jack Kerouac claimed to have written, in one go, *On The Road*. This was a solution to the problems of organization of the typing space that some writers encounter, when the flow of writing goes beyond the margins of the paper and gets lost in the void, and to the interruptions caused by changing the sheet in the machine. Arno Schmidt chooses to use A3 paper for the same reason, in order not to 'have to change paper too often'.

A mechanical literature?

Finally, returning to Nietzsche's assertion, does the use of a typewriter have any influence on the text to be? As there are no studies of this specific question, we are obliged to turn to the often contradictory observations of – what should we call them, 'writers', 'scriptors', 'typists'? – let us say, 'writers' using this instrument. Do the rhythm of striking, the attention paid to gesture, the complications of crossing out and correcting, the near impossibility of going back on oneself – in sum, the material, cognitive and practical constraints of typing – have repercussions on the actual form of the text and, if so, which? To what extent does the utilization of the typewriter, because of

---

[24] Rollin, *Ils écrivent*.

these very constraints, these mechanical laws, modify writing strategies and syntactic construction? Views seem to be split on this: some writers believe that the care paid to the material aspects of typing interrupts the flow of writing. One form this takes is exemplified by J. M. G. Le Clezio who commented that 'As I have never learnt to type properly I have to do it throughout with two fingers. So, through laziness, I end up suppressing adjectives here and there. This is how I improve my style without intending to.' Another is the belief that using a typewriter forces one to construct a phrase fully in advance, composing and correcting 'in the head'. Others, in contrast, insist on the greater freedom this instrument gives them. It is undeniable that writing on the machine generates, in comparison to writing by hand, a certain number of constraints that each writer handles in their own way: their approach puts life into the technique. To this are added creative, ludic, aspects: concrete poetry, 'visual texts', that combine and organize typed signs in constellations, in forms of alphabetical matter – carrying out that 'growing destruction of the word' diagnosed by Heidegger: the signs of the machine become signifiers in themselves.

This brief survey is intended merely to bring out certain aspects of the use of the typewriter in the production of literary texts. As the first, historic, stage in the interaction between genesis of a work and the machine, its importance seems to have been underestimated, and the strategies of utilization of this instrument remain very little known. But the fact that the typewriter brings 'the mechanical into the domain of words', connecting literary creation and publication, brings about, to use McLuhan's term, 'an entirely new attitude to the written or printed word'. And, if many writers have probably exchanged, in recent years, their 'machine' for a computer, how many of them are still using the latter basically as a typewriter? Should not the advent of IT lead us, indeed, to examine in a new light the issue of the relations between writing and the machine, relations attested to by the innumerable typescripts accumulated over a century? Is not the typewriter the only 'writing instrument' that creates a connection between hand and electronic writing? While it shows a certain impoverishment in relation to the true manuscript, and appears reductive compared to the graphic and semiotic riches of the handwritten text, writing by machine illustrates in a very distinctive way the tension between the limits of the instrument employed and the creative intervention of the writer. It depends on (or implies) strategies of organization of the page, of visual effects, a specific mode of relation between the semantic and the semiotic. One has only to think of practices, to cite just a few, as different as those of Valéry, Cendrars, Queneau, Perec, Ponge or Schmidt: the typewriter becomes, in itself and in ways different for each one, a means of creation.

The machine offered writers new possibilities: that of putting the text at a distance, of 'depersonalizing' it in order to allow a more objective process of critical reading; that of multiplying the levels and forms of redrafting, by alternating or putting after one another handwritten and typed versions; and finally that of playing with its specific characteristics, if only, as Joyce and Bachmann did, by using typing mistakes as the basis for neologisms or proper names. The typewriter, above all, changed the relation between production and product. This artisanal object constituted by the typescript, intermediate between manuscript and printed book, is in many cases the result of the work of specialist workers, 'typists'; it is also, more often than we might think, the fruit of direct work by the writer. A blank space in the history of writing, in the history of publishing and the press, the relation between machine and literature requires further exploration.

Further reading

Wilfred A. Beeching, *Century of the Typewriter*, Bournemouth: British Typewriter Museum, 1990 (1974).

Delphine Gardey, 'Mécaniser l'écriture et photographier la parole: utopies, monde du bureau et histoires de genres et de techniques', *Annales*, 1999, 3, pp. 587–614.

Delphine Gardey, 'The Standardisation of a Technical Practice, Typing (1883–1930)', *History and Technology*, 15, 1999, pp. 1–31.

Friedrich Kittler, *Grammophon, Film, Typewriter*, Berlin: Brinkmann and Bose, 1986 (translated as *Gramophone, Film, Typewriter*, Minneapolis and London: Stanford University Press, 1992).

Roger Laufer (ed.), *La machine à écrire hier et demain*, Paris: Institut du Livre/Solin, 1982.

'Machines à écrire. Des claviers et des puces: la traversée du siècle', Monique Peyrière (ed.), *Autrement*, 146, June 1994.

Ulrich Ott (ed.), *Literatur im Industriezeitalter*, Marbacher Kataloge 42/2, Marbach: Deutsche Schillergesellschaft, 1987.

Index